Contents

Acknowledgements

The author and publishers wish to thank the following who have kindly given permission for the use of copyright material:-

H W R Hawes for an extract from his book *Curriculum and Curriculum Development in Kenya,* 1976.

Institute of Social Studies for extracts from *Educational Innovations in Africa,* 1972, editor J A Ponsioen.

Longman Group Ltd. for extracts from *Curriculum and Reality in African Primary Schools,* 1979 by H Hawes.

Ministry of Education and Culture, Government of India, for extracts from the *Report of the Education Commission 1964-1966.*

President Julius Nyerere for extracts from *Education for Self-Reliance* and *Socialism and Rural Developments in Ujamaa: Essays on Socialism.*

The Open University for extracts from *The Curriculum: Context Design and Development* by R Hooper.

Oxford University Press Inc. for an extract from *The World Educational Crisis: A Systems Analysis* by Philip H Coombs. Copyright © 1968 by Philip H Coombs.

Sheed & Ward Ltd. for an extract from *The Pedagogy of the Oppressed* by Paulo Friere, 1972.

Spokesman for an extract from *Reflections on Education in the Third World,* 1975, by Keith Buchanan.

Taylor & Francis Ltd. for an extract from 'Secondary School Curriculum and Social Change in an Emergent Nation' by M K Bacchus, in *Journal of Curriculum Studies* Vol. 7 No. 2, November 1975.

Teacher College Press for an extract from *Children in Africa: A Review of Psychological Research* by Judith L Evans. Copyright © 1970 by Teachers College, Columbia University.

The British Council for extracts from *Developing a New Curriculum* by A G Howson, Copyright © 1972 by The British Council.

The Unesco Press for extracts from *Educational Trends in 1970* (ED/11EP/6/7) © Unesco 1970; *The Problem of Rural Education* by V L Griffiths (ED/11EP/6/7) © Unesco 1968; "Concerning Goals and Methods" by Bhuntin Attagara from *Prospects,* Vol. III, No. 1. © Unesco 1973; *Education in a Rural Environment* (ED/90/2) © Unesco 1974; *Educational Planning — A World Survey of Problems and Prospects* © Unesco 1970; *The Qualitative Aspects of Educational Planning* by C E Beeby (ED/11EP/9/2) © Unesco 1969, and from "Education and National Development" by Malcolm Adiseshiah in *Unesco Chronicle* Vol. XIII, No. 2, 1967.

West African Journal of Education for extracts from 'Understanding the African School Child' by E T Abiola and 'Some Guiding Principles of Education in Africa' by A B Fafunwa.

Every effort has been made to trace all the copyright holders but if any have been inadvertently overlooked the publishers will be pleased to make the necessary arrangement at the first opportunity.

Curriculum Development
A textbook for students

George Bishop

MACMILLAN

First published 1985 by
MACMILLAN EDUCATION LTD
London and Basingstoke
Companies and representatives throughout the world

ISBN 0–333–39118–7

15	14	13	12	11	10	9	8	7	
06	05	04	03	02	01	00	99	98	97

This book is printed on paper suitable for recycling and
made from fully managed and sustained forest sources.

Printed in Hong Kong

Introduction

In the past, curriculum development was often a case of groups of school inspectors conjuring up new syllabuses. For educational change to be effective it must be deliberately planned and rationally organized. Otherwise education can become, as it often does, a pragmatic affair, a case of hit or miss. Of course, what really matters in the long run in education is what actually goes on in the classroom – and outside of it. Even so, there must be a certain amount of philosophising and theorising; practice must be principled by ideas.

While accepting that some theory there must be, this book aims to concentrate on the action of curriculum reform. Instead of devoting overmuch time up in the sky in 'airy-fairy' land or in investigating 'never-never' land, the aim has been to keep both feet firmly planted on the realities of tropical terra firma. It is felt that this is what overburdened students and teachers, in the action and heat of overcrowded classrooms and often lacking adequate materials and facilities, want to know.

The book is divided into two main sections.

The theoretical bases of curriculum development

Chapters 1-7 deal with the theoretical bases, the foundations, underlying curriculum development. The chapters consider the main determining factors involved in curriculum development.

Chapter 8 deals with the various patterns of curriculum organization.

Chapter 9 discusses various teaching/learning strategies.

The action of curriculum development

Chapters 10-17 put this theory into action, covering the entire process of curriculum development from situation analysis to a formulation of objectives.

The actual writing and preparation of teaching/learning units is dealt with exhaustively. The very important role of the teacher in the whole business of innovation and implementation is followed by a final chapter on evaluation.

An Epilogue (Chapter 18) seeks to chart the main directions of change if education in Third World countries is to meet successfully the challenges of the future.

The lesson notes, syllabuses, etc. included in the book are given as examples which students and teachers, though in different places and in different situations, may yet find useful as models, as suggestions, which they can adapt and modify to their own particular situations.

1 Some General Curriculum Issues

The meaning of the word 'curriculum'

If an international symposium were to be held on prison reform or heart disease, it is unlikely that any participants would assume that the topic was space exploration or cancer. But even within a single country an educational term like 'curriculum' often has so many interpretations that it would be surprising if its meaning did not vary from one national system to another.[46]

There are many meanings attached to the word 'curriculum'. It is often loosely used to mean 'syllabus', or 'list of subjects', or 'course of study', or 'topics', or 'items of knowledge to be covered', or 'content', or 'organization of teaching and learning', or 'method', or 'time-table' and so on. All these are ingredients, only parts, of what we mean by 'curriculum'. The word has a much wider meaning. And curriculum development is more than just up-dating some subjects, like replacing the 'old' mathematics with the 'new'.

By curriculum is meant the sum total of all the experiences a pupil undergoes.

A curriculum is much wider than a syllabus: a syllabus is only part of the total curriculum. In its broadest sense, a curriculum is concerned not so much with prescribing the knowledge to be acquired as with the area of learning experiences to be organized by teachers, both within and outside the school, to enable pupils to adopt a positive attitude to learning, to acquire and apply knowledge and skills, and to develop their tastes and a balanced sense of values.

Determinants of curriculum

The determinants of curriculum are those factors which affect or determine the curriculum.

Curriculum is as broad as education, as large as life itself. No school is an island to itself; school is an integral part of society. So in considering questions of curriculum one must go beyond the confines of the school; one must look at society, at the kind of society one is trying to build. A curriculum does not develop in a vacuum; one must consider the values, the traditions, the beliefs, the whole culture, or way of life, of the society.

One must also consider the broad philosophical issues such as the aims and purposes of education. The politics, the ideology, of a country will have an influence on what is – or is not – included in the curriculum.

Curriculum decisions are thus not just about content or the most effective ways of organizing the teaching and learning of subject-matter. Curriculum decisions necessarily involve a complex network of social, cultural, philosophical, moral, political and ideological issues.

Language, being the means by which people communicate with one another, will naturally play a vital role in any curriculum.

Policies and strategies for the national development of a country's resources, plans for its future economic growth etc., will also influence the curriculum in schools by encouraging perhaps a rural bias in what is done in the schools or by giving the education provided in the schools a bias towards modern sector/industrial development.

The desire to provide universal primary education for all children – U.P.E. – also has its implications for the curriculum, as we shall see in Chapter 5.

One must also consider knowledge; not only the intellectual tools which have proved valuable to mankind and society in the past, but also the subject disciplines on which society and the world as we know it today depend and from which any worthwhile curriculum must draw.

Consideration must also be given to psychological issues, to the nature of human development, to theories of teaching and of learning. The psychology of individual differences teaches us, for example, not to expect identical results from all children just because they use the same curriculum.

Finally, one must bear in mind that decisions about curriculum inevitably involve financial priorities and constraints. Lack of money can be as complete a barrier to educational progress as lack of ideas or initiative.

At the Regional Conferences on Education convened by Unesco for African Member States, Nairobi, 1968, and for Arab States, Marrakesh, 1970, it was stated clearly that lack of finances formed one of the major constraints on the expansion and improvement of education.

President Nyerere, in his policy document *Education for Self-Reliance* (1967), recognised the constraints placed on education programmes by lack of resources:

> And the truth is that there is no possibility of Tanzania being able to increase the proportion of the national income which is spent on education; it ought to be decreased. Therefore, we cannot solve our present problems by any solution which costs more than is at present spent; in particular we cannot solve the problem of primary school leavers by increasing the number of secondary school places.
>
> These are the economic facts of life for our country. They are the practical meaning of our poverty. The only choice before us is how we allocate the educational opportunities, and whether we emphasise the individual interests of the few or

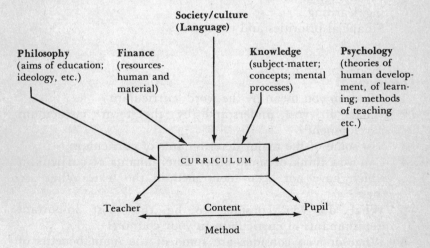

Fig. 1 The major determinants of the curriculum

3

whether we design our educational system to serve the community as a whole.[61]

The poorer one is in human and material resources the more wisely must one spend those resources. Strategies of curriculum reform will be shaped not only by what is desirable but also by what can be afforded; not only by what must be done but also by what must be done first.

These and some other determinants of curriculum are considered in greater detail in the ensuing chapters.

Summary

1 By 'curriculum' is meant *all the experiences* a pupil undergoes.
2 Factors which *determine the curriculum:*
   Society;
   Culture;
   Philosophical issues e.g. aims and purposes of education;
   Political issues;
   Language;
   A rural bias to education or education for modern sector/ industrial development?
   Knowledge;
   Psychological issues – child development, theories of teaching/learning;
   Financial priorities and constraints.

Questions

1 What do you mean by the word 'curriculum'?
2 What do you understand by the term 'curriculum development'?
3 List some of the major determinants of curriculum.
4 Can you think of some other determinants of curriculum which have not been mentioned in the text? What are these?
5 What do you consider to be the most important determinants of curriculum in your country?
6 What do you consider are some of the main benefits of education in your country?

7   What do you consider are some of the main problems of
    education in your country?
8   Briefly suggest how you would attempt to overcome some
    of these problems of education in your country.
9   In education, should we emphasise the interests of the few
    or should the educational system be designed to serve the
    many?

2   Some Determinants of Curriculum

Society/culture

A curriculum must be designed in the light of the major trends and developments within society and it must also reflect the major social and cultural needs of society. An educational system goes astray when it has no relevance to society.

Abdou Moumouri of the Niger, in his plea for a return to national languages and cultures, refers to: 'schools which bear no relationship to their surroundings', 'schools which are cut off from the life of the country and of society', 'unproductive schools which only train pupils for the civil service', 'which destroy national cultural values and personality and produce men who are foreigners in their own society'.[58]

In Tanzania, as in many developing countries, education is linked to national development and cultural renewal.

One of the basic tenets of society in Tanzania is 'ujamaa' – African familyhood and socialism. President Nyerere, in his 'Socialism and Rural Development', writes:

> The traditional African family lived according to the basic principles of ujamaa ... They lived together and worked together because that was how they understood life, and how they reinforced each other against the difficulties they had to contend with ... The pattern of living was made possible because of three basic assumptions of traditional life – mutual respect, sharing of joint production, work by all. These principles were, and are, the foundations of human security, of real practical human equality, and of peace between members of a society ...[62]

For President Nyerere, education was to play its part in re-establishing the advantages of traditional African democracy, social security and human dignity.

In *Education for Self-Reliance* he states: 'The education provided must therefore encourage the development in each citizen of three things: an enquiring mind; an ability to learn from what others do, and reject or adapt it to his own needs; and a basic confidence in his own position as a free and equal member of the society, who values others and is valued by them for what he does and not for what he obtains'.[61]

The philosophy of co-operation and self-reliance and independence is reflected in the curricula of schools in Tanzania.

Just as a particular society/culture influences the curriculum, so, too, a curriculum can influence and change traditional society and culture. One of the recommendations of the Government of India Report of the Education Commission (1966) reads:

The most important and urgent reform needed in education is to transform it, to endeavour to relate it to the life, needs and aspirations of the people and thereby make it a powerful instrument of social, economic and cultural transformation necessary for the realization of the national goals. For this purpose, education should be developed so as to increase productivity, achieve social and national integration, accelerate the progress of modernization and cultivate social, moral and spiritual values. (1.20 (6))

The Report (p. 615) touches on the almost exponential growth in knowledge and the resulting tremendous upheavals and changes in modern society.

In a modern society knowledge increases at a terrific pace and social change is very rapid. This needs a radical transformation in the educational system. Education is no longer taken as concerned primarily with the imparting of knowledge or preparation of a finished product, but with awakening of curiosity, development of proper interests, attitudes and values and building up of such essential skills as independent study and the capacity to think and judge for oneself. This also involves a radical alteration in the methods of teaching and in the training of teachers.[44]

The new stress in education must be not so much on producing an educated person as on producing an educable person who can learn and adapt himself efficiently all through his life to an environment that is ceaselessly changing. Since the contours of the future are as yet often vague and uncharted the need is for people trained to turn their hands – and their minds – to a wide range of occupations. Increasingly, 'knowing' is becoming less important than being equipped to 'find out for oneself'. Practical skills needed for today may well be redundant tomorrow. The need is for adaptable craftsmen rather than automatons set in their ways.

Hence the need to produce citizens who are more flexible, who have been taught general principles rather than specific skills so that they can readily abandon jobs which become redundant and obsolete and apply themselves to new industrial skills and techniques.

Education is not only an instrument for changing society. In addition to its culture-modifying role it has a culture-preserving one – to preserve all that is best and worthwhile in a nation's cultural and traditional heritage. The school has the task of making available to the young not only those facts and skills which will prove of value to the child in making his living in a sometimes uncertain future, but also to inculcate in him the traditional values of the past which will add meaning to much of his life.

Unless the preservation of culture is actively encouraged the culture soon disappears. Thus, as Professor George Milner points out:

In the Pacific, for instance, in less than a century and a half, the old Hawaiian culture has vanished, almost without a trace, and so has the culture of the New Zealand Maori, save in a few of its aspects such as wood-carving, funeral customs and food habits. Today, especially in French Polynesia and American Samoa, the trend is not only continuing, but accelerated under the violent impact of television and the change-over to a money economy.[56]

To give a sensitive understanding of a nation's cultural heritage it is necessary to teach its customs and traditions, its songs, dances, legends, heroic exploits and even its traditional culinary art and home remedies.

Moral and spiritual well-being

Along with the overall trend towards a more practical and less academic approach to education, most development plans for education in the developing countries also ensure that the moral and physical well-being of their pupils is not lost sight of. They recognise that the aims of development must be 'fullness of good rather than mere abundance of goods'.

Among the education development plans of nearly all Muslim nations is the preservation of the moral and spiritual values of Islam. One of the basic concepts underlying educational policy in Pakistan is the role of education in the preservation and inculcation of Islamic values as an instrument of national unity and progress. The same principles form an essential part of educational policy in Saudi Arabia.

The Indian Education Commission reported (p. 206) that a serious defect in the school curriculum was the 'absence of provision for education in social, moral and spiritual values ...' To remedy this it recommended that: 'the Central and State Governments should adopt measures to introduce education in moral, social and spiritual values in all institutions under their direct control. (1.75)'.[44]

The Guidelines of State Policy drawn up by the elected People's Consultative Assembly of the Republic of Indonesia in March 1978 lay down the active promotion of religious life not only in the country, but more specifically in schools by enacting that 'religious education be inserted into the curriculum of schools, from primary schools up to state universities'.

Questions

1 In what ways is your country helping to preserve its cultural heritage?
2 Are there any 'unproductive' schools or schools that should be abolished in your country's educational system? Elaborate.
3 Are there any circumstances in your education system that go against the cultural heritage of your country?
4 Is the traditional culture of your country disappearing? Is this a good or a bad thing? Explain.
5 Give an example of the culture-modifying role of education in your country, i.e. how education is changing the traditional patterns of life in your country.

6   Give an example of the culture-preserving role of education in your country, i.e. how education is helping to preserve and foster your country's national heritage.

7   Are there any things in your country's cultural heritage which you feel should *not* be preserved? How could education be used to do away with any such less desirable aspects of the national culture?

8   What provisions are made in the school curriculum for the moral and spiritual well-being of pupils?

Politics/ideology

> Curriculum development is a political activity in every sense. It is caught up with values, with what it is worthwhile, beneficial and useful to teach the young, and with how best to distribute educational resources both human and material.[83]

There is an inextricable relationship between education and national ideals and objectives. Many of the countries of Africa, on acquiring independence, saw and used the school as an important instrument to further the achievement of their political aims and to foster particular attitudes and values deemed necessary for national advancement and cultural identity. This is clearly reflected, for example, in the educational policies of Ghana in the 1950s.

One of the most striking examples of a political lead in the field of education is contained in President Nyerere's pamphlet *Education for Self-Reliance* (1967). For Tanzania the curriculum is a key element in its programme of national development and in its policy for the reform of society. The Tanzanian ideal of a new socialist man, enjoying equal rights with his fellows in a co-operating, work-orientated democracy, is to be achieved through education.

> This is what our educational system has to encourage. It has to foster the social goals of living together, and working together, for the common good. It has to prepare our young people to play a dynamic and constructive part in the development of a society in which all members share fairly in the good or bad fortune of the group, and in which progress is measured in

terms of human well-being, not prestige buildings, cars, or other such things whether privately or publicly owned. Our education must therefore inculcate a sense of commitment to the total community, and help the pupils to accept the values appropriate to our kind of future, not those appropriate to our colonial past.[61]

The direct influence of national and political goals in the educational policy of a country is further illustrated by the case of India. As the Report of the Education Commission (1964–1966) states (1.35):

Social and national integration is a major problem which will have to be tackled on several fronts including education. In our view, education can and should play a very significant role in it by:

1 introducing a common school system of public education;
2 making social and national service an integral part of education obligatory for all students at all stages. (Programmes of social and community service – public sanitation, village improvement, care of small children, help to old and sick – to be organised concurrently with academic studies in schools and colleges, as was the practice in the 'ashrams' and academies of old.) (8.79; 1.45)
3 promoting national consciousness. 'India is a land of diversities – of different castes, peoples, communities, languages, religions and cultures. What role can the schools and universities play in enabling their students to discover the "unity in diversity" that India essentially is and in fostering a sense of national solidarity transcending narrower loyalties?' (1.63)

The deepening of national consciousness can be fostered specially by two programmes:

1 the understanding and re-evaluation of our cultural heritage and
2 creation of a strong driving faith in the future to which we aspire. (1.66)

The problem of national integration is essentially one of harmonising such differences, of enabling different elements of the population to live peacefully and co-operatively and utilise

11

their varied gifts for the enrichment of the national life as a whole. (1.68)[44]

In Kenya, education is used 'as a tool to promote national unity so that the people can live and interact as Kenyans and not merely identify themselves with their tribal, religious or racial groups'.[48]

Questions

1 Your country probably has a National Development Plan. What are the main national ideals and objectives in this Plan?
2 In what ways are these national ideals and objectives reflected in the educational system in your country?
3 Do you consider that your country's educational system is helping to achieve the national ideals and objectives? Explain.
4 In what ways do you feel your country's educational system is not helping to achieve the national ideals and objectives? Explain.
5 How would you make your country's educational system more effective in achieving the nation's main ideals and objectives?

The importance of language

As we shall see, language plays a very important part in the educational system of any country. Language is the means by which we communicate with one another. When a country has one common language there is no great problem in communicating with each other. But when a country has many languages, problems arise. In Ethiopia, for example, more than 70 different languages are spoken as first languages. In Nigeria about 250 different languages are used. Which language is to be used as the national language? Which language is to be used in the schools? In Africa it is estimated that there are about 1000 indigenous languages.

The usual language policy is to teach first in the vernacular for two or three or four years, and then to switch to a national language. Teaching in the mother tongue provides the vital link between the home, the community, the local environment and the school.

In order to investigate the most appropriate language policy for the efficient primary education of Yoruba children in Nigeria, the University of Ife, in association with the Ministry of Education, set up the Ife Six Year Project. The Project confirmed what common sense would probably have suggested, namely, that children enquire, enjoy and participate when they are learning in a medium they understand (Yoruba) and are far more passive when they are struggling with the medium of a foreign language (English).

In a study made in Zambia, it was found that children who began their schooling in the vernacular language fared better in problem arithmetic when compared with children who began their schooling in the medium of English. In mechanical arithmetic there was no significant difference. That vernacular learners should fare better is understandable since success in 'problem' arithmetic depends primarily on perceiving the nature of the problem – which involves being able not only to read but also to comprehend the written word.

Much excellent work is being done by Curriculum Development Centres and Ministries of Education in most developing countries in the production of curricular materials in the mother tongue. As instances may be mentioned the Bureau of Ghanaian Languages, working with the Ghana Curriculum Development Division; the Curriculum Development Centre in Zambia; the Kenya Institute of Education, etc.

Both the Intergovernmental Conference on Cultural Policies in Africa (Accra 1975) and the Conference of Ministers of Education of African Member States (Lagos 1976) recommended that African vernaculars be used more and more as vehicles of instruction.

When language groups are large, education in the mother tongue is viable, as for example, the Hausa or Luganda or the Kikuyu. But when the numbers speaking the mother tongue are small or very scattered, problems arise – problems of providing suitable reading and instructional materials, of teachers who know the language fluently enough to teach.

But what, one might ask, is the vernacular in an urban setting? Urban areas attract from far and wide. Thus, in a city like Lusaka, it is not uncommon to find a dozen vernaculars in a single classroom, and a teacher conversant with none of them.

Among all the barriers to efficient teaching and learning perhaps those caused by the language problem are the most formidable. This is especially so when the teaching is done in a foreign language. Often the school and examination results in mathematics and science in developing countries are not as good as one would wish. These are the very subjects on which many countries rely for their economic and industrial development. This is not because the students are not as clever as elsewhere but often because the teaching and learning is done in a foreign medium such as English.

In order to accommodate mathematical terms and concepts many countries have found it necessary to extend their vocabularies. In Tanzania, for example, where Kiswahili is the medium of instruction in all primary schools, there has been a great deal of activity in developing and inventing new words and expressions to express concepts in mathematics. Thus, the word 'kitovu' which means 'a navel' was adopted as the term meaning 'the centre of a circle'. Again, because there was no word for 'the diagonal' of a rectangle, the word 'ulalo' was chosen. 'Ulalo' is the word used by makers of beds who, in cross-stringing a bed with cord, used the word 'ulalo' for 'the longest of all strings they used'.

The language question raises important implications for teaching. In teaching a subject in a foreign language, say, for example, teaching mathematics in English, we should heed this warning. Unless the linguistic concepts are presented in concrete and dynamic form, the language used by the teacher is often a mystery to the hearer. A story is told of young Johnny excitedly telling his father about his prowess in mathematics. 'Listen, daddy, three and two, the son of a bitch is five; four and three, the son of a bitch is seven'. From the ensuing complaint by the parents it was discovered that what the teacher had taught was 'three and two, the sum of which is five'.

Questions
1 Briefly describe any language problems, if any, that your country has.
2 How can these language problems be overcome?
3 Are there any language problems in the education system of your country?
4 How can these language-education problems be resolved?

5 Mention some of the language problems you have met in learning any particular subject at school.

6 What is the importance of the 'vernacular' in education?

Summary

1 *Society/culture and curriculum* A curriculum must be designed with relevance to the major trends and developments in society. Education must be linked to national development and cultural renewal.

Just as a particular society/culture influences the curriculum, a curriculum can influence and change traditional society and culture.

$$\text{society/culture} \rightleftharpoons \text{curriculum}$$

The tremendous growth in knowledge with its resultant upheavals and changes in society calls for an education aimed at producing educable, adaptable, flexible citizens.

Education is not only an instrument for changing society. In addition to this culture-modifying role, education also has a culture-preserving role – to preserve all that is best in a country's cultural heritage, along with its moral and spiritual values.

2 *Politics/ideology and curriculum* Education is inextricably bound up with a nation's ideals and objectives. The school is often used as an instrument to further a nation's political aims and to foster particular attitudes and values.

3 *Language and curriculum* Language is the means by which we communicate with one another. As such, it plays a vital role in curriculum. Problems arise when a country has many languages. Teaching and learning in a foreign language raises formidable barriers to efficient education. The language used by the teacher can often be a mystery to the pupil. Hence the importance of teaching in the vernacular, especially in the first few years of schooling. Teaching in the mother tongue provides the vital link between the home, the community, the local environment and the school.

3   Education and Economic Development

Education and productivity

It goes without saying that education is a key element in promoting economic and national development. An educated labour force will have a higher productivity than an uneducated one. But if a country is to achieve rapid economic development its education must be related to productivity. With a view to relating education to productivity some countries have recommended that work-experience be introduced as an integral part of all education, general or vocational.

The Government of India Education Commission Report details the programme of work-experience that is to be undertaken at the different stages of education (8.73).

> In the lower classes of the primary school work-experience might take the form of simple handwork, the objective being to train children to make use of their hands. In the senior classes it may take the form of learning a craft which develops technical thinking and creative capacities in the pupils. At this stage, some work-experience can be provided in real life situations, such as work on the farms at the time of harvesting or sowing or in a family production unit. Whilst productive work-experience in rural areas is largely built round agriculture, programmes oriented to industry and simple technology should be introduced in a fair proportion of rural schools.[44]

Non-productive education

The existing school systems in many countries are, however, not conducive to fostering economic development. In fact, they have

16

even held back development on occasions on account of their bookish nature, their high cost and their semi-mechanical imitation of external models which do not fit in with national needs.

The Report of the Indian Education Commission realised that if education was to contribute towards economic growth and earn a good yield on its investment the character of the education provided must also change.

> The present system (of education) is too academic to be of material help in increasing national wealth. ... The schools and colleges are largely unconcerned with the great national effort at reconstruction and their teachers and students generally remain uncommitted. (1.18)

> Most of the secondary schools offer a literary curriculum which fits a student for entry into a college and almost 'unfits' him for everything else.[44]

The Government of Sri Lanka also realised that the character of education had to change if it was to be a force in economic and national development.

> Whatever the national objectives and strategies for national development may be, the school is central to this activity in our societies. Our schools, however, remain insular. [The school] is insulated from the community, from work, from production, from the thoughts and aspirations of the masses from whose taxes we maintain this educational institution in splendid isolation. The school still maintains the idea of the scholar as one steeped in books and useless knowledge, aloof to all mundane matters and in fact above the life of the masses. This mandarin mentality is as abrasive as the white-collar one. In this context a good technician is considered not educated by our schools. Acquisition of skills is still not legitimatized by our schools.[79a]

Many schools have a prejudice against teaching practical subjects. Since the theorist has more snob prestige than the practitioner, schools tend to be snobbish against their pupils 'dirtying their hands'.

With a view to eradicating the stigma associated with studies that involve 'dirtying the hands', the Government of Pakistan decided:

> manual work for two hours a week which may be undertaken on a weekly or monthly basis is compulsory in all three stages [of secondary education]. This is intended to inculcate a sense of dignity of labour and to remove the widespread aversion which exists in our educated classes for work that dirties the hands. This will also correct the wrong notion that manual work is something inferior to intellectual work.[67]

Such policies might result in fewer philosophers but they would at least help the supply of engineers, scientists, doctors and technicians which are in short supply in all developing countries.

Over-production of the wrong type of graduates

One of the problems facing educational and economic planners in the developing countries is that of securing the right 'mix', or balance, of its graduates needed for optimum economic development. The educational systems in many Third World countries are over-producing certain types of graduates, for example, lawyers and arts graduates whilst under-producing others, such as engineers, technicians and nurses, needed for the development of these countries.

In many developing countries one of the main imperatives for economic development is the need to raise agricultural productivity. Yet there are many universities in developing countries without agriculture faculties. In those countries with agriculture faculties less than four per cent of the graduates are in agriculture; most of these end up behind desks 'administering'. This is because very often the pay is much higher for 'administering' than for 'doing' things.

Unemployment

National economies must be able to absorb the educated young people into productive work. However, the industrial and business sectors of most developing countries are unable to absorb the large numbers of school leavers seeking employment.

Educational systems and their outputs, especially in developing countries, have in recent years been growing two to three times as fast as the economy, hence faster than the number of new jobs available (especially of the type most students aspire to). This has given rise to the problem of graduate unemployment.

The imbalance between the growing output from the schools and the capacity of the economy to create new jobs to absorb the school-leavers is referred to as 'the gap'. This 'gap', unfortunately, continues to grow. In Kenya, for example, in 1970 two people with a primary school education or better were competing for one job available in towns or in government. Ten years later there were six people in competition for that job. Today, three million people are educationally equipped to join in the scramble for such jobs.

Professor Harbison states that Nigeria's educational system is almost exclusively oriented to filling city jobs in the modern sector. 'The values, subject matter and examination criteria at all levels of Nigerian education assume that school leavers want to become government civil servants, teachers, and employees of relatively modern and industrial and commercial establishments.'[30]

Yet Nigeria can only provide jobs in the modern urban sector for five per cent of the total labour force. Thus Nigeria, which once seemed to face insoluble manpower shortages, now begins to wonder how it will place its greatly enlarged supply of graduates.

The figures for Sri Lanka are really staggering. An ILO Report states that in the age group 15–19, ninety-two per cent of the adolescents with GCE 'O' levels are unemployed.

One way of preventing massive unemployment of the educated is to launch a propaganda campaign to convince all the young people who are trying to crowd through one narrow professional doorway that, in a growing economy, there are other openings available. These may for the moment lack traditional prestige, but are equally demanding of intelligence and education. But to convince the young a new look will have to be taken at salary structures and the rewards attached to the work of technicians, tradesmen, etc. The older generation of parents, too, who tend to hold academic education in awe and reverence, will also need to be converted. Professor Fafunwa describes such parental prejudice in his book *New Perspectives in African Education*: 'An African legislator summed it up succinctly when he said:

"Vocational education is urgently needed for our development and should be encouraged but it is not for my son".'[23a]

The need for technical manpower

In all developing countries a shortage of technical manpower is the weak link in the chain of economic and industrial development. A shortage of people suited to be technicians, foremen and supervisors, is one of the marked characteristics of under-developed countries.

This acute shortage of technical manpower has led many governments to embark on a massive switch from aimless general education to a more meaningful agro-technical education. These countries have also realised that any expansion of education must be related in its form and content to the nature and scope of the economic development of the country and to employment opportunities.

As a temporary measure the shortage of technical and professional manpower can be met by a 'lowering of standards'. This may seem a heretical statement. However, as Professor Lewis argues: 'When qualified manpower is in very short supply and when often vast areas of countryside have to be covered, two half-trained professionals could do more good than one fully trained professional.'[52a]

He justifies his claim:

This has been done, in fact, in many countries for generations, for example, the Central Medical School in Fiji which originally took in some entrants with little more than a primary school education, after a three year course turned out what were then known as 'native medical practitioners' who gave valuable service to the Pacific islands that would have had no hope of attracting fully trained doctors.[52b]

The faculties of arts, law and commerce in universities in the developing world tend to be flooded with students, while technical schools remain virtually empty, even though industry is crying out for skilled craftsmen. There are many strategies to tackle this problem.

One would be to limit the number of students entering the over-crowded faculties.

Another would be to offer more generous bursaries and scholarships to students going to technical schools or entering technical faculties than to those who go to the popular faculties.

Bringing the technical schools and colleges within the university system would enhance their prestige.

Another way to raise the social standing of technicians and technical sub-professionals would be to increase their emoluments.

But, if society as a whole looks down on any form of manual labour, and if, as so often happens in state services, the starting salary for a young man with the most miserable degree is higher than the top rate for a skilled craftsman, one can hardly expect students to flock to the technical jobs.

Professor M.K. Bacchus, referring to the situation in Guyana, puts the point most clearly:

The lesson obviously has not yet been learnt that changes in the curriculum of schools aimed at influencing students' occupational choices will not be effective if the basic reward structure is such that people are not likely to be attracted to these occupations in the first place. Given freedom of choice, people are always likely to opt for the type of education which, however irrelevant it might be from an educator's point of view, will lead to the more rewarding job in the society, as long as they have the ability to profit from the course.

The basic filip which can be given to encourage youngsters to enter into the technical and agricultural fields, which is the major purpose in the current proposals for curriculum reform in the secondary schools in Guyana, lies in the rewards which those who follow these fields of activity are likely to receive in comparison with other job holders in the society. Changes in school curriculum alone aimed at achieving such results are not only likely to be expensive but ineffective ... In short, if the Government wants to attract secondary school students to enter into the technical and agricultural fields it has first to begin by making a realistic appraisal of what rewards these fields offer in comparison to other occupational fields in the economy ...

The overall conclusion which can be made from evidence gathered for this study, is that the curriculum changes which took place were not very much influenced by the authoritative recommendations or professional encouragement of officials or advisers in the Department or the Ministry of Education as to the type of curriculum which they considered 'relevant to the needs of the Guyanese society', or necessary to 'produce well rounded individuals'. Instead they occurred in response to certain changes in the society which partly modified and widened the basis of recruitment to the economically more rewarding and socially more prestigious positions in the society.[7]

More science in the schools

In an age of increasing science and technology, many countries are strengthening and modernising their mathematics and science courses in order to produce more and better qualified candidates for higher level technical and scientific studies. The changing emphasis on a scientific and technological outlook has been reflected in the curricula of schools. Rapidly advancing technology has in many instances been one of the main pressures for curricular change.

Even at the primary level, there has been a great emphasis on the teaching of science. In 1965, the year of the Second Regional Conference of Ministers of Education, held in Bangkok, sixty-five per cent of primary pupils in Asia completed their first cycle of education without ever being exposed to learning experiences in science. Today, in all countries of the region, primary science in one form or another is one of the core subjects for compulsory study.

Wastage

The contribution that education can make to a country's development is vitiated by the enormous 'wastage' that occurs in the system itself.

Rémi Van Waeyenberghe of Unesco provides a sombre picture of wastage. He states that primary schooling has become:

the leading industry in countries of the Third World. This gigantic undertaking which absorbs at least one-fifth of the natural resources has an output of which three-quarters is waste and only one-quarter finished products ... Partly this is because the primary school is concerned above all with preparing students for secondary education. It is necessary to seek out and find educational structures better adapted to the needs and resources of the countries of the Third World.[14]

In India, forty per cent of pupils drop out in the first year and others lapse into illiteracy after one or two years. This drop-out is a tremendous waste of scarce resources. The costs incurred by developing countries from drop-outs and repeaters is sometimes increased by as much as six times the normal cost.

In many developing countries in Asia, Africa and Latin America the wastage rate between primary and secondary schooling ranges about the fifty per cent level. Fewer than half of those who enter primary school ever finish. Of those who do finish more than half take more than the 'normal' time for primary schooling.

Strenuous efforts are being made to alleviate the wastage problem. 'Repetition', for example, is on the decline in Ghana – but due to a deliberate policy of 'automatic promotion'. To overcome the wastage from 'drop-outs' many countries are fostering students' talents and channelling drop-outs into productive part-time non-formal education institutes.

Saudi Arabia has established ungraded elementary schools in which 'drop-outs' can continue their studies at their own pace.

Incentives – such as increases in salaries – can help to lessen wastage. In Somalia, for instance, the basic salary of diploma holders is forty times the national average: students are thus encouraged to stay at school till they obtain a diploma.

Alongside the educational television teaching for all pupils in the basic cycle of education in the Ivory Coast, there is a para-television teaching programme mainly for those who have 'dropped out' or 'failed'. This involves a programme of correspondence teaching in addition to T.V. teaching and is designed specifically to re-educate and re-animate these 'lost' pupils.

Summary
1 *Education and productivity* Education is a key element in promoting economic and national development.

But if a country is to achieve rapid economic development its education must be related to productivity. Some countries have introduced a form of 'work-experience' into their school curricula.

2 *Non-productive education* Many existing school systems hinder economic development because of their too 'bookish' character and the 'mandarin' mentality of students, disinclined to 'dirty their hands'.

If education is to contribute to economic growth the character of the education given must change.

3 *Over-production of the wrong type of graduates* needed for economic development (e.g. too many lawyers and arts graduates) can lead to graduate unemployment. Young people – and parents – need to be convinced that in a growing economy openings other than 'white – collar jobs' can be just as satisfying. However, young people will only enter the technical and agricultural fields if the rewards (e.g. salary) are comparable to those in other fields.

4 *Unemployment* National economies must be able to absorb the educated young people into productive work. Any expansion of education must be related in its form and content to the nature and scope of the economic development of the country and to employment opportunities.

5 *The need for technical manpower* In all developing countries a shortage of technical manpower is the weak link in the chain of economic and industrial development.

6 The changing emphasis on a scientific and technological out-look has led to *more science in the schools*.

7 *Wastage* The contribution that education can make to a country's development is vitiated by the enormous wastage that occurs in the form of 'drop-outs' and 'repeaters'.

Questions
1 In what ways is the education system of your country helping the economic and industrial development of the nation?
2 How can this help be increased?
3 In what ways is the education system hindering the country's economic and industrial growth?
4 How can this be prevented?
5 What activities in school would you consider were proving most effective in aiding the country's growth and development? Why?
6 What are some of the factors which cause an imbalance in the country's development?

7 What are the main reasons for any unemployment in your country?
8 How can the education system help to decrease unemployment?
9 What means is the government taking to increase its supply of scientific and technical manpower?
10 Are these means proving effective? Explain.
11 What are the main causes of wastage in the school system?
12 How can such wastage be prevented?

4 Education and Rural Development

A rural bias to education?

As a rule, in developing countries seventy to ninety per cent of all the people live and work in the rural areas. More than sixty per cent of the national economies derive from agriculture. Yet in many developing countries the educational systems remain unrelated to agricultural needs and to the demands of their societies.

The Report of the Education Commission of the Government of India bears this out (1.18): 'The educational system does not reflect the supreme importance of agriculture which is neglected at all stages and does not attract an adequate share of the top talent in the country'.[44]

The Government of the Philippines complained: 'Three-quarters of our elementary school children are malnourished or undernourished; yet it is difficult to get teachers to manage the vegetable gardens, teach agricultural skills and help carry out the Green Revolution'.[73]

To remedy this neglect of agriculture in the educational systems of developing countries many planners and educators have recommended that agricultural education as such should be included in the curricula of all schools, even at the primary level. For example, Malcolm Adiseshiah, a former Deputy Director – General of Unesco, recommends that: 'in primary schools, the teaching of elementary science, nature study with school gardens and livestock care, as well as craft education' should be taught.[3a]

Others propose that rural schools should have a special curriculum based on the needs of rural life and taught by a specially trained cadre of rural teachers. Such a proposal seems logical and sensible.

The fact is, however, that in the conditions obtaining in most developing countries, such proposals are quite definitely non-starters. The reason is not that such proposals ignore the needs of the rural areas, but that they ignore what parents want from the schools. Experiments with such pilot rural schools have often met with stern resistance.

C.E. Beeby, in his book *The Quality of Education in Developing Countries* explains why parents are often against any schemes, no matter how well-intentioned, to include any 'agricultural or rural bias' in the curriculum of the schools.

An Asian or African peasant whose meagre patch of ground cannot support all his sons, can scarcely be blamed for seeking for some of them the kind of schooling that will offer hope of escape from the land, and for looking askance at changes of curriculum or method that might bind them more closely to the farm or village that can offer them no future. This is one reason why well-intentioned schemes for giving an agricultural bias to primary schools have failed with such dismal regularity in most agricultural countries.[9]

Often a change to a more realistic and practical form of education more suited to the needs of the rural community is looked upon as a subtle attempt to fob children off with something inferior.

V.L. Griffiths says the same:

Whatever may be the official aims of education and the hopes of educators, the fact is that most parents look on the schools as a means of escape for their children from the hardships and privations of rural life. To establish special schools for rural children, where the curriculum deliberately attempts to keep them on the land, is to thwart their hopes and ambitions for their children and for their own old age. A recent survey in one of the more advanced of the developing rural countries showed that very few parents wished their children to become farmers. Experience would seem to show that in most areas special schools for rural children would be completely unacceptable ...

The tradition persists, and is unlikely to change until farming can show greater financial returns, stability, and ease than the white-collar jobs.[28a]

As against a 'separate' system of rural education, Griffiths argues for a less extreme group of suggestions:

> It is accepted that rural schools must follow very much the same syllabuses as town schools and that there must be, and must be seen to be, an equal chance for rural boys and girls to move up the educational ladder according to their ability, but rural science, rural studies, practical agriculture or gardening should be taught as alternatives to some of the regular items in the syllabus. In this way, those who did not succeed in getting white-collar jobs would at least be partially prepared to take part in the improvement of rural life, and they could continue their agricultural training in special vocational schools. In other words, the schools should have a double aim: education leading to salaried white-collar or technical employment, and education leading to unsalaried farming and an enlightened attitude to rural improvement. Parents, it is argued, would see the advantage of having the best of both worlds.[28b]

This seems a very reasonable compromise, with the result that many attempts have been made to carry this out.

Rural teacher-training colleges have been set up in a number of countries to train semi-specialist teachers; agricultural officers have co-operated in devising syllabuses and have sometimes been seconded to the education service to help supervise the programme; school gardens have been given widespread encouragement and school farms started where conditions appeared suitable. Science syllabuses have been devised which are largely based on rural material, and agriculture has been accepted as an examinable subject in school-leaving examinations.

'But', asks Griffiths, 'with what results?'

> One country which had enthusiastically taken up agriculture as part of its rural primary and middle school programme has completely abandoned it after a trial of about a decade. In another, no more than two per cent of school-leavers in a group of rural schools, teaching rural science, were found to go back voluntarily to farming. In another, a very large and populous country, eight years after the introduction of agriculture as an examinable subject in the School Certificate examination only eleven candidates entered for the paper. In another, the distinct curriculum of rural teachers' training colleges has been

abandoned. One could go on ... Parent want their children above all to get qualifications ... As for practical activities, such as the school garden – pupils work in it occasionally and as a labour gang, which makes them hate gardening.[28b]

In Nigeria, as in several developing countries, there has been a significant shift in emphasis in science away from 'rural science' to the 'process approach' – centred round the characteristic modes of thinking and working in science.

By way of a compromise Griffiths advocates supplementing the existing school curricula by introducing skills and techniques particularly relevant to a rural environment.

There are, for example, the simple skills that would be of value in a farmer's daily life – reading instructions, writing for advice, keeping records, calculating yields of local crops. It would not need any radical change in the curriculum (which would require a major reform) to introduce into the upper classes some training in skills of this type. As a first step it would be wise to scrutinise the content of books used by the children and the 'schemes of work' drawn up by teachers. If, as is likely, these are found to have little reference to rural life and its practical activities, it should be possible, without scrapping existing books and schemes to introduce supplementary material more closely related to the needs of the community around the school ...

With poorly educated and often untrained teachers it is little use expecting brief notes or sketchy outlines to be effective. The material must be worked out in detail for them by educationists experienced in the work of the primary school, and they must be taken through it, step by step, in short courses. The more this supplementary material can be made specific to a locality – perhaps with the help of local development officers – the more chance there is that it will be taught with a sense of realism and not treated as an academic exercise.[28c]

The Unesco pamphlet *Education in a Rural Environment* argues that what matters is not so much whether or not to give a rural or agricultural slant to education but rather to give the pupils an adequate background so that they can fit into the community and environment irrespective of whether this is going to be rural or urban, agricultural or industrial.

This was the policy adopted in the Bunumbu Community Teachers' College in Sierra Leone. The College produced a curriculum for a six year environmentally based course, but one that took into consideration the needs of all children in the country, rural and urban.

The planners argued that there should not be different curricula for town and country children. Instead that there should be a common curriculum for all children which stressed the realities of the social and economic life of Sierra Leone and which led to an appreciation of the skills needed for successful farming and a ready acceptance of manual work in town or country as an honourable way of life.

The aim of the College is to train 'community teachers' who, in turn, would teach children and adults.

Linked with the Teachers' College were twenty pilot schools which in turn were to become community centres and which mobilised the resources not only of the school teachers but of other 'teachers' within the community such as the Agricultural Officer, local craftsmen and parents. These schools were built by self help. To ensure their full co-operation in the project the headmasters of these pilot schools were given a one year training course at the College.

Migration to the towns

We must not educate people out of the ground which nourishes them.

One of the big problems facing developing countries is the drift to the towns, the escape of its young people to the bright city lights. And if, as often happens, the things that make for a 'better', more comfortable life – like ready supplies of water, electric light, proper sanitation, educational and medical facilities, prospects for employment etc. – are to be found more in the towns and cities, one can hardly blame the young people for deserting their rural homes and countryside.

As Professor Arthur Lewis has aptly pointed out: 'as long as we tax farmers in order to build tarmac roads, secondary schools, and hospitals not in the rural areas, but in towns, a young man who leaves school and goes back to the rural areas ought to have his head examined.'

The world's cities occupy only two per cent of the land. Yet fifty to sixty per cent of the population are found in them. In developing countries this percentage is even higher. This migration to the towns and cities has brought with it all the problems of overcrowding – disease, unemployment, crime.

In Kenya, it is estimated that one eighth of the urban population are frustrated job-seekers. The Kericho Conference of 1966 concerned itself with finding solutions, both educational and social, to the problems arising out of such massive unemployment. One attempt at a solution was the *village polytechnic*' movement. Primary school leavers, instead of being left to join the scrap-heap of urban unemployed, were to be absorbed into vocational training institutions in their own rural communities – village polytechnics.

In essence, the village polytechnic is an attempt to provide an education/training for young people in the rural and depressed rural/urban areas of Kenya. The aim of the polytechnic movement is education for self-employment, whether it be from improved methods of keeping bees or from making smokeless cookers. It was assumed parents and young people would want some academic education as well as practical training and so many village polytechnics attempt to provide this, thus balancing practical work with academic/theoretical studies. In nearly every case polytechnics are also developing courses which add elements of commercial training and agriculture to basic skill training.

Village polytechnics teach craft and technical skills to a modest level, using modest equipment in a modest environment. Most courses last for two years and are selected by the polytechnic on the basis of local need: no electricians are trained, for example, if a village is still years away from electrification. Students are generally expected to become self-employed within their community once they leave. Funds are raised locally for building materials and materials for courses are often purchased out of money earned by students working under contract to local firms.

The Kingari polytechnic, twenty miles north of Nairobi, runs classes in carpentry, metalwork, dressmaking and tailoring, shoe-making, masonry and typing and shorthand. All students also have to work in the *shamba*, the vegetable garden. The first classrooms were mud and wattle, built by the community. Now new classrooms are being added, constructed by the masonry students as part of their training programme. The principal describes how two of his pupils are now partners in their

31

own business, making water tanks, chicken feeders, watering-cans, house guttering, charcoal stoves and other items. The village polytechnic committee provided a loan of £150 to get them started. They paid it back within ten months, and are now able to save about £14 a month from their profits.

The village polytechnic graduates have proved that most young people who have a job that is paying well do not want to go to town. The key to the whole situation is employment. So long as young people have work and money enough for a decent living, they prefer to stay at home.

With a view to providing vocational training to those leaving school yet unable to find employment – a situation all too common in developing countries – a programme of training, teaching, and productive work was inaugurated in Botswana in 1963. This has come to be known as the Brigade Movement. In 1965 a group of twenty-five primary school leavers was recruited into the first Builders' Brigade at Swaneng. The three-year programme in instruction consisted of three elements: productive work and 'on-the-job' training; classroom instruction in vocational subjects; and classroom instruction in academic subjects. The brigade trainees received five hours each week of technical theory instruction in the classroom and the same amount of academic instruction, all the syllabuses being vocationally oriented. The rest of the working time – about thirty hours – was spent 'on-the-job'. The work produced by the trainees is sold and the proceeds used to defray the cost of their subsistence and instruction. The brigade is thus something of a mixture of training establishment, educational institute and economic enterprise. The brigade could be described as an institution offering primary school leavers a worthwhile technical or vocational training in such a way as to cover the recurrent costs of that training.

The builders' brigade was followed by a carpenters' brigade – engaged in making school desks, lockers etc. Today there are well over two dozen brigades in several centres, undergoing training in seven different crafts.

Rural transformation

If young people are to be encouraged not to leave their village communities then their rural life must be made more attractive.

The government must take a lead in this. But the local community itself can do much to improve its own conditions of life.

In many countries the emphasis now is on pupils acquiring competencies that not only might be useful later, but can be used right now. The students' learning activities are expected to be of direct and immediate social use to the communities in which they live. The take-off point is not some hypothetical problem of mere academic concern, but the solution of some real life (often survival) problem now.

A curriculum for rural transformation

For rural transformation at a village level one first needs to gather data at that level. From the data one then identifies the problems. These problems can then be used to develop a curriculum. It is essential to involve the active co-operation and participation of the community, the school and other agencies in this exercise.

Here are some examples of how real life community problems can be used as learning resources for the school curricula.[79b]

A Data ⟶	Problems ⟶	Implications for the curriculum
1 **Area 100 acres** Uncultivated land 25 acres. Elevation high. Suffers from frequent drought.	Lack of water for irrigation	What kind of irrigation technique or system may be taught and also constructed by the students?
2 **Occupations** Agriculture 11% Labour 04% Trade 08% Government Service 07% Private Sector 05% Masons and carpenters 02% Others 04% Unemployed 59%	Large unskilled labour force. Insufficient employment opportunities. Lack of drive to work among the people.	What employable skills may be taught in school? What learning would enable the students to be self-employed? What educational programme would change the people's attitudes towards work? What school products are marketable? What lessons would launch students into co-operative enterprises and initiate cottage industries?

A Data →	Problems →	Implications for the curriculum
3 Per-capita income 60.00 per month	Low production from land.	How may students help increase family income? How may the yield of the land be increased? What goods can be produced from the community resources? What natural resources of the community have not been adequately exploited? What other products may be raised considering the soil and climate of the village?
4 Health No. of houses without toilets 21 No. of houses with temporary pit toilets 17	Epidemics/ anaemia/bowel diseases.	What sanitary toilets may be constructed by the students within the income of the family? What toilet attitudes, habits and practices may be incorporated in the curriculum?

B Data from a village health and nutrition survey (illustrating how the data may be used to identify curriculum development problems.)

1 Breeding places for mosquitoes and flies are found in more than 65% of the houses surveyed. Knowledge and attitudes leading to the eradication of these breeding places should be included in the curriculum.

2 There is no proper disposal of garbage and refuse in some 65% of the households. The importance of proper disposal, the harm resulting from allowing refuse to accumulate should also be included in the curriculum.

3 Environmental pollution caused by animals and the resulting health problems should be given a place in the curriculum.

4 Adequate knowledge and healthy attitudes leading to better sanitary and toilet habits should be conveyed through the curriculum.

5 Tooth decay and Mosaic skin are some of the frequent

diseases prevalent in the sample surveyed. The curriculum should impart the necessary knowledge, attitudes and skills that could assist in eradicating these diseases.

6 The curriculum should give adequate emphasis to the development of healthy habits in oral hygiene.

Specifying rural transformation in this manner has many advantages. It leads to the identification of very concrete objectives. It indicates action which needs to be taken by different agencies. It indicates the different educational programmes which may be required for the various groupings of people by age or sex (children, adults, women, etc.). It also often indicates how inadequate the formal education system is in ensuring certain aspects of rural transformation.

The following Curriculum for Development gives an example of the kind of work which could be included in a curriculum for rural transformation.[79b]

Broad areas to be covered by a curriculum for rural transformation

Environmental sanitation
  Eradication of fly and mosquito breeding places
  Disposal of garbage and refuse
  Ventilation of houses
Environmental pollution
  Water pollution
  Air pollution
  Pollution by animals
Personal hygiene
  Health habits
  Oral hygiene
  Sanitary and toilet habits
Community welfare programme
  Problems of irrigation
  Purification of drinking water
  Problem of unemployment/under-employment
  Problem of deforestation
Food production and utilization
  Food production
  Food storage
  Food preservation
  Judicious planning and consumption of meals

Functional literacy

In 1964 Unesco launched the concept of 'functional literacy' as a method of training for development. This is not to be confused with just cracking the codes of reading and writing. Teaching reading and writing just for the sake of literacy is absurd, as evidenced by the failure of the many night classes and social education programmes. It has to be linked with real life situations.

Functional literacy differs from so-called traditional literacy in that instead of being an isolated operation it is specifically geared to economic and social objectives. The learning of reading, writing and counting is integrated with occupational, vocational training. It is also selective in that it is intended for those groups which, on becoming literate, would make the most effective contribution to development and progress. The teaching methods and materials are closely associated with the needs of the environment, for example: the adoption of new cultivation techniques, the introduction of new crop varieties; production and marketing (crops, self-management, agricultural credit facilities, co-operatives); technological adaptation in industry; nutrition, hygiene, child-care for women. In this way the learner is not a 'pupil' but a participant in a global training strategy, a useful productive member of the community. As a result of one such functional literacy project Tanzania hoped that the whole population of the United Republic would be functionally literate by 1976.

An excellent project, utilising part of the military budget and facilities, was the *Literacy Army* established by Iran. After undergoing a four-month training course in military barracks, all secondary school graduates had to teach for fourteen months each in rural schools, especially in remote villages. These literacy corpsmen were responsible for leading the villagers in various social and developmental activities and for the teaching of children and adults. Their major responsibility was the establishment of elementary schools and the improvement of rural community living.

Iran has also shown commendable enterprise in its efforts to bring education to people who would otherwise be left out, namely, people living in remote, isolated areas, and desert nomads. This it has done by means of peripatetic teachers and mobile schools, which move with the migratory tribes.

Summary

1 *A rural bias to education?* In predominantly agricultural countries the school curriculum should at least reflect the importance of agriculture.

Many poor parents look askance at schemes for an 'agricultural' bias to education: they want their children to escape from the land, from the hardships of rural life.

As against a 'separate' system of rural education, a compromise is to supplement the existing school curricula by introducing skills and techniques relevant to a rural environment.

What matters most is to give all pupils an education that will fit them to their communities and environment, irrespective of whether this is going to be rural or non-rural, agricultural or industrial.

2 *Migration to the towns* Young people desert their rural homes and drift to the towns because the amenities (water, electricity, sanitation, educational and medical facilities, prospects for employment, etc.) are better there. This migration brings with it problems of over-crowding, e.g. disease, unemployment, crime.

These problems are being overcome by such strategies as 'village polytechnics', the 'Brigade Movement', etc.

The key to the problem of migration to the towns is employment. If young people have work and money enough for a decent living they will stay at home.

3 *Rural transformation* If young people are not to leave their village communities, then rural life must be made more attractive.

The real-life (often survival) problems of rural communities can be made the basis of many worthwhile school activities.

4 *Functional literacy* Teaching reading and writing just for the sake of literacy is fruitless. It should be linked to real life situations, to development.

Questions

1   Is there a rural/agriculture bias to the curriculum in your schools **a)** at the primary level? **b)** at the secondary level?
2   Do you think having a rural/agriculture bias in your schools is proving of benefit – or would prove beneficial – to your country and its people? In what ways?

3   What do you consider are the main factors against having an agriculture/rural bias to the education in your schools?
4   Do you consider there should be any agriculture/rural bias to the school curriculum? Explain.
5   What are some of the alternative suggestions to having a 'separate' system of rural education in the schools?
6   Does your country suffer from what is called 'the drift to the towns'? What are the disadvantages – and advantages, if any, – caused by such drift?
7   Do you feel such migration to the towns should be stopped? Explain why. How would you prevent such migration?
8   Mention some of the major problems caused by over-crowding in some of your big towns or cities. How can these be overcome or lessened?
9   In what ways is your government trying to make life more attractive for people living in the rural areas?
10 Describe one or two significant ways in which local communities themselves are attempting to improve the conditions under which they live.
11 Does your country suffer from the problem of youth unemployment? What are the main causes of this? How can unemployment among young people be lessened in your country?
12 Describe a few real-life problems you are aware of which could be included in the school curriculum.
13 Describe what your country is doing to eradicate illiteracy. How could these efforts be made more effective?

5 'Education for All' – Implications for the Curriculum

Everyone has the right to education. Education shall be free, at least in the elementary and fundamental stages. Elementary education shall be compulsory. Technical and professional education shall be made generally available and higher education shall be equally accessible to all on the basis of merit.

(Universal Declaration of Human Rights Article 26.)

Basic education is the primary object of any plan of development. Indeed, hunger for education is no less than hunger for food; an illiterate is a person with an under-nourished mind.

(Pope Pius XII. Encyclical 'Populorum Progressio'.)

Universal Primary Education

The initial precept of virtually all educational systems is that each child should receive full-time instruction in school. In the 1950s many newly-independent countries embarked on programmes of Universal Primary Education. The main response of educational systems in developing countries to the challenging circumstances arising after their independence was to expand themselves as rapidly as possible – by and large in the old image – in a desperate effort to keep up with expanding demand. Thus most nations have followed a strategy of linear expansion of their existing educational systems, aimed at enrolling a larger number and proportion of the youth population at each level.

And the numerical results achieved have been dramatic. In the great majority of nations gross enrolments have more than doubled at every level in the past ten to fifteen years. But this dramatic increase in enrolments has brought with it huge problems. As Coombs points out, the figures hide: 'the vast social waste and human tragedy in the high rate of drop-outs and failures ... and the large number of costly 'repeaters', and, most important, they say nothing about the nature, quality and usefulness of the education received'.[17]

This typical response to the overwhelming pressure of demand for education led to scarce resources – classrooms, teachers, books etc. – being spread thinner and thinner over more and more students, until in many instances education became a caricature of itself and a travesty. Expansion was often so rapid that unqualified teachers were frequently far more numerous than qualified or upgraded ones.

Bhuntin Attagara of Thailand argues forcibly for quality rather than seemingly impressive statistics.

> Yet in so many developing countries a disproportionate amount of effort and funds are expended to give more children more years of irrelevant and inefficient schooling at the expense of upgrading the teaching staff, the content and method of instruction, teaching materials and educational leadership. Expanding quantity with only a corresponding marginal return of quality is a little bit like adding zeros after the decimal point – the number may look impressive, but it does not add up to very much.[5a]

As Coombs points out: '*more* education has come to mean *worse* education. The youngsters are not getting as good an education as they used to ... as reflected, for example, in the high proportion of poorly qualified teachers, bulging enrolments, leading to severely over-crowded classrooms, and the widespread shortage of textbooks and other teaching materials.'[17]

The open-door strategy of education, letting everyone in who wishes, allowing them to stay for as long as they like and go as far as they please, may satisfy social demand and conscience. At least, it may appear to do so, but if done in a hurry it leads to a drop in quality, resulting in storms of protests at high drop-out rates, poor quality and waste of public resources.

Despite the considerable efforts made throughout the Third

World towards giving all people at least a primary education, to bring millions of young people to a place in the sun, more and more millions are condemned each year to do without it. Today, only half the world's population ever attends school.

Bhuntin Attagara describes the position of Thailand.

Providing universal elementary education alone, say for six or seven years, has proved for many of us to be a quantitative exercise in futility. Promises are made and broken, new target dates replace solemnly pledged old ones, new headlines are concocted probably for people with poor memories, and all the while birth rates soar and so do educational budgets in their futile and doomed attempt to keep the percentage of children in school from dropping – even though simple statistics clearly indicate that the mass of children out of school continues to rise.[5a]

This inability to achieve anything like universal primary education is due to many factors – the population explosion, paucity of resources and galloping costs.

Strategies for economy

The Report of the Uganda Education Commission, 1964, poses the seemingly insoluble question: 'When over half the nation is illiterate and the people clamour for education; when teachers are in short supply and inadequately trained; when government and industry demand trained recruits; when unemployment is widespread and increasing; when the country is poor, what policy should the government pursue?'

All developing countries, despite their richness in ideas, have one thing in common in their poverty, in inadequate resources for the requirements of education both in terms of money and men.

When resources are limited and the competing demands for these are many, one tries to get the best value for one's money. This has led to a search for new strategies in education.

1 Cutting down the curriculum to 'life skills' only
Among the strategies to provide quality primary education at a significantly lower cost, one solution explored was that of paring down the normal curriculum to 'life skills' only – to what is relevant and absolutely essential.

41

2   Reduction in the length of schooling

There are many strategies one can use to secure the same or better education with no increase in time or costs. Tests carried out in the Soviet Union on half a million pupils have shown that the normal four year period of primary education can be reduced to three years without any loss of standards. Research on how young children learn, together with enlightened teaching methods, has enabled the time of schooling to be reduced without any fall in achievement.

Some countries, unable to provide more schools, have experimented with the idea of converting the four year primary school course to a two year course, thus enabling double the number of children to be taught. Whilst it may be possible in a country like the U.S.S.R. to reduce the years of primary schooling from four to three, many educationists believe that there is a critical mass of educational exposure below which the effects of any schooling soon dissipate away. Professor Capelle, who was closely involved with education in Africa over a period of twenty years, states: 'I do not believe, from my experience in Africa, that it is possible to go lower than a four year period of schooling for children.'[10a]

Professor Elvin is of the same view: 'There is a good deal of evidence that a primary education of a very short time – say one year – is likely to be wasted effort . . . For my part I would sooner have half the number of primary schools with four years than twice the number with two. But the limits change as you go up, and I would say I would sooner have all the schools for four years than half the schools for eight years.'[10b]

India, faced with a vast mass of illiterate children, attempted to achieve functional literacy in less than four years. But this was not successful. Dawood reports: 'We have tried to educate children within a period of one or two years, and we find that they lapse into illiteracy. We have come to the conclusion – I wish it was otherwise – that in less than four years it would not be possible for the education that you impart to become effective. If it could be otherwise, probably the problem of India could be solved more easily.'[10c]

However, one should bear in mind the observation of Professor Torsten Husén, of Stockholm Teacher College, that there is no linear relationship between the number of years of schooling and the outcome. Four years does not pay off twice as much as two.

On the other hand, if you have four years of bad teaching, it is worse than two years of bad teaching, because it discourages motivation among other things.

Husén gives an example from his native Sweden to show that it is not the number of years of schooling that is critical; it is the quality of the schooling that matters.

> In my own childhood experiences in sparsely populated areas in my country, the children went to school every second year. While they had six years of compulsory elementary schooling, they actually went to school only three years – every second year from the age of 7 up to the age of 13. This paid off almost as much as if they had had full-time schooling from the age of 7 up to 13. I bring this to notice because the over-all assumption that we as educators often have is that learning does not take place without teaching. Or to express it in a more operational way, there is an assumption that nothing happens in the brains of our students if there is not a person sitting behind a desk exposing them to a verbal stimulus. This is one of the false assumptions upon which much of what is happening in our schools and universities is based.[10d]

One of the great heresies of our time is that someone who really wants to learn can only do so in a conventional classroom, sitting still before a teacher and a blackboard. What children learn in school is a more important measure than the time they spend in class. This being so, as Hawes argues, 'a shortened school day or some version of shift work, in reasonable conditions, may prove more profitable to a longer one in conditions where learning is severely hampered' due to over-crowding, etc.[33a]

This is what Botswana and Lesotho are doing. Faced with a lack of buildings and staff they have recognised 'short time' attendance as preferable to over-crowded classes. Thus in many schools the lower classes operate on half-sessions, the groups attending for two and a half hours a day instead of five hours. In this way the children enjoy more space and equipment and attention from the teacher.

3 The shift system
This is another way of getting more children into school without building additional schools. In the *double-shift* system children spend half the time in school and then another group of children takes their place. Thus, in Ghana for instance, the first shift attends school from 7.20 a.m. to noon; the second shift lasts from

12.20 to 5 p.m. By thus 'staggering' the attendance of the pupils the teacher is able to spread his services to double the number of children. In metropolitan Kano in Nigeria, the second shift begins from 1 p.m. and the children follow the same curriculum but with a different set of teachers. But this means, of course, an increase in the number of teachers.

In the Philippines, where there has been a rapid increase in population, attempts are being made to reduce costs by using an 'in-school-out-of-school' programme. The pupils are in school one week, carrying out the normal school programme. The next week they spend out of school and learn from kits which are sequenced self-learning tasks based on the community. During the week when one group is out of school another group is in school.

Many schools in developing countries, especially in the more remote areas, are one-teacher schools. Several strategies exist for coping more efficiently in such a situation. One method is to reduce the number of grades the teacher has to handle at the same time by dividing the grades into two shifts. Another strategy is to combine different grades in different subjects in such a way as to lighten the teacher's burden yet to use his time to the best advantage. This is called *plural-class* teaching. Another strategy is the old monitorial system, where the more able pupils of the senior grades are trained as monitors and then do some teaching in the junior grades under the teacher's supervision.

One might ask why so much attention is devoted in this book to matters such as the length of time children spend in school etc. These are logistical problems: how do they concern the curriculum? Any well-constructed curriculum should take cognisance of such logistical considerations. Whether the children will be in school for two or three or four years or longer, whether they will be in school in the mornings or afternoons, their ages, the speed with which they should be able to cope with content at their different stages of development, and so on, are all matters which should be reflected in the design and construction of an appropriate curriculum.

Another look at U.P.E. – from quantity to quality

In many developing countries today the concern is not so much with the quantity of education as with quality. Many countries

44

are paying close attention not just to how many children are in school, but to what is going on in the schools. Despite the difficulty of limiting universal free primary education and cheaper secondary education, countries are now planning for realistic targets that will still safeguard quality.

Nepal, for example, planned to have only sixty-four per cent of its primary school-age children in school in 1976. The planners put in a significant amount of money for quality education. Similarly, they put a ceiling on the percentage of pupils in each cycle of education and developed an achievable educational enrolment pyramid.

Selection for secondary and higher education

Many are called but few are chosen.

At the opposite extreme from the 'wide-open' system is the policy whereby everyone (if it can be afforded) is given a chance for primary education, but a severely selective process limits who goes on from there. In this way, elementary education serves to screen the academically bright, the students in secondary and higher education can be held down to a manageable number, and quality can be more readily maintained. The strategy is designed to produce an 'educated elite' which will provide society with its essential leadership.

This is what Tanzania is doing. The President justifies such a policy in his *Education for Self-Reliance*:

> The implication of this is that the education given in our primary schools must be a complete education in itself. It must not continue to be simply a preparation for secondary school ... For in Tanzania the only true justification for secondary education is that it is needed by the few for service to the many ... Further education for a selected few must be education for service to the many. There can be no other justification for taxing the many to give education to only a few.[61]

Such selection for secondary schooling is usually done by means of 'objective' tests of ability, by examinations, etc.

But, despite all attempts to make the selective system as fair and democratic as possible, in actual practice many other factors intervene such as class, religion, income, race and political affiliation. Factors such as the socio-economic and cultural background, the motivation of parents and of children, are often more important than pedagogical factors in determining the selection. The selection procedures invariably tilt the scales on the side of children with a good vocabulary and a culturally rich environment.

Equality of opportunity in education

Dawood describes how equality of opportunity in education varies, in India, for example; 'between one state and another, between several districts in the same state, and what is more important, between one sex and another. The rate of literacy and primary education among women is very, very low. In backward areas, because of social customs such as the purdah system, women do not come into schools.'[10e]

Equalization of educational opportunity has been one of the major objectives of successive Five Year Plans of the Government of India, and considerable headway in this direction has been made through programmes of expansion of educational facilities at all levels of education. The 'scheduled castes', about fourteen per cent of the total population of India, formerly occupied the lowest rungs of Hindu society and were regarded as 'untouchables' (Harijans). However, there has been considerable improvement in their situation in the last twenty-five years. Enrolments from these castes have increased at all stages in education at a much faster rate than for the country as a whole so that the gap between them and other communities is being rapidly bridged.

With a view to equalizing educational opportunity twenty per cent of places at Jawarhalal Nehru University, Delhi, are reserved for scheduled castes and tribes. Furthermore, in the entrance examination twenty per cent marks are awarded for 'deprivation' to disadvantaged students from backward and isolated areas or from very low income homes. Thus, rich, well-educated candidates from urban centres can only score a maximum of eighty per cent.

Jamaica has also adopted a policy of positive discrimination towards schools in the more inaccessible rural areas.

Non-formal (out-of-school) education

> In developing countries, the lost leaders of tomorrow are the
> bright and ambitious youngsters of today, who, by accident
> of birth and place, are deprived of access to the stuff of
> learning in any digestible form.[16a]

Non-formal education, in the form of 'adult education', 'continuing education', 'on-the-job training', 'accelerated training', 'farmer or work training', 'extension services', or some such form of education, provides the chance to the 'lost leaders of tomorrow' to find themselves.

Correspondence education, radio and television, are also all being used effectively to help give everyone the opportunity to reap the benefits of education.

When speaking of non-formal education one should not forget the education of the home. The largest and most effective kind of non-formal education takes place where children learn skills from parents and neighbours. Skills involving simple science and technology like ploughing, irrigation management, blacksmithing, carpentry and even shop management are all effectively learned in a very practical way within the family. The importance of this education cannot be stressed too much.

All countries, no matter how poor, can capitalise on non-formal education.

Basic education for all

Most developing countries are involved in the seemingly unavailing struggle to provide education for more and more children and also at the same time provide some form of education for the large numbers of adults who have received no education at all. Today there are still 870 million adult illiterates in the world; the world illiteracy rate is 20 per cent. One way of co-ordinating the dual obligation of getting children into schools and providing programmes for adults has been the notion of basic education.

> The starting-point for all planning should be to provide basic
> education for all, regardless of age or sex. This should not be
> taken to mean a specified number of years of schooling but

rather a specified level of knowledge and aptitudes, an awareness of social realities and a specific level of ability in the individual to make use of the manifold sources of knowledge offered by society. This level would not be the same for a child as for an adult. Nor would it be static; it would rise as the country becomes more 'developed'.[89a]

In the Bunumbu Project in Sierra Leone, referred to in Chapter 4, teachers are trained to provide both children and adults with basic education. Central to the thinking of this Project is the concept of community centres linked to schools. The Bunumbu Community Teachers' College has been developed not only as an education centre but also as a community centre for the area.

The concept of basic education is not a new one. It was an alternative form of schooling designed by Mahatma Gandhi, whereby peasants in the rural communities could transform their societies.

Hawes interprets basic education as follows.

Basic education is an idea and not a system.
It is not conceived as three years, four years or six years, but rather as a set of basic skills, knowledge and attitudes which will enable learners to take charge of their own lives and set them free to learn further.

Basic education involves the acceptance of different paths to learning towards its goals.
Hence different structures, contents and educational materials can be used. To apply this concept to older adults is possible. It is, however, most profitable to consider basic education in relation to a) children in formal primary schools, b) children, youth and young adults following alternative paths towards the same general goals. Such paths would include accelerated patterns of formal schooling for older children as well as many varieties of part-time and non-formal education. Implicit in the concept of alternatives is the idea that there is a certain basic education 'core curriculum' which may be covered in a number of alternative ways.

Basic education is very basic.
It relates to situations as they are, to the 'minimum survival needs' of a majority of learners, many of whom are studying in difficult conditions.

*Basic education is not to be considered as terminal in con-
trast to some other form of education which leads to further
study, and not as rural in contrast to urban education.*
On the contrary, it must be thought of as providing the
maximum degree of mobility for the learner to meet changing
situations and to continue his education to the best of his abilities and opportunity. Provision of basic education should open
doors for learners rather than close them.
*Basic education must be conceived in the context of
partnership . . .*
between various educational agencies e.g. the family, the
school, non-formal education, the community.[36a]

An attempt to put the concept of basic education into practice
is the Kwamsisi Community School Project, near Korogwe, in
north-east Tanzania. At the start an assessment was made of the
developmental needs of the village. This was followed by determining the learning requirements of various groups – the school
children, the adolescents and the adults – to meet these developmental needs. Specific curricula and programmes, along with
appropriate learning materials, were then designed for the differing learning needs of the different groups. The objectives of
the Project were to implement the policies set out in the Arusha
Declaration and in *Education for Self-Reliance.* These objectives
are:

1   The development of literacy and numeracy.
2   The development of social citizenry with particular emphasis
on:
a)   self-reliance;
b)   social and human equality;
c)   skills, values and attitudes necessary for good health, hard
work and better life in the Ujamaa village.

As in the Bunumbu Project there is a conscious attempt to
achieve the closest integration between school and community
education. The work of the school and of the community as reflected in the day care centre, the carpentry workshop, the dispen-
sary, the experimental projects in poultry-keeping and in tobacco
growing, the functional literacy programme, etc. are seen as
complementary to one another. Persons with special skills in the
services mentioned above teach the skills in the school; the school
teacher reciprocates by teaching the adults in the community.

Similar 'community learning systems' or 'community learning centres' have been established in many parts of Tanzania – and also in other parts of Africa, e.g. the Namutamba Project in Uganda, the Ipar Project in Buea in Cameroon and many others.

This new concept of basic functional education stresses health and nutrition, the development of employable skills and rural development. Science, as an integral part of this education, focuses on preparing the learner to deal with real problems, in particular those brought about by the impact of technology on the physical, cultural and socio-economic environments.

Lifelong education

Prominent in education discussions and proposals today is the notion of lifelong education. There is nothing new in the idea of continuity of the educational process. But the concept today means more than just the practice of adult education, usually in the form of evening classes. The traditional pedagogy and psychology that told us that the capacity to learn was limited largely to youth, that old horses are fit only for putting out to pasture, has been shown to be wrong. We keep on learning all our lives. The concept of lifelong education thus rejects the view of a formal schooling which occurs once and only once in a person's lifetime.

The Education Planning Commission of Alberta Province, Canada, has centred its education reforms on the notion of lifelong education. It states why.

We believe that the school-dominated, classroom-centred, full-time teacher oriented, eight hours, eight or ten-month system is an expensive one, and apart from the demands of further population increases, very little additional investment should be placed in this form of education ... Society requires the acceptance of the belief that education is life and life is education; the belief that people will spend periods throughout their lives in some structured learning experience.

In 1972, the Faure report *Learning to Be* crystallised certain educational axioms that were to pave the way for the concept of lifelong education. These have been summarised by Hawes as follows:

50

1   that schooling is just a part of education;
2   that education cannot be conceived of as taking place at certain ages, stages, times and places. It is always unfinished business;
3   that educational opportunities formal and non-formal must relate to each other both horizontally (e.g. school, home, mosque, media, work experience) and vertically throughout the different stages of a learner's life;
4   that there are many paths to learning, no one path being better or worse than another, only more efficient or more appropriate;
5   that methods, materials and delivery systems must also vary to suit purposes and means available.[36b]

Slowly the concept of primary or elementary education is giving way to that of a basic cycle of education of flexible duration intended to provide enrichment for life.

In many countries of Africa, Asia and Latin America the demand is growing for a form of basic education for the masses as a first phase in lifelong education.

The authors of *Learning to Be* propose lifelong education as the master concept for educational policies in the years to come both for developed and developing countries.

Many countries have already begun to implement such a policy. The Government of Indonesia has taken the concept of lifelong education as a master concept in reorganizing and reforming its educational system. We saw in an earlier chapter how the 'village polytechnics' of Kenya are training young people in the rural areas not only to acquire skills to transform them from 'job-seekers' into 'job-makers' but also to face the changes they will meet in the course of their lifetimes. The Government of Nigeria, in its National Policy on Education, has decreed that 'lifelong education will be the basis for the nation's educational policies'.[60]

The following quotation from Coombs applies to all changing societies, developed or developing.

Lifelong education is essential in a rapidly progressing and changing society for three primary reasons: 1 to ensure the employment mobility of individuals, and to make unemployable 'drop-outs' of the past employable; 2 to keep already well-trained people abreast of new knowledge and technologies essential to their continued high productivity in their respective

51

fields; and 3 to improve the quality and satisfaction of individual lives through culturally enriching their expanding leisure time. In this perspective, the continuing education of teachers at all levels, is of special strategic significance; if they fail to keep up with the frontiers of knowledge they will be giving yesterday's education to tomorrow's citizens.[16b]

Summary
1 *Universal Primary Education (U.P.E.)* Everyone has a basic right to education. Most developing countries have followed a policy of linear expansion of their education systems and have achieved impressive results.

But this dramatic expansion has led to scarce resources – class-rooms, teachers, books ·etc. – being spread thinner and thinner over more and more students, leading to a fall in the quality of education. The population explosion, inadequate resources and galloping costs have compounded the problems. Half the world's population still goes without education.

2 Strategies for economy
a) paring the curriculum to life skills only, to what is relevant and absolutely essential;
b) reduction in the length of schooling. With enlightened teaching methods the time of schooling can be reduced without any fall in standards. It seems there is a critical mass of four years at least of schooling if the schooling is to be effective. It is not the number of years but the quality of the schooling that matters;
c) the shift system.

3 Countries are now taking another look at U.P.E.: the emphasis is on quality rather than quantity; not just on how many children are in school but what is going on in the schools.

4 Selection for secondary and higher education is usually done by examinations, 'objective' tests of ability, etc. These tests, however, often favour children with good vocabularies and who come from culturally rich environments.

5 Equality of opportunity in education should be a target for all educational systems. Sometimes it is necessary to discriminate positively in favour of disadvantaged groups, e.g. women, children in isolated rural areas etc.

6 Non-formal (out-of-school) education in the form of 'on-the-job' training, adult education, correspondence education,

education by radio/television, etc. can bring education to many who, by accident of where they were born, would be otherwise deprived of it.

7   Basic education implies a set of basic skills, knowledge and attitudes which will enable learners to meet life's changing and challenging situations. It stresses health and nutrition, the development of employable skills and rural development.

8   Life-long education means what it says – that education is a life-long process: we keep on learning all our lives.

Questions

1   To what extent has your country achieved U.P.E. (Universal Primary Education)? What are the factors preventing such achievement?

2   To what extent does your educational system suffer from the problems of a) drop-outs, b) repeaters, c) failures? How is the government trying to reduce these?

3   Has there been a fall in the quality of education resulting from your country increasing enrolments in the schools? Explain.

4   How can a government help to prevent a fall in the quality of education?

5   Should a government go for quality or quantity in its educational system? Give some of the arguments for and against.

6   All countries in the world lack the resources they would like to finance their educational systems. How is your government trying to cope with giving as many children as possible an education with insufficient resources?

7   Describe how an increase in population could adversely affect the quality of education in a country. How could such a fall in quality be prevented?

8   List some of the major 'strategies for economy' in education used by governments.

9   Can you suggest another 'strategy for economy' in education that has not been mentioned in the textbook?

10   Are the 'strategies for economy' in education proving effective in your country? Explain.

11   What procedure does your country use for selecting pupils for secondary and higher education? Does this procedure work

effectively both for the country and for the children in the schools?

12 Is there any lack of equality of educational opportunity in your country? How could this be remedied?

13 What are the main types of non-formal education in your country?

14 In your country do you have anything that resembles the 'basic education' described in the textbook?

15 What steps, if any, are provided for 'life-long education' in your country?

6 Knowledge as a Determinant of Curriculum

Education, whether it be formal or informal, has a purpose. That purpose is to transmit from one generation to the next the accumulated wisdom and knowledge of the society, and to prepare the young people for their future membership of the society and their active participation in its maintenance or development.

(President Nyerere, *Education for Self-Reliance*)

Obviously, the cultural heritage, the knowledge and wisdom accumulated by any society over the years will provide an important source for decisions such as what is to be included in the curriculum. This curriculum, as an instrument of society for educating the young, will naturally reflect the ideals and values, the knowledge and skills, the attitudes, deemed significant by that society.

But this knowledge is vast. It is estimated that knowledge is doubling every ten years (this is not true, unfortunately, of wisdom!). This means that new ways of teaching, learning and understanding must be found if the new generation is not to be submerged intellectually beneath a mountain of facts.

Since one cannot transmit the entire 'repertoire of knowledge' one must make a selection, a listing of priorities deduced from philosophical, sociological, cultural and psychological considerations.

Philosophical criteria for selection of content

Since one cannot teach everything, one must select from the vast stores of knowledge possessed by each nation and society. One must consider philosophical questions such as what knowledge is considered most worthwhile, what are the permanent human qualities one wants to transmit to the younger generation, what is the purpose of education? Different societies will differ in their answers to such questions.

For Professor Paul Hirst one of the primary aims of education is the development of a rational mind. For him knowledge consists of 'forms of thought'. These 'forms of thought', with their distinctive and characteristic logical structures, constitute the distinctive disciplines – or forms (domains) of knowledge – we call 'subjects'. For Hirst knowledge differentiates into seven distinctive forms, namely, mathematics, science, literature, fine arts, history, religion and philosophy.[39]

But Hirst's case for the special characteristics and educational virtues of domains of knowledge or subjects does not mean he is justifying the traditional grammar school curriculum with its separate subjects in water-tight compartments, with its academically oriented teaching. He is not advocating the mere acquiring of pre-digested 'knowledge' from 'authorities'; he emphasises acquiring the forms of thought 'from the inside'; the teaching must be structured into a questioning, inquiring mode; the key concepts and ideas must be utilised for stimulating the mind; the forms must be used creatively and critically.

In his *Realms of Meaning* (1964) P. H. Phenix identifies four principles for the selection and organization of content:

1   The knowledge to be taught/learned must be drawn from the disciplines, from the fields of discipined enquiry.
2   From each discipline or subject the key, seminal ideas representative of that discipline should be chosen.
3   The content is chosen in order to exemplify the characteristic methods of enquiry of the discipline, for example, the 'scientific method'. (Much of the science work in schools is, however, far removed from the spirit of scientific enquiry.)
4   The content, the materials, must stir the imagination.

In Phenix's classification of knowledge, there are six 'realms of meaning', representing the fundamental intellectual achievements of mankind, with their own typical methods, leading ideas and characteristic structures. These are:

1   *symbolics* – language, mathematics;
2   *empirics* – physical, biological and social sciences;

56

3   *aesthetics* – music, art, literature;
4   *synoetics* – 'personal knowledge', i.e. philosophy, psychology;
5   *ethics* – morals;
6   *synoptics* – integrative subjects such as history, religion.[69]

Professor Skilbeck's criteria for choosing and organizing what should form the curriculum, what the learning tasks should be, are[65d]:

1   They must be *meaningful* to the learner, they must connect with his experience;
2   They must be *structured* into a pattern or system, and not be a set of separate, discrete elements;
3   They must be *inviting*, so that the learner is stimulated to hard work;
4   They should be *activity-based*, with the child himself involved in the processes of inquiry and creativity, instead of being a mere spectator on the touch lines.

The knowledge component of the curriculum must be organized so as to provide scope, sequence and integration.

Scope. It is not enough to determine only the content or subject matter that should be covered: the mental powers, the skills, attitudes, values, that should emerge from the learning situations are equally important. It is not enough to learn and know science; one must also appreciate the scientific habit of thinking. It is not enough to know history, but also to appreciate the processes a historian uses. Mastery of content and manipulative skills by themselves are not enough; the mental operations or processes, like understanding the underlying principles, must also be involved. The word scope therefore refers to both content and mental processes.

Sequence refers to the ordering or arrangement of content and accompanying mental powers into a sequence of teaching-learning episodes. Sequential development involves building upon previous experiences. Sequence provides continuity of learning.

Integration. Hilda Taba argues for more than a vertical relationship within subjects; she also emphasises a horizontal relationship between the main areas of knowledge.[81] Integration refers to such relationships between various areas of the curriculum at the same time.

In order to achieve co-ordination between various disciplines and between different levels of a particular discipline the Institute of Education in Dar es Salaam established a system of horizontal and vertical panels. Thus a secondary or teacher training panel (horizontal) would co-ordinate and moderate activities in various disciplines for a particular educational level. A vertical panel in a particular subject would moderate the overall sequential development of that subject. The Institute would co-ordinate the work of the various panels.

For Taba ideas were the basic threads for establishing integrating relationships. She recommends organizing the curriculum around ideas and learner skills rather than subjects and content topics.

Wheeler's criteria[92a] for the selection of subject matter and of learning experiences are like Taba's. He, too, argues for integration, for what he calls:

Pattern – an inter-relatedness of activities and experiences on a vertical plane (within a given subject) and on a horizontal plane (among several subjects).

Balance of breadth (horizontal coverage) **and depth** (vertical coverage). 'A sufficient range of ideas (to ensure breadth) should be chosen which have greatest applicability and greatest power to transfer, and enough time should be spent on each to ensure depth.'

He warns against too wide a coverage leading to superficiality.

Continuity and sequence – the continuous development of basic ideas; a progress from simplified wholes to more complex wholes, which are related logically, scientifically or perceptually.

Certain other criteria for Wheeler are:

Validity Is the knowledge authentic and valid as we near the twenty first century? One consequence of rapidly changing knowledge is the equally rapid obsolescence of subject matter used in schools.

Do the learning experiences actually contribute to the desired outcomes? For example, if initiative is an objective then pupils must be given opportunities for exercising initiative.

Comprehensiveness Do the content and learning experiences provide for a wide range of educational objectives?

Significance Is the content logically central enough to apply to a wide range of problems? In history, for example, it is possible to have a curriculum studded with historic facts. But if the curriculum does not put across the basic ideas, for instance, about historic causation and effect, then the curriculum lacks significance.

Consistency with social realities Change, rapid change, is characteristic of the world we live in. The material and experiences selected must help develop minds which can cope with change. Often what is selected is based too exclusively on what has stood the test of time.

Relevance and applicability to life situations in the present or future.

In many countries much of what is taught is irrelevant to the pupils' backgrounds, needs and aspirations. This is evident still in some of the former colonial territories. Many developing countries have found that the curricula they have inherited are hopelessly irrelevant to the life of their country.

Much of what was taught in the former British colonies was a carbon copy of the system in Britain. In his *New Perspectives In African Education* Professor Fafunwa remarks that: 'Pupils at the secondary school level know more about the complicated physical geography of the British Isles, the remote continents of Australia, North and South America and Asia than the continent of Africa itself'.[23b]

Fortunately, children in the former British colonies are no longer subjected to the details of Henry VIII's amorous adventures. But it was not so very long ago that girls in the former Gilbert and Ellice Islands, located on the Equator, where the temperature seldom drops below 85 degrees, day or night, winter or summer, had to knit pull-overs in order to meet the requirements of the Cambridge Overseas School Certificate Examination.

However, a more enlightened approach is now apparent; content is selected for its relevance and fitness to the emerging needs of students and to the society it is intended to serve.

A good example of relevance in the selection of appropriate teaching-learning topics is provided by this brief extract from the Geography Syllabus for Primary Schools (Standards III–VII) in Tanzania.

Geography Syllabus for Primary Schools (Standards III–VII)

Introduction

The main aim of this syllabus is to implement the needs of Primary Education in Tanzania in relation to our Policy of Ujamaa and Self-Reliance.

Main things to be taught

Topic	
Tanzania Workers	**1 Uses of maps**
	a) The position of Ngorongoro-Region, District, route to Ngorongoro from District Headquarters.
Game Wardens of Ngorongoro-Arusha.	b) The geography of the area along the route from home to Ngorongoro.
	c) The geographical study of Ngorongoro: physical features, rainfall, vegetation of the area in comparison with that of the school's village.
	2 Discussion, use of pictures, diagrams etc.
	a) Types of birds and animals of Ngorongoro.
	b) Animal requirements.
	c) Game Wardens and their studies.
	d) Daily routine (activity) of a Game Warden.
	e) The importance of this National Park (emphasis on tourism and the importance of the tourist industry).
	f) Some study on other National Parks of Tanzania.

A person who has exerted considerable influence in the design and development of curricula is the American psychologist, Jerome S. Bruner. Bruner regards subjects rather as structures of knowledge and inquiry; subjects have not only a content but also a form. As he says: 'Every subject has a structure, a rightness, a beauty. It is this structure that provides the underlying simplicity of things, and it is by learning its nature that we come to appreciate the intrinsic meaning of the subject.'

In his *Theory of Instruction*[13] Bruner argued that the curriculum should be organized around fundamental concepts and relationships. Because, he asserts:

1 Understanding fundamentals makes the subject more comprehensible to the learner; to learn structure is to learn relationships – how things are related.
2 organizing knowledge in terms of principles and ideas facilitates memory. Detail is more easily recalled. Research has

proved that unless detail is placed in a structured framework it is soon forgotten. 'An unconnected set of facts has a pitiably short half-life in memory.'

3   mastery of general principles, understanding something as a specific instance of a more general case, is helpful to 'transfer of learning', to learning in the future, in other contexts.

4   emphasis on fundamentals reduces the gap between 'elementary' and 'advanced' knowledge in a subject. Bruner has shown how eight year olds can be taught the principles of quadratic equations by exploring with wooden blocks and balance beams. Ideas, 'as simple as they are powerful', can be presented progressively on different levels in a 'spiral' curriculum.

A 'spiral' curriculum involves the continual reintroduction – a reiteration or repetition – of more powerful ideas and principles, not simply additively by adding new ideas but qualitatively by presenting the same fundamental ideas, e.g. the concept of 'energy' in science, in different, more complex representations.

Bruner is not so much concerned with the capacity of the child's mind as with unlocking that capacity by the use of appropriate materials and techniques. Bruner starts 'from the child' (i.e. relating things to the child's previous experience) rather than 'from the subjects'. But in order to unlock the child's capabilities, intellectual techniques must be mastered.

Bruner argued that any theory of instruction must be concerned with:

1   the nature of the knowledge to be learned;
2   the nature of the learning process;
3   individual children.

For Bruner a theory of instruction had four major features:

1   predispositions to learning, e.g.
arousing curiosity,
keeping interest alive and the exploration going,
direction – so as to prevent the enquiry from becoming random, the exploration from aimless drifting;
2   the structure and form of knowledge;
3   sequence – the way-in to a subject and its sequential development;
4   re-inforcement or 'feed-back'.

For a long time there was a conflict between those who argued that teaching should stem from the 'logic of the subject matter' and those who argued that learning should be 'psychologised' or 'personalised', i.e. related to the learner's own experience. Bruner resolved the dichotomy of 'nature of subject matter' versus 'nature of learner' by his notion of 'translation' – *the task of instruction is to translate the subject matter's basic ideas, i.e. its structure, into language appropriate to the learner.*

Bruner's views have exerted – and continue to exert – considerable influence on curriculum development.

Bruner's revolutionary hypothesis that any subject can be taught effectively to a pupil of any age in some intellectually honest fashion, if note is taken of the pupil's level of development and if the subject is presented in terms which he can readily grasp, has formed the basis for many new curriculum projects. The Nuffield Mathematics Project has shown that concepts and principles previously only attempted at sixth form level can be tackled in a simple but acceptable form in the primary school. Almost any concept can be understood at different levels. Take the example of respiration. Children of six can think of respiration: breathing in and breathing out, as if the body is acting like a pair of bellows. When they reach ten or eleven, children can look on respiration in a different sense, but it is still intuitive. They know that the motor car burns petrol, and by simple analogy can appreciate that the body burns the gas called oxygen. But it will require formal thinking before they can understand the various exchanges that go on, and the various changes that occur in the blood.

To develop curricular materials based on the 'structure' of a subject involves employing persons who know that structure best – often university professors and even those working on the frontiers of knowledge in that subject. This involvement of university professors and professional scientists in the development and design of curriculum and materials is now a regular feature of most curriculum development programmes.

Sociological/cultural criteria for selection of content

On sociological grounds the knowledge deemed relevant to the curriculum will relate to relevant contemporary issues of society and of the world at large, for example, conservation of resources, disease and malnutrition, overpopulation. As Nyerere and others argue, if we want students to be able to meet important human issues adequately, then such issues themselves must form the stuff of the curriculum.

This idea was developed in the United States in 1957 by Smith, Stanley and Shores who advocated a 'common culture core curriculum' in terms of 'broad social problems and themes of social living'. The existing, somewhat traditional demarcations of 'subjects' were to be used merely as resources in investigating and re-interpreting cultural/societal issues.

A curriculum has to guide and orientate pupils towards the culture in which they will live their lives. This will embrace the customs, values, beliefs, techniques, institutions and patterns of social living, etc. of the society. This does not imply that the cultural map must be a still-life from the past, regimenting the young into passive acceptance of prevailing social customs and mores. The map should signpost the way to the present and to the future, allowing freedom to innovate, to experiment, to create.

In Britain, there are two approaches to the notion of the curriculum as a selection from the culture of a society.

For Raymond Williams the curriculum is cultural selection. A child must be taught:

1   the accepted values and mores of his society;
2   general knowledge and the attitudes appropriate to an educated man;
3   a particular skill, so that he can earn his living and make a contribution to society.

Dennis Lawton argues for selection from the culture of what seems most significant and from the body of knowledge and experiences. Such a selection leads him to five 'cores' of the curriculum, corresponding to Hirst's 'forms of knowledge'. These five areas or cores are:

1   Mathematics;
2   Physical and Biological Science;
3   Humanities and Social Studies (history, geography, classics, social sciences, literature, religion);
4   Expressive arts (music, drama, physical education, painting, pottery);
5   Moral education.[51d]

Often not sufficient attention is given to including the culture, the traditions, of the home, of society, in what goes on in the schools.

E.T. Abiola deplores the increasing dichotomy – 'the great divide' – between the world of home and the world of school. 'One of the greatest calamities involved in the present educational system in Africa is that it is an unfortunate break from the process of cultural development at home. It is almost meaningless to the child who is being educated, and it is taught by those who have little understanding of what should be imparted to the child.'[1]

He goes on to refer to a matter of increasing concern to developing countries, namely, the almost schizophrenic development of children arising from a 'clash of cultures'.

The African school child is in a process of transition from a traditional society, to an assumed westernized mode of living. This process of transition creates problems arising from the clash of cultures, – a clash between a village economy and a monetary one; between an extended family consciousness and a nuclear family one; between a polygamous attitude and a mono-gamous substitute; between comprehensive inclusive living and occupationally oriented existence; between imported secular religion and traditional belief system; between group living with its authority and constraints and a self-oriented existence. These conflict-systems affect parental and societal values and ideals, and through this, the type of socialization processes embarked on at home, at school, and in society at large.

With such conflicting patterns of behaviour and expectations, and with intellectual life cut-off from the rest of living, it is difficult for the adolescent child to know what ideals to serve.

He is very outspoken about the teaching in the schools:

Education at school has been of the mechanical variety ... teachers in particular are commonly ill-trained, rigid in ap-proach and authoritarian in their relationship with their pupils ... Knowing themselves to be inadequately equipped and inse-cure in their status, they are fearful of venturing into the unknown where they might neither be able to cope with un-familiar methods, nor retain the firm control of the class that goes readily with mechanical routine.

Coombs expresses similar sentiments:

In rural areas especially their schools are called upon to launch a child from a static, ancient and impoverished environment into a dazzling new world of modern ideas, outlooks, knowledge and gadgets. At the same time, however, they are cautioned not to alienate the child from his own cultural heritage, or from the practical development needs of his own neighbourhood. How can they meet these diverse and often clashing expectations? To do so would tax the wisdom of the world's finest teachers in its best-endowed schools. But these are not found in rural areas of developing countries.[16c]

International understanding

In a world daily contracting as a result of the revolution in communications, the need for teaching international understanding and multicultural awareness becomes daily greater. At a Conference held in Kansas State University in October 1970, Dr Franklin Parker, Professor of Education, West Virginia University, deplored 'the current neglect of teaching of international understanding.' He went on: 'Frankly, the educational systems of most of the world's nations are notoriously nationalistic and ethnocentric. This is true despite an increasing dialogue of international programmes.'[68]

The Fiji Education Commission Report (1969) stressed the need for international understanding in the curriculum. 'The curriculum must not be parochial. It should be Fiji–orientated in form but universal in value.'[26]

Psychological criteria for selection of content

Decisions about content of courses cannot be taken without careful regard to the abilities and interests for whom they are designed.[39]

When it comes to choosing suitable subject matter and appropriate teaching/learning experiences for the curriculum, regard must be paid to the interests and needs of children; to the special characteristics of children at different ages; to the stages of human development; to factors such as stimulation, maturation, motivation, which bear on intellectual development; to the nature of the learning process; to how knowledge can best be sequenced and organized for efficient learning and teaching; to new ways of knowing and of teaching, and so on. An understanding of both the structure of the academic disciplines and the structure of learning and teaching are essential.

Whilst children's needs and interests will not be used as overall criteria in selecting content, attention will be given to such interests and needs, to their differing abilities and aptitudes by:

1   allowing the details of a course to vary according to the different groups of children or individuals;
2   providing for different learning rates;
3   providing a flexible curriculum, i.e. providing wide and varied learning experiences to cater for individual differences and to whet the wide and varied appetites of children;
4   providing variations in the methods of teaching.

These psychological factors are important enough to warrant a separate chapter and are considered in detail in the next chapter.

Summary
It is estimated that knowledge is doubling every ten years. Since one cannot teach everything, one must select.
1   *Philosophical criteria for selecting and organizing content, the knowledge to be taught, the learning activities to be fostered.* We must decide:
    what knowledge is most worthwhile to pass on?
    from each discipline or subject the key ideas should be chosen;
    the characteristic method of enquiry of the subject should be encouraged (e.g. the 'scientific method').
The knowledge must:
    be meaningful to the learner;
    be relevant to the society in which he will live;
    be structured into a pattern or system;
    be arranged into a sequence of teaching-learning episodes;
    have breadth (inter-connected or integrated with other subject areas) and depth (going to the heart of the matter);
For Bruner subjects have not only a content but also a form or structure. The curriculum should be organized around this

structure, around the fundamental concepts and relationships, because:

a) understanding fundamentals makes the subject more comprehensible to the learner;

b) organizing knowledge in terms of principles and ideas facilitates memory;

c) mastery of general principles is helpful to 'transfers of learning' – learning in some other context.

Ideas can be presented progressively on different levels in a 'spiral' curriculum.

Bruner argued that in teaching we must be concerned with **a)** the nature of the subject to be learned, **b)** the nature of the learning process **c)** the nature of the individual children.

The task of teaching is to translate the basic ideas of the subject, i.e. its structure, into language appropriate to the learner's stage of development.

2 *Sociological/cultural criteria for selection of content* – i.e. relevant, contemporary issues of the society/culture, e.g. disease, malnutrition, conservation of resources, overpopulation, multicultural awareness, international understanding.

3 *Psychological criteria for selection of content* – the needs and interests of children, their development, the nature of the learning process, methods of teaching/learning etc.

The differing needs, interests, aptitudes, capabilities of children can be catered for by:

a) providing variations in courses, i.e. flexible curriculum;

b) providing for different learning rates;

c) providing variations in methods of teaching.

Questions

1 By what criteria would you judge whether a subject or topic should be included in a school curriculum?

2 List what you consider are the eight most important subjects that should be included in any school curriculum. Say why.

3 Are there any subjects in the curriculum which you feel should be excluded? Say why.

4 What does the word 'scope' mean in curriculum development? Give an example.

5 What is meant by 'integration' in curriculum development? Give an example.

6   List some of the topics taught in a particular subject that you feel are 'irrelevant'. Say why.

7   What 'relevant' topics do you feel should be included in the school curriculum? Explain why.

8   Briefly say why Bruner has made an important contribution to education.

9   What is meant by a 'spiral' curriculum? Give an example.

10   Bruner lays great emphasis on the 'structure' of a subject or topic. By reference to one subject or topic illustrate what Bruner means.

11   Bruner has said that any subject can be taught to a pupil of any age in some honest fashion at any level. Do you think he is exaggerating or not?

12   Give one example of a topic which is taught at high school level which is also taught in a simple way in the primary school.

13   Describe any large cultural/societal issues that are taught in your schools.

14   Does the teaching in your schools help to widen the gap between the 'world of home' and the 'world of school'? In what ways can the school help to bridge this gap?

15   Describe anything that is done in the schools to increase international understanding and co-operation.

16   How can you cater for the differing needs, interests and abilities of children in constructing a curriculum?

7 Psychological Factors as Determinants of Curriculum

> Curriculum development must draw on a continuing stream
> of basic research, particularly in the area of learning.[91b]

Theories of human development, theories of learning, the pedagogical principles derived from psychological theories, must all be
considered in determining the curriculum.

Among the earliest influential theories of human development
was that of the famous American philosopher and mathemati-
cian, A.N. Whitehead.[95A] He believed that in the process of
human development all children went through three stages:

a stage of Romance (or make-believe), followed by

a stage of Precision, and finally

a stage of Generalisation.

Jean Piaget's stages of development

The Swiss psychologist, *Jean Piaget*, has gone further in his
attempt to categorise more precisely the stages of human development.

Piaget observed and recorded in minute detail the spontaneous
reactions of many children to a wide variety of situations. From
this he formulated his theories concerning the reasoning of the
child, and the language and mode of thought of the child.

Piaget identified the following stages of *cognitive development*:

1 *The sensori-motor stage* (applicable to children up to two
years of age approximately). No abstract reasoning is possible at
the infant stage. The thoughts of infants are 'intuitive', closely
linked with actual physical action and immediate observation.

The infant is unable to think about or imagine the consequences of an action unless he actually carries it out; he is unable to draw logical conclusions from his activities and experiences.

2 *The pre-operational or pre-conceptual stage* (between two and seven years of age approximately). The child learns to manipulate things mentally, but only objects and materials that can be manipulated concretely. Mental operations develop with active exploration of things in his immediate environment. The child can appreciate the variety of living things and objects around him. He develops the ability to discuss and communicate. He can recognise such common shapes as □, ○, △. He can recognise regularity in patterns. He is able to group things together according to a given criteria, e.g. shape, colour, living or non-living.

3 *The stage of concrete operations* (ages seven to eleven approximately). The child can now perform more varied and powerful mental operations. Problems are solved in a more ordered and quantitative way. He is able to visualise objects from different angles; he can visualise the shape of cross-sections. He can classify living things and non-living materials in different ways.

4 *The stage of formal operations or abstract thinking* (ages eleven to fifteen approximately). The child is now able to think about abstractions; he is no longer tied to the concrete and to the here and now. He is able to use hypothetical reasoning. Abstract logic and mathematics are now at his disposal. He is able to distinguish observations which are pertinent to a solution from those which are not. He is able to undertake 'controlled' experimentation.

All children pass through Piaget's stages of cognitive development in the same order but at a different rate. Each child, in his own way, at his own rate and in his own time and in his own individual style, passes through these stages in the same order. Learning is an individual matter.

The age at which a given stage appears varies from child to child. There are many factors, such as the child's intelligence, his previous learning experience, and his social and cultural background which affect his 'pace'. This means that no two children will be acquiring a concept at exactly the same moment in time. Thus in a classroom it can be imagined that though the majority of children will be within a certain norm, there may be a great deal of variation from child to child. This does not mean that an individual programme is needed for each child. It would seem to imply more *flexibility* in the way in which the curriculum is taught, that is different teaching methods. These teaching methods should allow the child to develop at his own pace within the classroom situation. The idea of smaller groups within the class, the children in each group working together on a specific topic, and even sometimes individual work, is also a possible solution.

This would in many cases entail a modification in the scheduling of the timetable of a school day. It follows that if children are working as a group or as individuals, at their own pace, then they should be given the amount of time they need in order to finish a task, rather than having to leave it uncompleted as the end-of-lesson-bell rings. If this is the case then ultimately the idea of 'the integrated day' should be considered. Such ideas are more feasible at the primary level where the constraints are less. Their application to the secondary level might present certain problems in view of the present type of curricula.

Both pre-service and in-service teacher education would be affected by such changes as they entail providing teachers with experience not only of new methods of teaching but also of different ways of organizing the school day.

Implications for the curriculum

Piaget's theory of cognitive development has very important implications for the curriculum.

Readiness

Each stage of development builds on an earlier one and forms the foundation for the next. Concepts are acquired in sequential hierarchies and therefore certain concepts are fundamental for the acquisition of those that follow. In planning a curriculum, we must take these stages of development of the learner into account. The planning of a curriculum should be considered from the logic of the child rather than the logic of the subject matter.

There is no use 'hurrying up' or 'getting on' with a particular topic or concept (so as to 'finish' some section of the syllabus) until the earlier cognitive stages have first been mastered. Time is the servant, not the master, of the child. You cannot force the child to develop understanding faster than his absorption of the related experiences; he will 'learn' when he is 'ready', that is, when he has reached the appropriate stage of intellectual development.

But one need not accept the situation passively: teachers can stimulate children into readiness – the learning process can be speeded up or slowed down by appropriate or inappropriate learning situations.

This notion of *readiness* is a very important one in curriculum work.

Sequential learning

Linked to the notion of 'readiness' is that of *sequential learning*. This involves awareness of the stages of development, of 'learning hierarchies', through which the learner must pass as he advances from one concept to a more sophisticated one and the corresponding sequencing of the teaching/learning experiences and of the materials and resources used. The task of the teacher is to figure out what the learner already knows and how he reasons so as to ask the right question at the right time so that the learner can build on his own knowledge.

In other words, the object is to select experiences just the right step ahead of the learner to challenge him without frustrating him. In the Piagetian school the teacher does not transmit ready-made knowledge; by guiding the child's experiences he helps the child construct his own knowledge, lets him discover truth by letting the object or experience give the answer. Piaget believed the pupil has to re-invent or re-discover science rather than merely follow its findings. 'You don't teach children to think; you give them something to think about.'

Failure to appreciate the significance of the notions of 'readiness' and 'sequential learning' can have serious consequences, as the report on Aspects of Science Education in the Asian Region (1977) demonstrates.

Contrary to popular views, Asian junior science programmes can be said to reach a high academic standard. Indeed, the content of many programmes is much more difficult than that to be found in the programmes of countries such as the United

States of America, the United Kingdom, France and Australia. Unfortunately, many concepts are introduced at inappropriate stages: some advanced concepts such as displacement volume are introduced early, while other simpler concepts are found later in the programmes. For this reason I think it very important that trainee science teachers be introduced to the techniques and findings of Jean Piaget . . .

It is important that teachers and curriculum developers can be made aware of the problems that come from introducing concepts too early. If you introduce an experience that is 'too advanced' for the intellectual level of the children, they may ignore it. But, on the other hand, they may distort it, and then assimilate the distorted concept. We then have the problem in later teaching where children have false preconceptions which block proper learning.[91c]

It was precisely to minimise such errors resulting from failure to recognise the psychological development of children that Mysore State, as long ago as 1959, appended the following note to its 'Primary School Curriculum. Std. I and II'.

1 The psychological foundations of the age group are given at the beginning so that teachers can see the content of the syllabus in relation to the child's need.
2 Physical maturity and the extent of development of sensory organs of this age group are given so that teachers may know the types of activities they may devise.

Piaget's contributions to pedagogy

Piaget's classification of intellectual development is sometimes criticized as being negative in that it tells us more about what we *cannot* do at various stages and ages. But there is no doubt that such a classification of cognitive development is of tremendous help and importance to anyone concerned with the design and development of curriculum. It alerts us to several psychological and pedagogical pre-conditions that must be taken into account.

Mention has been made of the need to consider factors such as readiness and sequential learning. Piaget's ideas have contributed many other important elements to teaching/learning theory. Among these might be mentioned:

1   the need, in general, to pass from the concrete to the abstract; concrete experience first, the word later;
2   the process of forming a concept takes much longer than had been previously thought;
3   one must cross the line between ignorance and insight many times before real understanding comes;
4   Within each subject or discipline there are progressively more complex concepts. And on both logical and psychological grounds one needs to progress from the simpler to the more complex. This is what is done in a 'spiral curriculum'.

Many developing countries are today engaged in studying at first hand the psychological development of their own children. The Bangkok Institute for Child Study, for example, is engaged on a systematic study of the socio-psychological growth and development of Thai children.

Studies have been carried out in many non-European countries to investigate whether the developmental stages postulated by Piaget were applicable to non-European children. Abiola found that cognitive development in Nigerian primary school children conformed to Piaget's developmental stages.[1] A study carried out on a sample of children in Sri Lanka confirmed the same stages of development.[80] A series of studies in Thailand relating to such subjects as conservation of mass, weight and volume, tended to confirm the existence of the developmental stages postulated by Piaget.[80] A study on the science and mathematics concepts of Thai children, aged 7–12, carried out in Penang, 1975, confirmed Piaget's theory of the concrete operational stage of intellectual development at this age range. Other examples of agreement with the Piagetian stages of development are given in Appendix 7A to this chapter.

Which, one supposes, all goes to prove what is called the 'psychic unity of mankind'.

The importance of parental and environmental stimulation

Mention has been made that Abiola found that cognitive development in Nigerian primary school children conformed to Piaget's developmental stages.

However, though the stages of development were identical,

Abiola found that the development of basic aspects of perception of time and space were hindered by the lack of parental stimulation. The Nigerian child tends to play by himself and misses the mother's reinforcement value for cognitive adequacy. Abiola points out how the lack of toys, picture books, etc. fails to provide cognitive stimulation. The problem is aggravated by the fact that the language of instruction in many English and French-speaking African countries is different from the home language and this bilingualism undermines the school-child's assimilation.

Dr S. Biesheuvel also referred to the importance for intellectual development of stimulation provided by the parents, the home and the environment.

> For the ultimately full deployment of our manipulative and perceptual skills, adequate stimulation from without and appropriate interaction opportunities with the environment are necessary. If the material culture, or child rearing habits do not provide these opportunities, the period of maximum developmental receptivity passes, and subsequent learning is far less effective than it could have been.

Child rearing practices can have an important effect on intellectual development.

Marcelle Gerber and R.F.A. Dean, who did their work in East Africa, mainly among the Baganda people, found that at the age of six months the African child was two or three months ahead of his European counterpart. By the age of three the European child had caught up. Gerber attributed this to the effects of weaning which appear to be accompanied by a change in the mother's attitude towards the child. After weaning the child is given less attention and the mother is no longer available constantly, nor is she as indulgent or accepting of the child.[22a]

Children on whom care and affection are bestowed develop more rapidly intellectually than those to whom proper parental attention is denied.

Parental care and the home/family environment are very important factors in human development.

Cultural stimulation

Professor Vernon emphasises that the degree to which a child's intellectual potential is developed depends to a large extent on the stimulus he receives. Abiola showed how lack of toys, picture books, etc. can retard cognitive development. The lack of picture books and other pictorial stimuli can be a serious handicap in the development of three-dimensional pictorial perception, which in turn can adversely affect school-work since so many text-books make use of diagrams and pictorial representations.

The lack of toys and other such stimuli can retard the development of manipulative skills. But despite the lack of manufactured (Western) toys, the ingenuity and inventiveness of some African children in improvising their own toys must be recorded.

Biesheuvel notes: 'The infinite pains which children have been shown to take over the construction of toys, the resourcefulness that goes into the design and construction of wire models, indicates that curiosity and interest are latent, that there is much that can be exploited to evoke behaviour marked by spontaneity and inventiveness.'[72a]

And a specialist in African anthropology writes: 'Everywhere we found children using the pith from a stalk of millet, bits of wire or discarded tins to make themselves 'lorries', 'cars', 'aeroplanes' or musical instruments with an amazing precision and the most complex control systems.'[89b]

Use of pictorial material

Visual media are used extensively and increasingly in the educational systems of many Third World countries. This has certainly been so in the Ghanaian educational system, on the assumption that such media are readily understood. It was in order to test the validity of this assumption that Mundy-Castle[72b] carried out a study of Ghanaian children aged five to ten years in an attempt to find out how they responded to depth cues in pictorial material.

An unequivocal result of this study was that very few children responded to the depth cues in the pictures; there was no evidence of consistent three-dimensional interpretation.

He suggests this is because, 'cognizance of depth cues in pictures is a function of culturally-determined familiarity with pictorial material.'

The children used in his study had had little or no formal or informal experience of pictorial material.

Other cross-cultural studies of pictorial depth perception tend to confirm Mundy-Castle's suggestion that cognizance of depth cues in pictures is a function of culturally-determined familiarity with pictorial material. W. Hudson (1967), from studies of adolescents and adult samples with a variety of cultural and educational backgrounds, confirmed that persons unfamiliar with pictorial symbols and perspective as practised in Western culture tended to be two-dimensional in their interpretation of pictorial material. He found that in the normal course schooling was not the principal determinant in pictorial perception. Cultural isolation tended to nullify any effect of schooling. Informal instruction in the home and habitual exposure to pictures played a much more significant role.

Appendix 7B describes a piece of research on visual perception carried out in Kenya as a result of certain difficulties encountered in a rural health education project.

Miss Maclean points out (1960) how posters used during a health campaign in Nigeria proved quite inappropriate. The posters which were designed after the Western style, and which depended for their impact upon economy of presentation, were not understood. A.C. Holmes (1964) also found that health posters used in Kenya were not successful through lack of understanding of the convention of perspective. He found that the amount of detail in a picture influenced comprehension. Too much or too little detail were both detrimental.

J.L.M. Dawson, working in Sierra Leone (1963), and P.E. Vernon, working with English and West Indian children (1965), came to similar conclusions – that depth perception in pictorial material is enhanced by cultural familiarity with such material. Hudson (1960) found that lack of cultural stimulus may prevent or retard the development of three-dimensional pictorial perception.

In Western culture orientation with reference to the four main points of the compass, or to vertical-horizontal axes, is commonplace. But in many parts of Africa and other countries (Samoa, for example) people live in rounded huts; they see curved trees and hills. They see little furniture, or squares and rectangles. Segal, Campball and Herskovits (1963) show how such children from an 'uncarpentered' environment find difficulty in perceiving visual illustrations drawn by people familiar with straight lines and right-angles.[72c]

The child who has few construction toys, or toys at all, and who sees few diagrams or schematic representations of things may have difficulty in interpreting what he sees in Western textbooks.

Psychological tests

Children in developing countries are often subjected to psychological tests of ability and educational attainment devised in and for other cultural settings. The children very often are quite unfamiliar with the materials and cues used in the tests and so any results will tend to be invalid. Arthur Crijns concluded from his work at Pius XII College, Roma, Lesotho, that Western tests were not applicable to Africa because they were alien in cultural content and probed abilities valued in Western cultures which may not be operative in African intellectual behaviour.[22b]

Health and Nutrition

These are vital factors in human development. Lack of proteins and vitamins can seriously retard intellectual growth. Pre- and post-natal protein deficiency is rife in many developing countries; such a deficiency leads to central neural damage which in turn impairs intellectual development. Kwashiorkor, a disease which results from malnutrition, is common in Africa. It is caused by deficiency of protein in the diet during the child's second or third year. In both children and adults the disease causes mental apathy and slowness and feebleness of movement. The cognitive development of children is retarded; they lose all normal curiosity and desire for exploration that is natural to the child and seem to show no interest in their surroundings.

A culture which taboos the drinking of milk and offers no other protein substitute will exhibit some of the psychological characteristics noted above.

Ill-health is one of the great obstacles preventing the developing countries from realizing their full potential.

Summary
The stages of child development, according to *Piaget*.
1   *The sensor-motor stage* (up to 2 years of age): no abstract reasoning is possible at this infant stage.
2   *The pre-operational/pre-conceptual stage* (2–7 years): mental operations develop with active exploration of things.
3   *The stage of concrete operations* (7–11 years): problems come to be solved in a more ordered and quantitative way.

4   *The stage of formal operations or abstract thinking* (11–15 years): the child is no longer tied to the concrete; he can make abstractions.

All children pass through these stages in the same order but at different rates. Learning is an individual matter. The age at which a given stage appears varies from child to child. This implies the need for flexibility in teaching and in organizing the school day.

The curriculum should be planned from the logic of the child rather than the logic of the subject matter.

A child will learn when he is ready i.e. when he has reached the appropriate stage of intellectual development.

What is learnt must be sequenced, from simpler to more difficult concepts.

Parental and environmental stimulation are very important.

Lack of cultural stimulation (e.g. lack of picture books, etc.) can retard intellectual development. Unfamiliarity with pictorial representations can cause problems in interpreting diagrams, maps, etc. in textbooks.

Psychological tests of ability etc. developed for one cultural setting may be invalid in other cultural settings.

Health and nutrition are vital factors in development. Lack of proteins and vitamins can seriously retard intellectual growth.

Questions

1   In what ways would you consider Piaget's work important for developing countries?
2   Briefly describe Piaget's four stages of intellectual development.
3   Why is it important that teachers be aware of and know Piaget's four stages of intellectual development?
4   Individual learning/tuition is a fine ideal. What are the factors that would prevent this happening on a fairly large scale in your country?
5   How could the educational system be changed at not too much additional cost to permit more use being made of individual learning in schools?
6   What is meant by 'readiness'? Give an example to show how failure to appreciate 'readiness' can result in ineffective teaching/learning.
7   What is 'sequential learning'? Give an example of 'sequential

learning' in the teaching/learning of any subject or topic.

8 Piaget advised going from the concrete to the abstract. Give an example of how you would make use of this principle in drawing up a class lesson.

9 Should logical or psychological factors play the bigger part in developing a school curriculum?

10 Mention some of the parental/home conditions which might retard the intellectual development of children.

11 Mention some parental/home conditions that would stimulate the intellectual development of children.

12 Should psychology be taught to student teachers in training? Explain why.

13 Mention some difficulties you or your pupils have experienced in perceiving visual/pictorial material because of unfamiliarity with such material.

14 To what extent is ill-health/lack of nutrition an obstacle to education in your country?

Appendix 7A
Researches in the cognitive development of children

Rochelle, working with Congolese primary school children in 1966, found that the different types of problem-solving behaviours manifested by these children appeared in the same sequence as those of European children irrespective of the cultural environment.

In 1961 Price-Williams[72d] carefully worked through a series of Piaget's tests with Tiv children in central Nigeria. He found that if familiar materials like earth and nuts were substituted for the materials used by Piaget in his tests on the concept of 'conservation' in European children, then there was no difference in age norms between the two groups.

By 'conservation' is meant the fact that the magnitude of a property, such as length, weight, volume, area, etc. does not change as a result of a change in configuration. Thus a wooden stick does not change in length because it is moved to a different position. Realisation of 'conservation of length' is achieved by children at about the age of seven.

'Conservation of substance or quantity' is not appreciated before the age of eight or nine. Prince recounts some experiments carried out in Papua/New Guinea.

It was a revealing experience to take two identical balls of plasticine, to show them to a class and to roll them up until the class agreed they were identical, and then to deform one and to find out that even at Grade 6 level at the top of the primary school there were children who were convinced that the change of shape had produced a change of quantity in the plasticine.

Similarly, when two equal glasses of water were filled to a level to which all the class agreed was equal, and one then poured into a different shaped container, there were Grade 6 children who decided that the change of container produced a change in the quantity of water.[71]

R. Ogbonna Ohuche, of the University of Sierra Leone, carried out tests with children of the largest ethnic group in Sierra Leone, the Mende. His results confirmed Piaget's principle of the conservation of quantity applied to the Mende and also that this concept only came to be appreciated by children once they had reached the age of seven; below seven they could not appreciate conservation of quantity.[64]

The notion of conservation of surface or area develops at about eight or nine years of age. Again, experiments show that there are no differences in development of conservation concepts between the children tested by Piaget in Geneva and non-European children.

Conservation of volume is perceived about the age of eleven or so. 'Two balls of clay are shown to displace equal amounts of water. Then, with one ball changed to a pancake-shape, comes the question: "What about now? Do both push the water up by the same amount, or does one push the water up more than the other?"'[72e]

Children below eleven will think the different shapes will push water up by different amounts.

The concept of conservation of weight also only develops in children about the age of eleven. Conservation of weight develops later than conservation of substance or quantity. Goodnow suggests the reason is that 'quantity is under immediate visual perception, weight is not.' He instances an interesting example of one of the boys explaining conservation of weight. 'He pointed out that sometimes when he bought rice it came in a bag like

 , and sometimes in a bag like . But

it was always the same weight: he knew because he had carried them.'[72f]

Appendix 7B
Visual perception in a Kenyan population

The research was a systematic attempt to analyse the factors tending to favour or impede the recognition of simple drawings of familiar objects. It was carried out in Kenya on a population

representing a wide cross-section of age and level of formal education and sophistication.

In the first part of the work,[75] diagrams of familiar objects were presented to the respondents, who were asked what they thought they were. In the second stage those objects which had been misidentified most frequently were drawn in a natural setting with two or three other objects related in common experience, to test whether such a setting would increase recognition. Some interesting, and sometimes unanticipated, results emerged. The references are to diagrams shown.

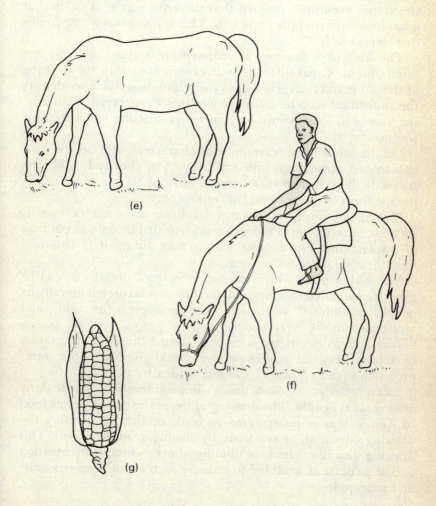

(e)

(f)

(g)

Many of the respondents did not look at even a simple diagram as a whole, but focused on a single feature and based the whole interpretation on that. The tortoise a) was identified as a snake (by only looking at the head, this misidentification being made even by those who had correctly identified a drawing of a snake just beforehand), or as a crocodile, rhinoceros or pineapple (by focusing on the shell pattern), or as an elephant (by only looking at the feet).

A single wrong detail can accordingly cause major misinterpretation. The goat b), perhaps the commonest domestic animal in Kenya, was frequently identified as a cow; the baffled researcher eventually realized that the artist was at fault, in that goats have tails that turn upwards. The drawing was wrong in this one respect only.

The idea of a drawing as representing a type, or class, was often absent. Great difficulty was experienced with the drawing of the old man c), largely due to the respondent trying to identify the individual who he assumed was being portrayed. Similarly, the dancer d) led to confusion, since no particular tribal costume was portrayed.

On the other hand, cartoon stick characters, and isotype symbols caused surprisingly little difficulty. A mother and child were correctly identified in stick cartoon form by 94 per cent, and in isotype form by 96 per cent, of respondents.

Placing an object in a natural context does not necessarily increase recognition. A horse e) was identified by only 58 per cent of respondents, but a horse with a man riding it f) brought identification up to 88 per cent.

Pictorial symbols which can be interpreted literally or can be given an extended meaning will tend to be interpreted literally by people of limited education. For example, the skull and crossbones motif, very widely used in Kenya both on poison bottles and on electricity poles, was given a literal interpretation by 48 per cent, but only 18 per cent could give a symbolic interpretation such as 'poison', 'danger' or 'death'.

Interpretation is sometimes 'impressionistic', particularly among rural people. The drawing of the maize cob g), staple food in Kenya, was misinterpreted as bird, or fish (by turning the drawing sideways), or as a man (by turning it upside down). This drawing also illustrated the finding above, where concentration on the pattern of seeds led to answers such as tortoise, crocodile and pineapple.

8 Patterns of Curriculum Organization

> The separate lessons and subjects are single pieces of a mosaic; and what matters most is not the numbers and colours of the separate pieces, but what pattern they make when put together. Some of the most urgent questions which all secondary schools are having to ask themselves just now are about the total patterns of the curriculum for all their pupils. They are finding that it is not enough to tinker with the separate pieces.[15]

The way a curriculum is conceptualised in theory and then designed, organized and developed for practical implementation depends on a country's particular philosophy of education, on its national, social, cultural, economic, developmental aspirations, on where it considers the main stream of emphasis should lie. Should cultural and societal needs or the demands for economic development determine the nature of the curriculum? Should the curriculum be geared to the interests of the child or should it be based on the disciplines of knowledge? Should the emphasis be on generalism or on specialism? Should there be a common curriculum for all students or should there be different curricula for different students? How much emphasis should be given to psychological and pedagogical considerations, such as learning theory, methodology; how much to situational (local) considerations, e.g. urban, rural, ethnic, community schools? Depending on one's answer to such basic questions of curriculum as to what should be taught, why, to whom, in what manner (i.e. how), where, will our conceptualisation of the pattern of curriculum take shape. These conceptualisations of the design and organization of the curriculum have important repercussions on other key processes of curriculum – namely, the day to day implementation implications, the role of the teacher, methodology, diffusion of innovation, evaluation, etc.

Cirriculum conceptualisations

David Hamilton[29a] has analysed *curriculum conceptualisations* into three main categories, corresponding to some of the basic questions of curriculum development mentioned above – what, where, to whom and in what manner? His three types of curriculum conceptualisation are:

1 Those with an emphasis on curriculum content, on knowledge, on what should be taught.
2 Those with an emphasis on the curriculum situation, on the local learning milieu, on the where; whether rural, or urban etc.
3 Those which emphasise the organization of the teaching/learning process, the structure and sequence of learning, the organization of materials; which emphasise the to whom and how.

As we shall see, these different curriculum emphases give rise to different patterns of curriculum design, development, diffusion, evaluation.

Emphasis on curriculum content

Arising from philosophical considerations about the structure of knowledge, the disciplines of the mind, knowledge is treated as having intrinsic value, with the learner a more or less passive recipient of externally derived information.

Innovation strategies that emphasise content usually arise from a concern to:
  update the curriculum,
  reaffirm cultural and moral values of society (i.e. the cumulative knowledge of the past),
  provide vocational orientation (looking to the future).

Evaluation of knowledge-based curricula is easy since the goals (the inculcation of specific knowledge or skills) are attained when the material of the curriculum is transferred into the pupil's mind. The 'objectives' approach to curriculum development fits

86

in readily with a knowledge-based curriculum since the curriculum output can easily be compared or checked against a preconceived blueprint of objectives.

Knowledge-based curricula are also easily amenable to large scale development and dissemination programmes; mass production techniques can be used to further mass education.

Emphasis on curriculum situation

Where the emphasis is on the curriculum situation, the main aim is that the curriculum accurately reflects the life-world of the child; the concern is with the overall fit between the curriculum and the situation, rather than with the achievement of learning objectives. Knowledge is regarded as relative to the specific situation rather than a universal absolute. The concern is not so much with detailed specification of content and organization (as embodied in syllabuses and teachers' guides) as with flexibility of interpretation and implementation. This means that such curriculum development must usually be on a small scale. As Hamilton says: 'If a content emphasis can be described as an engineering approach to curriculum development, then the situational emphasis is much closer to gardening. Curricula are devised according to soil type, and then close attention is paid to preparing the ground.'[29b]

The situation-based curriculum adopts a goal-free approach (i.e. without pre-specified goals and objectives), studying actual outcomes rather than predicted ones, and so avoids falling into the difficulty of having to specify objectives and criteria in advance. But this also makes the evaluation of such curricula more difficult.

The emphasis on the 'local' situation, on where the action is, encourages local or community-based curriculum development and relies, for putting it into practice, on the spread and diffusion of ideas by local catalytic agents.

Emphasis on organization of teaching/learning process

Where the emphasis in the pattern or design of the curriculum is on the organization of the teaching/learning process, much attention is paid to learning theory, and the ideas of Piaget and Bruner loom large. Much attention is paid to the general processes of learning rather than to particular bits of knowledge.

Enquiry, rather than knowledge, becomes the focal point of organization and the goal of education is *learning how to learn*. It is more concerned with the results of research into learning and teaching, with the sequence of learning, with the organization of materials, than with details of content and with devising assessment (e.g. examination/test) procedures to the point of forgetting what the whole business is about – the education of children. The acquisition of knowledge is treated as a means to an end, rather than as an end as in the content approach.

With such curricula, however, evaluation can be doubly difficult because both 'content' and 'outcome' are not their primary concerns – the learning process is the main concern.

These conceptualisations must not be seen as water-tight categories, distinct and separate from each other. Any good curriculum would draw from all these emphases, using different emphases depending on the demands and needs and circumstances of particular local situations. Most patterns of school curriculum borrow and adapt from these broad areas and develop patterns of curriculum organization suited to their own particular situations and requirements.

We shall now examine some of these patterns of curriculum organization.

Some patterns of curriculum organization

The common-core curriculum

The common-core curriculum is an example of a content-based curriculum. A common body of fundamental knowledge and skills is taught to all pupils.

According to Professors Hirst and Peters a knowledge and understanding of various modes of experience are central to education and human development. It follows then that all children must reach some basic competence in each of these modes, in each of these significantly different and important kinds of knowledge and understanding. In other words, they advocate a liberal education for all.

These modes of knowledge are:
Mathematics
Physical Sciences
History and the human sciences

Morals
Religion
Philosophy
Literature and the fine arts.

Obviously, not all children will reach the same level in these subjects, some will go further in certain areas than others.

No one may opt out of a discipline or subject merely through lack of interest. Whilst a choice of topics is allowed within each area, based on pupils' interests, aptitudes and abilities, no choice is permitted within the separate disciplines until a basic minimum of understanding is reached in them all. In other words, they propose general education for all throughout the secondary stage. If a person is less able in a subject, say, mathematics, then far from being allowed to give it up in favour of something with which he can cope, he should be given more, perhaps differently orientated, teaching in the discipline, so that he becomes able at it.

This compulsory core may, – and should be – supplemented by optional courses, according to the special interests and abilities of pupils, the demands of vocational training, etc.

Differences in ability and aspirations is catered for by employing different methods and approaches in the teaching.

The idea of a liberal education for all is fine, but not all children can cope with the demands of a liberal education. As John White points out:

> it is pointless insisting that children should get on the inside of pure mathematics, theoretical physics, philosophy, etc. if they lack the natural ability to do so. This is why uniformity of educational provision will not do. The central objective should be to tailor the curriculum far more closely to what each individual can manage. Those of lower ability tend to be given a 'watered down' version of an academic curriculum which only leaves them bored and frustrated.[95]

Specialised curricula

As against a common-core curriculum for all, others have advocated specialised curricula, calling for differentiation of studies based on the abilities, intelligence, aptitudes and interests of the learners.

Professor G.H. Bantock, in his *Towards a Theory of Popular Education* (1971), advocates a dual curriculum. For the non-academically minded, Bantock advocated an alternative curriculum based on the affective-artistic side, on an 'education of the emotions.'

Bantock's differentiation of the curriculum was not to be just a 'watering down of the high culture classical humanism curriculum' appropriate to an elite, but instead a radically different curriculum (for the masses) consisting of activities based on 'first-hand experience', on the 'face to face interests of the people'. In this way, he would avoid 'the trivialities implicit in much of the so-called vocational and life adjustment work done as a sop to the less able.'

An example of differentiation of curricula is provided from Tanzania. Until 1974, the secondary course was: 'mainly academic, similar to the colonial 'grammar school' pattern. At the beginning of 1974, however, it was decided that all secondary schools should be designated 'agricultural', 'technical', 'commercial', or 'domestic science'. The schools are not intended to be 'vocational' but to provide a basic secondary with an important practical component.'[82a]

The comprehensive school idea originated from trying to provide a secondary level education for as many children as could benefit from it with a curriculum that catered for a wide variety of abilities and interests.

The comprehensive school is usually based on a 3-3 system:

1   in the first three years - a general education for all;
2   in the next three years - a specialised education, where children choose courses in accordance with their individual abilities, skills, aptitudes and interests.

It provides for general education, specialised education and vocational training under one roof.

Because of the large number of specialist staff required comprehensive schools tend, necessarily, to be large, with a minimum of about 600 pupils to be viable. Whilst the comprehensive school allows for maximum differentiation on an individual basis, it retains the class or form or standard as a basic social unit. The comprehensive school can be an effective instrument for promoting social integration.

Professor Fafunwa suggests that educators in Africa should consider closely the comprehensive school idea.[23c] He points out, however, that at the moment many of the secondary schools in Africa are not large enough (about 300 pupils) to provide the wide range of facilities necessary for a comprehensive education.

Fafunwa proposes the following basic curriculum for the first three years of secondary school:

Languages
African and world literature
General Science
Mathematics
Social Studies (history, geography and civics)
African music and art
Physical Education
Any one of: Agriculture, Home Economics, Commerce and
   Industrial Arts.

At the end of the first three years each pupil's ability will have become evident through proper guidance and counselling, and at this material time children who have academic interests will be placed in that section while those with vocational, technical interests will be likewise placed.[23d]

A child-centred curriculum

Childhood has a meaning and a value in itself, apart from its value as a step on the way to maturity. The better the child, that is, the truer he is to his child nature as such, the better man will he make when the proper time comes.
(Sir John Adams, *Evolution of Educational Theory*,
Macmillan 1915.)

Someone once remarked that 'the schooling industry is a mammoth conspiracy against children'. As against a subject/content-biased curriculum many people argue that the particular educational virtues and characteristics of subjects should give way to the interests, the developmental needs (i.e. growth), the capabilities of the child.

John Dewey argued for a child-centred curriculum. Instead of fitting the child to the school curriculum, the curriculum should be adapted to the child. A subject has meaning only if it is translated to the child's own experiences and meets his growing needs. Thus a child masters a difficult subject like speaking because the child needs that form of expression.

It goes without saying that what is taught must be interesting and meaningful to the child, as against being interesting only to the teacher. This does not always happen. Often the

91

child-centred curriculum ends up as a teacher-centred curriculum.

Several objections arise if education is to be guided solely by the interests, the needs, etc. of children, by what has been called 'childrens' narcissistic whims'. For example, how do we know the future needs of children; which needs have educational priority? One must distinguish between 'learner-centred' education and 'child-centred or interest-dominated' curriculum. Education is concerned about learning about culture and about the rules of its various aspects: if a child is to be educated then he must learn the rules, whether they interest him or not. Admittedly, interest will certainly lend motivation to the child, but in the long run he will need such subjects as reading, mathematics, etc., even though he may have no interest in them. There are certain things a child needs to learn even if they do not interest him.

Temporary interest and immediate need of children can also be criticised on the grounds that education can degenerate into a hodge-podge of bits and pieces, ephemeral and unrelated. In the interests of a temporary relevance a more permanent and deeper comprehension is sacrificed. This does not mean, of course, that in education one may not use temporary expedients to stimulate interest in learning.

No one would disagree that the interests of children should be used to influence methods of teaching, to stimulate and motivate. Where the disagreement arises with some progressives is when they advocate that children's interests and needs should influence not only the methods but also the objectives and the whole pur-pose of education. The teacher must not opt for what is merely interesting, but must judge what is valuable and then, by method, make it interesting and tempting. The importance of children's interest lies in the sphere of method, rather than of content.[55]

The revolt against child-centred 'progressive' education

Lastly, a different sort of religion has been recently peddled; but one, to be fair, which is derived from a misunder-standing of educational theories: a vague belief that small children should do their own creative thing, so that the roles of the teacher are merely to create a nice environment and pat their charges on the head each time they produce a lousy painting or poem.[31A]

Many educators feel that the pendulum has swung too far towards child-centred progressive methods and that there should be at least a partial return to more structured instruction, especially in such basic subjects as reading and mathematics.

Many feel that a philosophy based solely on the children's needs and interests is a 'blue-print for utter chaos'. John Merritt states that practical investigations are the favourite for the 'progressive' teacher. But, he remarks: 'the investigations carried out are often monumental in their pointlessness.'[40a]

Romantic theories about 'creativity', 'discovery methods', 'unfolding children's capacities' and so forth are all very well, but, as has been pointed out many times, some important skills like writing and word recognition and numeracy can only be mastered by systematic practice.

In many countries, especially in the U.S.A., there has been a reaction against the 'progressive' school; the fall in standards in reading and writing and numeracy has been laid at the door of the 'play-way' method of teaching, and a return has been made towards a subject-divided curriculum, towards formal structured reading, towards an 'essentialist' curriculum.

Beevers suggests[11a] that the permissive methods of progressive education could be resented in some developing countries and lead to conflict between parents and teachers, between the school and the community. He makes the very valid point that in many instances it may be important that sociological research should be carried out before a new curriculum or new methods are introduced.

For example, in Sierra Leone, where tribal culture lays stress on conformity, on authority, on discipline, on group reliance, and where individual initiative is discouraged, a child-centred, 'progressive', method might prove difficult to introduce. In Malawi, the President has taken a somewhat extreme stand against 'modern methods' in education and has forbidden their use.

Subject-centred versus child-centred education

The dilemma: logical (subject-centred) versus psychological (child-centred).

Is the curriculum to be subject-centred or child-centred? Is it to be a subject-based curriculum or a needs – and interests-based curriculum? Should the learning groups be based on 'subjects' (information) or based on the interests and needs of children (psychological/social)?

There is really no need for any dichotomy between the logical and the psychological. The 'child' and the 'subject' are two limits which define a single process. Teachers should teach subjects and they should teach children. The art of teaching lies in bringing the two into contact – the current interests of the pupil and the socially developed traditions of thought and behaviour.

The structure and key concepts of a subject economise the workings of the mind – the memory is less taxed because facts are grouped around some common principle; observation is assisted because we know what to look for and where; reasoning is directed; the path along which ideas march is laid out instead of hopping from one chance association to another.

But this subject matter also needs to be psychologised, i.e. it must be made relevant to the child's interests and needs; the subject matter must be translated into the experience of the learner; the material must be translated into life terms; it must be developed within the range and scope of the child's life.

A compromise between a subject-centred curriculum and one based on the 'interests' of children, i.e. a child-centred curriculum, has been suggested by organizing curriculum along interdisciplinary themes or topics, since themes and topics are close to how young children think and because these provide considerable scope for pupil-initiated learning. In using a theme, a topic, an important general concept, such as 'power' or 'energy', for example, pervading several subject disciplines, is developed. Another theme could be 'local government'. This would, in a country like Tanzania for example, involve teaching and learning about the political processes of the country, how TANU, the national party, puts over its policies, the implications of 'self-reliance', etc.

For the teacher who wishes to adopt the 'theme' approach Midwinter suggests the following method of action:

Pick your theme. Draw up, in consultation with the children, your flow-diagram of the points of interest and concern that commend themselves as natural and spontaneous manifestations of the theme. Organize the work-load accordingly and programme the production so that it has some pattern or notion of ensemble, in order that, eventually, the entire group will witness and benefit from the final outcome.[40b]

> Integration should be the marriage of true minds, not an administratively decreed cohabitation between essentially different people speaking several languages, all desperately trying to make the thing work.[65a]

Historically, subject matter was divided into separate subjects, nicely ordered in sequence and packaged for teaching to young people at various age levels. It was only towards the beginning of this century that other patterns of organizing the curriculum were suggested: the grouping together of subjects similar in content, the breaking down of barriers between subjects to form broad fields such as general science, social studies, etc.

In contrast to the fragmentary nature of the traditional, subject-divided curriculum, integration is a re-grouping of ideas and knowledge between subjects and disciplines so as to provide a new and intellectually reputable curriculum. Integration does not mean a fitting together of bits and pieces from different subjects but rather making use of the unique contribution of the individual subjects.

The 'unit' of the curriculum is not so much a subject as an idea.

Either the main topics, ideas, concepts, theories in a single discipline may be used as the 'integrating thread' (e.g. 'energy') or the methods of thought and work and types of enquiry (e.g. the scientific method) may serve as the 'integrating thread.' But when all is said and done it is the learner who achieves or does not achieve integration. Integration can be encouraged by the way the content and teaching/learning experiences are presented, but in the end the learner himself must see and appreciate the relevant relationships; integration is up to him.

Thailand provides six years of universal primary education for its children. But instead of this education consisting of a host of subjects the new curriculum is divided into only four integrated subject areas: basic skills, life experience, work experience and character education.

Sri Lanka has also re-designed its primary school curriculum as an integrated curriculum around ten or eleven themes. These eleven themes are:

1 Our houses and the people who live in them.
2 Things we eat and drink.
3 Things we wear.

4　Things which help in work.
5　How we live in mixed communities.
6　The world around us.
7　Our school and its neighbourhood.
8　People who help us.
9　How we travel and communicate.
10　Our earth and the sky above it.
11　Things we see and hear.

As a result of a National Workshop on Primary Education held in Ibadan, Nigeria (26 April–8 May 1971) the Nigeria Education Research Council recommended a Social Studies Programme to replace the separate subjects Geography and History. The Report points out that:

> The Social Studies syllabus is not a fusion of the two former subjects and syllabus framers stress that anybody who thinks of it this way has missed the point of the new policy.
> What has been attempted has been to isolate the knowledge, the skills, the attitudes and values that a child of primary school age can be reasonably expected to acquire and which will help him in the process of becoming a useful citizen and one who understands the environment in which he lives.[59]

The Social Studies syllabus committees, instead of haggling over lists of topics for inclusion in a syllabus,

> made an honest attempt to achieve a real degree of integration.
> The processes involved a number of related steps;
> 1　Identifying the aims of the programme as a whole.
> 2　Examining and listing characteristics, needs and problems of learners at three stages: lower, middle and upper primary.
> 3　Listing themes and sub-themes (units) for each class of the primary school.
> 4　Developing each of the themes on a grid with the following headings: a) Topic; b) Main objectives; c) Concepts to be developed; d) Attitudes and values to be inculcated; e) Skills and abilities to be acquired; f) Facts to be taught; g) Ways of learning and teaching; h) Teaching and learning materials to be used; i) Evaluating the learning.[36c]

Integration is easier said than done. Professor Kerr lists the difficulties encountered in some earlier attempts at integration.

Our treatment in schools during the 1940s and 1950s of general science and social studies has taught us to be cautious about grouping disciplines together. Certainly, during the general science movement we were more concerned with the informational content of courses than with underlying concepts and methods of enquiry. Teachers were not adequately prepared for the change through in-service courses and continued to think and teach in terms of biological, chemical and physical topics. The textbooks and the examination papers continued to reflect sharply the separate disciplines. The lesson is that unified courses must evolve slowly out of those principles and methods from the separate disciplines which are inter-related and fundamental.[40c]

A Nigerian delegate to the National Workshop on Primary Education, held in Ibadan, referred to above, illustrates the complexity of integration.

You have blue bits and you have yellow bits and it's going to be much easier for you to put them together one on top of the other so you have a blue and yellow syllabus. But you have to design a green syllabus. You also have blue teachers and yellow teachers. You will need to turn them into green teachers . . . and that will be even more difficult.[36c]

Strategies for integration

1 *Correlation of subjects* by establishing cross-links between different subjects. This has been done, for example, in the Nigerian Cultural and Creative Art Syllabus, which integrates Music, Dance, Drama and Fine Art.
2 *Integration through themes, topics, concepts*, as mentioned above.
3 *The centre-of-interest method* (the Decroly method) of integration. In a village in a developing country, for instance, the centre-of-interest could well be the understanding, management and improvement of the village.

The African Primary Science Programme (APSP) and the Science Education Programme for Africa (SEPA) have produced a whole series of 'units', based on topics and centres of interest, aimed at developing basic scientific and mathematical skills that cut across the traditional subject boundaries. The units are in use in Kenya, Ghana, Nigeria, Sierra Leone, Tanzania and Lesotho.

Several of the countries, notably Kenya and Ghana, have modified the units to their own local situation. The African Primary Science Programmes take the environment as their starting point and focus of attention.

Integrated studies, extending beyond subject boundaries, call for greater flexibility in school organization and for new and more demanding roles for teachers.

Exploration of themes, exploration of the local environment, pursuit by individuals or groups of their own-initiated enquiries, all these will call for flexibility in the normal timetabling arrangements and in the normal grouping of pupils. In some schools half-day and even full days are timetabled for the various activities to be pursued.

Integrated studies involves a change in the normal role of the teacher. In the Humanities Curriculum Project (U.K.) the role of the teacher was radically transformed from that of information-giver to debate-leader. Integrated studies is generally a new experience for teachers. From being a specialist in his subject the teacher now needs a deep knowledge of a range of subjects and of their significant concepts. But such teachers are in short supply. At Countesthorpe College in England an inter-disciplinary approach is used. But, 'very little integration is taking place between science and other things. Between the sciences there are problems with teachers not having enough knowledge in the other fields to integrate.'[31]

The report goes on to touch upon another factor which adds to the difficulty of integration, namely, subject specialists who 'view themselves and their disciplines and knowledge with the jealous eye of a threatened priesthood' and 'defend the boundaries of their specialist subjects against the marauding pedlars of integration'.[76]

Traditional loyalties die hard; it is subjects which give teachers their professional identity. They see themselves as historians, geographers, linguists, mathematicians, scientists. An integrated curriculum takes away from them their specialist role (or so it appears to them) and so teachers may resent swapping a subject expertise for the right to participate in a generalised approach to human problems and issues.

Team-teaching

In team-teaching, 'teams' of teachers co-operate in teaching a common theme or topic to single or combined classes. The individual teachers play a variety of roles and are expected themselves to acquire an 'integrated' overview of the theme, topic or problem as well as offer specialist skills, concepts and modes of enquiry.

Reconstructionism

By contrast with the traditional, subject-orientated and the 'progressive', child-oriented approach there is another strategy, *reconstructionism*, which requires the subject matter to be treated not in terms of subject disciplines or centred on the child but in terms of contemporary cultural issues and problems e.g. health, population etc. For reconstructionists, the curriculum is a programme of action to bring about changes in culture.

In developing countries, dissatisfied with existing society (often hang-overs from what President Nyerere calls the colonial heritage), reconstructionism looks for a renewal, a reconstruction, of the social order through education. Nyerere realises he cannot implement his programme of rural socialism without drastic changes in what the schools teach and how they teach it. He is opposed to any curriculum that elevates acquisitiveness and urban sophistication over co-operation.

In a nutshell, reconstructionism:
1 avows that education, properly organized, can be a major force for planned change in society;
2 favours a social-core curriculum based on rationalistic, democratic, communitarian values, as instanced by Tanzania's programme of rural education;
3 avows that learning is an active, social process involving projects, problem-solving, guided but not dominated by teachers, adaptable and flexible.

Summary

Our conceptualisations of the pattern of curriculum will depend on our answers to such basic curriculum questions as to what should be taught, why, to whom, in what manner (i.e. how) and where.

Such conceptualisations of curriculum tend to emphasise:
1 curriculum content or knowledge (the what);
2 the local curriculum situation (the where);
3 the teaching/learning process (the to whom, and how).
Some patterns of curriculum organization

The common-core curriculum: a common body of fundamental knowledge and skills is taught to all pupils. All pupils are to be given a certain quantum of general education. (Differences in pupils' abilities are catered for by different methods and approaches in teaching).

Specialised curricula – different studies according to the abilities, aptitudes and interests of the learners.

The comprehensive school provides a wide curriculum to cater for a wide variety of abilities and interests.

A child-centred curriculum. Instead of fitting the child to the curriculum, the curriculum is fitted to the child – to his interests, needs, capabilities.

Should education be subject-centred (logical) or child-centred (psychological)? A compromise can be made by organizing the curriculum around themes or topics.

Integration is a regrouping of ideas and knowledge from different subjects to provide a new intellectually reputable discipline, e.g. social studies.

Reconstructionism deals not so much with subjects or the child but in terms of contemporary issues and problems.

Questions
1 In your school curricula is emphasis placed on content, or on the local situation, or on the teaching/learning process?
2 Describe parts of the curriculum in any particular subject which emphasise **a)** content, **b)** the local situation, **c)** the teaching/learning process.
3 In your educational system is the education 'general' or 'specialised'? Do you think this is a good or bad thing?
4 State some of the advantages and disadvantages of the 'core' curriculum.
5 Discuss the advantages and disadvantages of a 'specialised' curriculum.
6 What are the main advantages of a 'comprehensive' school?
7 What are the main disadvantages of such schools?
8 Do you think your country should operate a 'comprehensive' system? Explain why.
9 Dewey said that instead of fitting the child to the curriculum we should fit the curriculum to the child. Explain why you either agree or disagree with him.
10 Give an example to show how children's interests can be

catered for by the method used in teaching a particular topic.

11   What is 'progressive' education? Do you think your country should adopt it?

12   What are the reasons why a child-centred/progressive education may be resented in some Third World countries?

13   Should the curriculum be logical (i.e. subject- centred) or psychological (child-centred)? Argue your case.

14   Give an example of teaching using a 'theme'.

15   What is meant by 'integration' in the curriculum?

16   Give an example of integration in the curriculum.

17   What are the advantages, if any, of integration?

18   What are the disadvantages, if any, of integration?

19   Describe how the principle of 'reconstructionism' could be put to effective use in designing a curriculum.

9   Teaching/Learning Strategies

I hear, and I forget,
I see, and I remember,
I do, and I understand.
(Chinese proverb).

Psychological and pedagogical principles

The phrase 'teaching strategy', rather than 'teaching methods', is used since the latter has traditional undertones of merely training the pupil in skills. Teaching strategy implies the deliberate planning and organization of teaching-learning experiences and situations in the light of psychological and pedagogical principles with a view to achieving specific goals. These principles were touched on in an earlier chapter. They are briefly reviewed again.

Obviously, any teaching/learning strategy must take note of a) the age and ability of the learner. Piaget's stages of sequential intellectual development are very important in this regard. It is well to bear in mind that these stages can be uneven: in one area of his thinking a child may be at one stage; in another area, at another stage. Different strategies must be adopted for children of different abilities: the very able must be stretched, the less able not fobbed off with a diluted academic treatment.

Other important factors in the psychology of learning are b) motivation and interest. Pupils' motivation and interest in what they learn can be enhanced by ensuring the matter they experience is relevant to life, has some bearing on the social conditions, the environment, the world around them. With this in mind many schools now use, as against the straight didactic method of expounding facts to be learnt, a variety of teaching/

learning approaches – a topic-centred approach, interdisciplinary enquiry, problem-solving, projects, life-adjustment courses and so on. The greater the variety of experiences offered the more likely is the child to find activities that will assist his learning. Care must be taken to ensure, however, that such 'real experience' education does not degenerate into watered-down courses consisting of a pot-pourri of trivia.

It is the teacher's job to make the teaching/learning situations and experiences interesting. It is the task of the teacher to make even dull old ditchwater sparkle like champagne.

There should be c) insightful learning as against rote learning. Relationships and principles are more important than facts and applying what is learned is more important than merely learning it. The student should not just learn subject matter but should learn from the subject matter. Facts alone are not enough. Since education is also a preparation for facing the problems of life, children must be trained to think for themselves and to understand, especially in a world of wishful thinking, of prejudice, of conclusions drawn from little or no evidence. With rote learning we descend to verbalism, to 'magic' instead of 'logic'. The graduates of rote learning become B.A.s – Believe Anything!

It is important that there should be d) active involvement and participation rather than passive reception (just listening, watching, etc.). The pupils must play the game instead of just watching from the side-lines.

Bearing in mind these principles, a useful sequence of instruction should be along the following lines:

1 Motivation. The student must want something. And children are innately curious. Use those two criteria to develop the teaching/learning situation.

2 Cue – to gain the student's attention. The student must notice something – something pinned on the board, something in the organization of the material, something different, a special emphasis, a change of voice, etc.

3 Response – during the lesson the student must do something, i.e. active participation. The student must use his newly acquired knowledge, transform it, apply it.

4 Reward – the response needs to be rewarded. The student must achieve something. Success is one of the strongest motivating forces for further effort. Things must be arranged and organized so that most days a child goes home with the taste of success on his tongue. To ensure success, ensure that the work

and the tasks are not beyond the pupils. Provide a background of success, not failure. The work must be sufficiently challenging, but it must also provide sufficient experience of success. Confidence is vital to learning.

Some strategies of teaching/learning

The didactic method: the 'jug and mug' method

This was the predominant method of teaching in the past; unfortunately, it is still only too common today. In this method of teaching the teacher, the fount of wisdom, is the 'jug' who fills with knowledge (facts) the child, who is the 'mug', speaking metaphorically. The teacher expounds, lectures, holds forth – and inevitably bores. He instructs, he provides information and seeks to ensure that this is learned. The result is that schools are full of teaching and no learning. In contrast, in infant schools, where the emphasis is on play, on purpose, on activity, hardly anything is taught but at every minute valuable lessons are being learnt.

This observation by George Bernard Shaw in his book *Education and the Social Order*, though written half a century ago, is still not without some significance. He argues: 'Even a boy's interest in mechanical devices can be killed by too much instruction. If you teach a boy the principle of the common pump in lesson time, he will avoid acquiring the knowledge you are trying to impart, whereas if you have a pump in your backyard and forbid him to touch it he will spend all his leisure touching it.'

Paulo Friere, the revolutionary Brazilian educator, launches a blistering attack on the traditional, didactic, jug-and-mug technique.

A careful analysis of the teacher-student relationship at any level, inside or outside the school, reveals its fundamentally narrative character. This relationship involves a narrating subject (the teacher) and patient, listening objects (the students). The contents ... tend in the process of being narrated to become lifeless and petrified. Education is suffering from narration sickness ...

Narration (with the teacher as narrator) leads the students to memorise mechanically the narrated content. Worse still, it turns them into containers, into receptacles, to be filled by the teacher. The more completely he fills the receptacles, the better a teacher he is. The more meekly the receptacles permit themselves to be filled, the better students they are.[27]

This Report of the Ministry of Education of Thailand describes the 'bucket theory' of teaching that used to prevail in that country. The description would apply to many countries.

The most salient impression that is gained from a cursory observation of teaching methods in Thai schools is the emphasis on learning for the sake of passing examinations. The influence of this point of view pervades the entire educational system – from primary grades, through the universities. Among the consequences of this emphasis is the heavy reliance on rote methods of learning by the student. It is an application of the 'bucket theory' of knowledge. According to this theory, the beginning pupil starts his educational training with an empty bucket of knowledge and each successive teacher tries to pour as much as possible into the bucket. The person who completes his schooling with the largest quantity (of factual knowledge) in his bucket is presumably the best educated.[84]

Coombs gives a harsh, but true, picture of what passes for education in many parts of the world, both developed and under-developed.

The learning techniques . . . remain the same: the rote method, the technique of cramming, and, once the examination menace is passed, of forgetting all those useless impedimenta. The examination system is not an evaluation of a student's personality and intellectual equipment, his powers of thinking for himself, reflection and reasoning. It is a challenge to resourceful deception and display of superficial cleverness.[16d]

Reliance on the 'jug-and-mug' technique of teaching, over-reliance on dictation of 'notes' or blindly copying notes from the blackboard, emphasis on rote memorisation with a view to passing examinations, endless practice in answering multiple choice questions, cramming – all these practices are hardly in line with the psychological and pedagogical principles of teaching/learning mentioned earlier.

One can say, in some mitigation, that the actual physical

conditions of schooling in some countries make it difficult to adopt more enlightened and progressive methods of teaching. With large, noisy, overcrowded classes, with hardly room to move, it is difficult to employ alternative methods of teaching such as group and activity methods, the enquiry approach etc.

In search of other strategies

One of the most characteristic features of education during the past two or three decades has been the demand for a 'new look' at education, for a change not only in what is taught but also how it is taught.

The traditional type of teaching is no longer adequate. The pupil is an individual to be developed wholly, i.e. intellectually, physically, aesthetically, morally, emotionally. Today's teacher, instead of being a mere tradesman bartering his knowledge, must be a craftsman.

There is no simple solution to the business of teaching. What is certain is that we must work out scientifically what strategy or strategies would be most appropriate, at particular stages, in particular situations.

The following are some considerations to be borne in mind. In all teaching we must consider:

1 content – the nature of the subject, with its particular 'structure' (Bruner), its peculiar 'realms of meaning' (Phenix), its characteristic method or discipline;

2 the nature of the pupil – his
age – 'milk for babes, beer for the older!'
maturity,
background.

What other factors?

3 one's objectives;

4 the teacher himself, his capabilities, his experience, his particular specialisms, his interests;

5 the facilities – or lack of them – in the school; the equipment, teaching aids and other teaching material.

It is a natural instinct to search for the most pleasant and satisfying way in anything we do. So why 'fight' the pupils? Admittedly, we should not let the interests and characteristics of children dictate what is done in education but we should consider these in deciding on our teaching strategies. Let our strategy flow with the stream of children's interests and characteristics rather than battle against the stream – usually unsuccessfully.

What are the interests and characteristics of children?
1   They are very active. Believe it or not, but they are interested in any mental or physical activity.
2   They are interested in things close to them; in quick goals.
3   They like to explore and make discoveries themselves.
4   They are interested in things that move, e.g. toys.
5   They like solving problems, provided the problems are at their level.

Thus a sensible teaching strategy would be one that emphasised finding out, with the pupils investigating and discovering facts for themselves, using their own eyes and hands and brains. Instead of saying 'Here is something to be learned' we should say 'Here is something to find out', 'Here is a problem to be solved.'

So one method **not** to use would be the *lecture method*. It has many disadvantages.
1   Pupils are not brought face to face with nature. Someone else – the lecturer – extracts the significant relationships.
2   It is all teacher and no pupil.
3   Also, too much talk and chalk by the teacher often means disciplinary problems.

It would be true to say that the present system of examinations is to a large extent responsible for this 'steam-shovel' approach.'

This is not to say the lecture method must never be used. It has its place, for example, in bringing out the romance of a subject and presenting it on a grand scale. The lives of the great scientists can be used to humanise the teaching of science instead of it being presented as a sordidly materialistic subject.

In stark distinction to the lecture method is the *discovery (heuristic) method*.

In discovery/enquiry-based teaching the teacher creates situations, from which the pupil discovers for himself the principles or knowledge the teacher wishes him to learn.

The pupil attacks the subject in the attitude of the discoverer. For dogma the teacher substitutes discovery; for passive receptivity, he/she substitutes activity. The pupils are taken on a voyage of discovery, with the teacher piloting (not pushing or shovelling) he pupils.

This strategy has several advantages.

1 The child plays the game himself instead of merely being a spectator on the touch lines.

2 It is a good antidote to spoon-feeding.

3 Admittedly more mistakes will be made by the learners, but better that than that everything is done for them, including their thinking. We learn best from our mistakes.

The disadvantages are:

1 We cannot expect children to discover all the things they need to know. So it is inappropriate in an extreme form.

2 It is all pupil and no teacher. This is in accord with the 'mathetic' (Greek 'mathet' = pupil) principle of today where the emphasis is not so much on teaching as on learning by the pupil. The shift is from the teacher as answer-giver to the teacher as problem-poser. The teacher is a resource rather than a source or fount of wisdom.

3 It takes time. But are not fewer facts by good methods better than many facts by poor methods?

Open-ended enquiry methods are all very will but unless they are carefully supervised and regulated they can often lead to confusion and frustration from an apparent lack of clear progress and achievement on the part of the pupils. Children like the security of a situation they can understand as against being left helpless in an 'enquiry-based' learning situation.

In theory learning by discovery, by experience, by activity, ought by logical right to dominate the entire conduct of the teacher in the classroom. But this does not dispose of the problem of just where to strike the balance between open-ended enquiry methods and the mastery of those skills and facts which teachers know that children need to learn.

A modified heuristic approach is the *problem solving method.*

Education is a preparation for facing the problems of life. The teacher must aim to nurture 'active wisdom'.

As against the didactic, jug-and-mug methods of the educational 'oppressors' Paulo Freire argues strongly in favour of its replacement by a problem-solving strategy in order to liberate the 'oppressed' – the students. He argues that the didactic method – the banking concept of education, where students are mere 'depositories' – is an insult to human dignity and an affront to the human personality. The problem-posing concept of education, on the other hand, respects the individuality of the student.

Ideally, the pupils themselves should pose the problems. But this often leads to the selection of problems that are too trivial, or too difficult, or just unmanageable in the circumstances. So the teacher's wisdom and guidance are necessary. But this can be done by judicious prompting and suggestion rather than by magisterial decree.

Dewey believed that most of education could be learning tasks organized within a problem-solving framework.

W.H. Kilpatrick, a disciple of Dewey, applied this problem-solving technique to integrated teaching in the primary school and developed what is today called the project method.

The *project method* involves a study or investigation by small groups or teams of pupils of particular themes and topics. In this method a voyage of discovery is decided on. As far as possible the pupils should be encouraged to do the planning and carrying out, with the teacher merely steering the boat clear of any rocks. The teacher should be concerned to see that the children do their thing, not his or hers. How often are class exhibitions and projects simply products of the teacher's professional ego rather than the children's understanding and interests?

The criticism is sometimes made that so often projects are 'soft options' having little worthwhile knowledge content.

Whilst the curriculum should be based on pupils' interests, this does not mean that any nefarious interests of children are sufficient grounds on which to base curricula. Not every interest has educational potential. The teacher must choose those that have 'theoretical mileage'.

The advantages of the project method are:
1   high pupil interest;
2   it is a good training in resource and initiative.
The disadvantages are that
1   it can degenerate into purposeless fooling around or pointless passing of time. It was for these reasons that the method came to be discouraged in the U.S.S.R.;
2   it takes up time. But does this matter?

Activity methods form another counter to the jug-and-mug techniques of teaching. Instead of the classroom being a 'sit-stillery', children are encouraged to be active, to do things.

However, one must beware of two misconceptions or misrepresensations of the notion of activity:
1   one is the notion of activity as an end in itself and not as a means to an end;

2 the second is the notion that practical activities are suitable only for the less able. This is a great heresy.

Sometimes, the *lecture demonstration method* is used. It has been shown that when children:

1 observe demonstrations carried out by the teacher they gain more marks in the immediate future;

2 carry out the work (e.g. experiments) themselves, they gain more marks in the long run.

The ideal strategy would seem to be a judicious blend of practical work by the pupils themselves augmented with demonstrations by the teacher.

Warning: If you are going to give a demonstration, make sure that it works (or else be prepared for strong discipline!) So test the experiment or demonstration beforehand and ensure it will work before the actual demonstration in front of the class.

Sometimes, despite all precautions, the demonstration does not work. What then? Cultivate calmness of composure and a sense of humour.

To ensure your demonstration achieves its desired purpose:

1 The class must be clear as to the purpose of the demonstration. Tell them why the demonstration is being performed, but do not tell them the anticipated results beforehand. Let them use their own eyes and brains.

2 The demonstration must be on a fairly large scale so as to be visible to all.

3 The demonstration should be simple and not consume overmuch time.

So which teaching/learning strategy do I use?

There is no one strategy for teaching. The teacher must consider all the relevant circumstances and decide which strategy would serve the purpose best in those conditions and circumstances.

There are many teaching/learning episodes that cannot be reduced to a 'content' which is then taught by a 'method'. Unpredictable, unexpected events – such as a sudden swarm of locusts, or an eclipse, or an earth tremor, or something far less spectacular yet worthy of interest – can all be made the occasions for worthwhile educational ventures. It is the teacher's job to fan a spark of passing interest into a steadily burning flame.

110

Opportunism is the salt of good teaching and seasoned teachers seize on any such 'teachable moments'. Good teachers judge success from the light in children's eyes; they adapt or modfy their lessons to keep that light shining.

Planning the lesson

I have a lesson of 45 minutes (or maybe, a double period). What do I do in that time?

Since teaching means 'inciting to learn' and bearing in mind the characteristics of young children noted earlier, I would in general settle, as far as possible, for a strategy that involved discovery by the children. Avoid the didactic, lecture method, which for the pupils means 'one end dumb, the other end numb'.

So begin with a challenging problem; and investigate it as a voyage of discovery with the class. (An example of such a teaching/learning strategy in science is given in Appendix 9A).

Since variety is the spice of life, break up the 45 minutes into several activities:

1   oral – carefully planned questioning, etc.;
2   a short exposition by the teacher about the task or problem;
3   practical work by the pupils, especially as most pupils 'think with their fingers';
4   written work, e.g. calculations, by the pupils, including applications of what they have done. Just as there is no teaching if there is no learning, pupils must be able to apply what they have done or discovered or worked out.
5   recapitulation, including dealing with any difficulties, misconceptions. A summary of what was accomplished.

See Appendix 9B for a lesson plan in Mathematics incorporating these suggestions.

Other variables in teaching strategies

Teaching strategies are closely linked to and determined by several variables besides the teacher and the learner. Obviously, the facilities available – or not available – such as teaching materials and equipment, laboratory apparatus, specialist workrooms, etc. will all influence what is done in the school and how it is done. The media of communication, too, will have an influence. The availability of audio-visual aids – from simple flannelgraphs and chalk-boards to more sophisticated hardware such as radio, film and television, will also influence teaching strategies. The lay-out and design of the classrooms, too, can be an important determinant in the pattern of teaching – whether formal class teaching, group discussions, teaching in small groups, individual programmed learning etc. Finally, the very tone and climate of the school can have an exhilarating influence or a deadening influence on the teaching within it.

Summary

Teaching strategy means the deliberate planning and organization of teaching-learning experiences and situations in the light of psychological and pedagogical principles with a view to achieving specific goals.
Any teaching/learning strategy must take note of:
1   the age and ability of the learner;
2   motivation and interest;
3   insightful learning – relationships and principles are more important than facts;
4   active involvement and participation.
Some strategies of teaching/learning
1   The didactic method: the 'jug-and-mug' technique;
2   The lecture method;
3   The lecture demonstration method. If you must demonstrate, make absolutely sure (beforehand) that the demonstration works.
    Avoid these as much as you can.
Other teaching/learning strategies. The pupil of today is an individual to be developed wholly – intellectually, physically, aesthetically, morally, emotionally. Hence the need to adopt other teaching/learning strategies, making use of the interests and characteristics of children.
    A good teaching strategy is one that emphasises finding out, with the pupils investigating and discovering facts for themselves, using their own eyes and hands and brains. For example:
1   The discovery (heuristic) method: the teacher creates situations from which the pupil discovers for himself the principles or knowledge the teacher wishes him to learn.
A modified heuristic approach is:
2   The problem-solving method.
3   The project method/the topic method. Here teacher and class

112

decide on a particular project or topic, which is then investigated.

4   Activity methods.

There is no one strategy for teaching. The teacher must consider all the relevant circumstances and decide which strategy would serve the purpose best in the conditions and circumstances. *To help plan your lessons.* Whenever possible begin with a challenging problem and investigate it as a voyage of discovery with the class.

1   Oral – carefully planned questioning.
2   A short exposition by the teacher about the task or problem.
3   Practical work by the pupils.
4   Written work by the pupils, e.g. calculations, applications of what they have done.
5   Recapitulation/summary.

Questions

1   What is meant by a teaching/learning 'strategy'? Describe one or two important teaching/learning strategies.
2   List and briefly discuss some of the important factors in the psychology of learning.
3   It is said that different teaching/learning strategies should be used for children of differing abilities. Give one example of this.
4   Give one example of how you would 'motivate' your pupils in a particular lesson.
5   Do you agree that in education teaching and learning 'facts' only is not sufficient? Explain why.
6   Give an example of how you would encourage children to 'think for themselves' in the course of a lesson.
7   Give an example of how you would teach a particular topic so that it is 'logic' not 'magic'.
8   Give an example of how you would make use of children's curiosity to teach a particular topic.
9   Discuss the importance of 'success' in learning.
10   It is said that schools are often full of teaching but little learning. Explain this statement. How could you change such a situation?
11   Is there any place for 'rote' learning in the schools? Explain.
12   Discuss the advantages and disadvantages of examinations.
13   To what extent do the physical conditions in the schools,

such as overcrowding, etc., prevent effective teaching/learning? Can you think of other 'physical' factors that prevent such effective teaching/learning?

14 What do you suppose is meant by a 'new look' in education? In what ways do you feel your educational system could do with a 'new look'?

15 What are some of the important factors a teacher should bear in mind in working out a strategy of teaching?

16 List some of the chief characteristics of young children. How would you use these characteristics as an ally in your teaching?

17 What is the 'heuristic' method? Give an example from your teaching or learning.

18 What are the advantages of the 'discovery' method in teaching/learning? Is this method used in your schools? Elaborate.

19 What are some of the disadvantages of the 'discovery' method? How can these be overcome?

20 Discuss the statement that 'it is better to teach fewer facts by good methods than many facts by poor methods'.

21 What are the advantages and disadvantages of the 'problem-solving' approach in teaching/learning?

22 Give an example of the use of the 'project' method.

23 List some of the advantages and disadvantages of the project method.

24 Write out a lesson plan indicating how you would proceed in teaching a particular topic to a particular age group.

Appendix 9A

An example of a 'guided discovery' lesson in science

(For pupils at the top of primary school or starting secondary school.)

Aim: That pupils understand the concept of centre of gravity and how it explains equilibrium ('balancing').

Apparatus: Corks, nails, forks, centre of gravity toys (home-made), wooden stick or pole, home-made plumbline, piece of

114

cardboard to demonstrate stable, unstable and neutral equilibrium, paper clips, nuts or bolts, thread, wire.

The children should be asked before-hand to equip themselves with: one pencil, one pair scissors, one stone, one sheet of cardboard.

Plan: 1 Introduction: The Problem: 'Why do things balance?'
a) Distribute cork to each member of the class.
'Can you balance a cork on the point of your pencil?'
b) Provide each member with either two nails or two forks.
'Now can you balance the cork on the pencil point?'
'Why?'

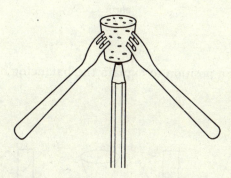

2 Demonstrate
Balancing 'toys', e.g. nodding bird, prancing horse, Humpty Dumpty, etc. shown on accompanying work sheet.
'Now can you explain why things balance?'
3 Demonstrate the point of balance on the wooden stick or pole.

This point is called 'Centre of Gravity' (C.G.) – where all the weight may be considered to be concentrated.
4 Brief discourse on meaning of force of gravity and weight.
a) Why does a ball thrown up always come down?
b) Is a man in Australia upside down?
c) Sir Isaac Newton's theory (very simply) about gravity.
d) Earth satellites; space ships; weightlessness;
e) Plumb-line – the weight comes down as close to the earth as possible. Why?

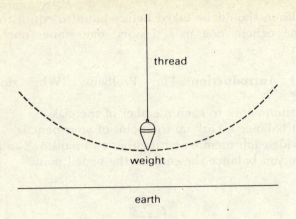

thread

weight

earth

5   Still not in a position to explain the balancing of the toys. So **demonstrate**:

Stable equilibrium
C.G. *below* point of
suspension (0)

Unstable equilibrium
C.G. *above* point of
suspension (0)

Neutral equilibrium
C.G. *at same level* as
point of suspension (0)

'Now can you explain why the toys balance?'

Answer: Things balance when their centre of gravity is below the point of suspension.

6   **Some light relief!**
If possible: show pictures illustrating 'balance'; perform a 'balancing trick'!
7   Distribute work and questions sheet to each member of the class.

116

Work and questions sheet
A.   *Things to do and make*
1   "centre of gravity" toys

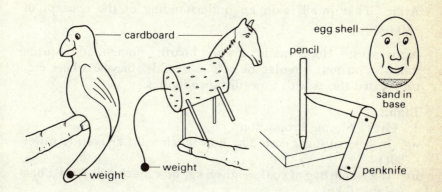

2   Cut out these shapes from a sheet of cardboard: **a)** a square,
b) a rectangle, **c)** a circle, **d)** a triangle.

Using a plumb-line find the centre of gravity of each.
How can you make sure that is the centre of gravity?

Result:
a)   The centre of gravity of a square is where the . . . cross each
other.
b)   The centre of gravity of a rectangle is where the . . . cross.
c)   The centre of gravity of a circle is where the . . . cross.
d)   The centre of gravity of a triangle is where the . . . cross.

3   Cut out an irregular shape from a sheet of cardboard. Find its
centre of gravity.

4   Find the centre of gravity of **a)** a hoop, **b)** a box, **c)** a chair.

B.   *Questions*
1   Why is a tail put on a kite?
2   Why do ships carry ballast?
3   Draw an egg in **a)** stable, **b)** unstable, **c)** neutral equilibrium.

117

Appendix 9B
Lesson Plan (Mathematics)

Form V   Time: 1½ hours
                                               (11.00–12.30)
                                               Date:

Aim: That pupils gain an understanding of the concept of variation.

Apparatus: Home-made graph board; home-made spring balance; various circular objects – tin lids, bicycle wheel etc; duplicated sheets with time/distance figures.

Plan:
1   **Oral**   Simple Proportion:
a)   If ¼ kg of sugar costs 20c, how much will 1 kg cost? (Answer 80c)
b)   If a whole bag of coal weighs 8 kg, how much will ¾ of a bag weigh? (6 kg)
c)   If 10 men take 2½ min to sing the National Anthem, how long will 20 men take? (!)
d)   A car travels at 50 k.p.h. How long will it take to go 200 kilometres? (4 hours)
e)   If one man takes 3 sec. to fall down a precipice, how long will 9 men take? (!)
f)   A girl walks 4 kilometres in 1 hr. How far will she have walked in 2½ hrs? (10 kilometres)
g)   Miriam can drink a bottle of Coca-Cola in 1½ minutes. How long to drink 1 dozen? (!)
h)   If 1 m of cloth costs 2.50 how many metres can you buy for 10.00? (4 m)
i)   John, who is 5 years old, is 1.5 m. tall. How tall will he be when he is 20? (!)
(**Others:** If Henry VIII had 6 wives, how many did Henry II have? If it takes 3 mins. to boil an egg, how long for 5 eggs?)

2   **Blackboard**
Beef costs 3.00 a kilo.

Cost	3	6	9	12	15	18	21	24	27	30
Wt.	1	2	3	4	5	6	7	8	9	10

Question

Do you notice anything special about these figures?
Yes; if we double the weight, the cost is ...? (doubled)
if we treble the weight, the cost is ...? (trebled)
if we halve the weight, the cost is ...? (halved)

We say that the cost varies directly as the weight. $C \propto W$

3 Demonstration (Hooke's Law)
Demonstrate home-made spring balance.
If I double the weight, what happens to the extension?

Question

Does the extension vary as the weight? (*Hooke's Law*).

4 Refer back to the table of cost and weight of beef.

Question

Anything else special about the figures?

Hint: $\dfrac{C}{W}$?

Yes, $\dfrac{C}{W}$ is always the same or $\dfrac{C}{W}$ is constant.

Anything else special?

Draw the graph Cost vs Wt.

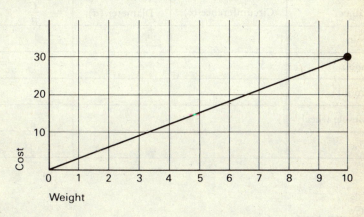

Yes, the graph of Cost against Wt. is a straight line, which goes through the origin.

Questions
e.g. What is the cost of 5½ kg? How much do I get for 19.50?

5 Summary - on blackboard, class providing the information.
The cost varies directly as the wt. i.e. $C \propto W$
a) if when we double (treble etc.) one, we double (treble) the other;

b) if $\dfrac{C}{W}$ is constant;

c) if the graph of C against W is a straight line.

6 If the diameter of a 50 cent coin is 2 cm what is the diameter:
a) of a 10 cent coin? b) of a 20 cent coin?
Does the diameter vary as the value?

7 Practical work by the class
Problem: Does the circumference of a circle vary as the diameter?
How can we find out?
a) doubling? b) is $\dfrac{C}{d}$ a constant? c) graph.

Distribute tin lids, hoops, wheels etc.
Children to fill in this table, using say 5 objects.

Object	Circumference (c)	Diameter (d)	$\dfrac{C}{d}$
coin			
hoop			
tin lid			
bicycle wheel			
disc			

Is $\dfrac{C}{d}$ constant?
(Yes $\dfrac{C}{d}$ = a constant, which is called π. $\dfrac{C}{d} = \pi$ or $C = \pi d$.

More problems
a)   How could you find the circumference of this (wheel or coin) taking only one measurement?
b)   If the circumference of a circular track is 440 metres, what is the diameter? (Use $\pi = \frac{22}{7}$ Ans. 140 m.)

If $C \propto d$, then the graph C against d should be a straight line. Let's see if it is.

Put a table of suitable values of C and d on board, *using measurements made by children.*

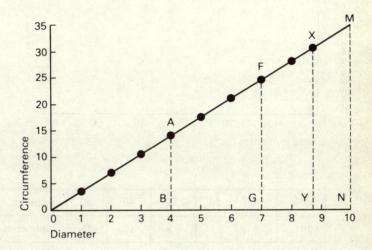

Questions
What is the circumference if diameter is 7.2?
What is the diameter if circumference is 28.5?

8   Mention the slope or gradient.

What is the slope of our graph? e.g. $\dfrac{AB}{OB}$

Is this the same as $\dfrac{FG}{OG}$, $\dfrac{XY}{OY}$, $\dfrac{MN}{ON}$?

What is special about this slope?
Yes, it is the same as the constant (π).

$\dfrac{y}{x} = c$; or $y = cx$, c being the slope.

121

What is so unusual or wonderful about the slope?
Let us do this problem together.
Distribute sheets with time/distance figures.

Walking

time	10	20	30	40	50	mins.
dist.	1	2	3	4	5	kilometres

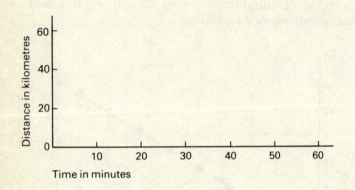

Bicycle

time	10	20	30	40	50	mins.
dist.	3	6	9	12	15	kilometres

Car

time	10	20	30	40	50	mins.
dist.	8	16	24	32	40	kilometres

Train

time	10	20	30	40	50	mins.
dist.	10	20	30	40	50	kilometres

Aeroplane

time	10	20	30	40	50	mins.
dist.	60	120	180	240	300	kilometres

122

Questions

1 Is distance $\propto$ time? In each separate case:
a) if we double one, do we double the other?
b) is the graph a straight line through the origin?
c) is $\dfrac{d}{t}$ a constant? (i.e. $\dfrac{d}{t}$ = constant = velocity)

2 What is the velocity of a) the cyclist? b) the plane? etc.

Hence significance of the slope.

3 What is the distance covered by the car after 45 mins?
4 How long will it take the train to cover 50 kilometres?
5 Where do you think the slope of a) a jet, b) an express train, c) a motor bike, d) a runner, etc. would be?

Classwork & homework

For example:
1 Graphs using data provided on duplicated sheets.
2 Textbook, p. 24. Question No. 1.

Looking ahead: i.e. lessons to follow:

Variation directly as the square i.e. Area $\propto$ height^2 ($A \propto h^2$)
Variation directly as the square root i.e. time $\propto \sqrt{\ }$ length (pendulum)
Inverse variation

10 The Process of Curriculum Development

It is easy to get submerged or drowned in detail; to see things in their right perspective one needs a panaromic view. Otherwise we can become like the fabled blind men who tried to describe an elephant, one holding the trunk, the other the tail. Each one of them is clutching a different limb of the truth but neither of them is seeing the whole.

We need first to see the whole process of curriculum development on a broad canvas, before getting down to the specifics. 'Frameworks' of the curriculum development process provide us with such broad canvases. They enable us to see the wood rather than the trees; they provide us with the total picture.

Frameworks of curriculum development

This is Wheeler's simple framework of the curriculum development process.

1. The formulation of aims and objectives.
2. The selection of learning experiences (activities) – determining the centres or focal points to be used for organizing these experiences, so as to assist in the attainment of the aims and objectives, having regard to the nature of the learners, and to the principles of learning.
3. The selection of content – determining not only what subject matter should be covered but what mental powers and capacities, such as thinking, skills, attitudes, values, etc. should emerge from the learning activities.
4. Organization and integration of the learning experiences and content and methods so as to constitute a practical guide to action in the classroom.

5 Evaluation of the effectiveness of stages 2, 3 and 4 in achieving the aims and objectives enumerated in 1.

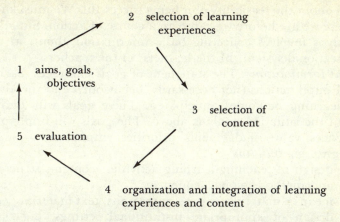

Fig. 2   Curriculum development as a continuous process[92b]

Another framework of the curriculum development process is that of Professor Skilbeck.

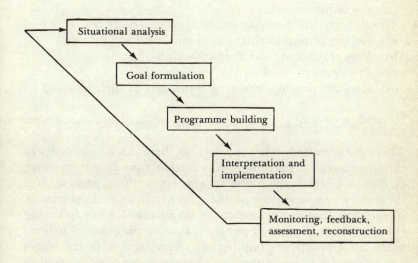

Fig. 3   The curriculum development process[65b]

He begins, logically, with

1 *Situation analysis*   This involves finding out the context in which the curriculum development process is to take place and about the feasibility of it being successful. We must know where we are before we can plan a course of action. Situation analysis involves collecting basic information about: **a)** the educational system; **b)** the learners; **c)** the teachers.

2 *Goal formulation*   The statement of goals embraces teacher and pupil actions (not necessarily 'behaviour') and the kinds of learning outcomes anticipated. These goals will 'derive' from the situation analysis above. The goals will imply preferences, values, judgements, priorities, emphases.

3 *Programme building*
   a) design of teaching-learning activities: content, structure and method, scope, sequence;
   b) means – materials, e.g. resource units, text materials, etc;
   c) design of appropriate institutional settings, e.g. laboratories, field work, workshops;
   d) personnel deployment and role definition, e.g. curriculum change as social change;
   e) timetables and provisioning.

4 *Interpretation and implementation*   Problems of installing the curriculum change, e.g. in an on-going institutional setting where there may be a clash between old and new, resistance, confusion, etc.

5 *Monitoring, feedback, assessment, reconstruction*
   a) Design of monitoring and communication systems.
   b) Preparation of assessment schedules.
   c) Problems of 'continuous' assessment.
   d) Reconstruction – ensuring continuity of the process.

He adds a caveat.

There is a temptation to suppose that there is a logical order in the five stages of this model. It is certainly possible to produce elaborate systems diagrams of the curriculum process. Yet there may be sound institutional and psychological reasons for intervening first at any one of the stages and for not following the arrows on those increasingly elaborate diagrams. Furthermore, in a practical planning operation, the different stages can be developed concurrently. There is plenty of evidence that teachers do not, in fact, proceed in a linear fashion from goals to evaluation. The model outlined encourages teams or groups of curriculum developers to take into account different elements and aspects of the curriculum development process, to see the process as an organic whole, and to work in a moderately systematic way.

This model differs from the previous model in these respects:
1   It identifies the learning situation, not materials production and change strategies, as the major problematical area of curriculum development. It encourages developers to think educationally about the situation which is to be changed, not about how to implement pre-designed models and techniques of change.
2   It encourages curriculum developers to enter the model at whatever stage they wish. For example, the real problem as perceived by the teacher may be inadequate examinations, or poor text materials – either can be the starting point for curriculum thinking.

Dr. Dave provides a much more detailed framework of the curriculum development process, which is shown on page 128.

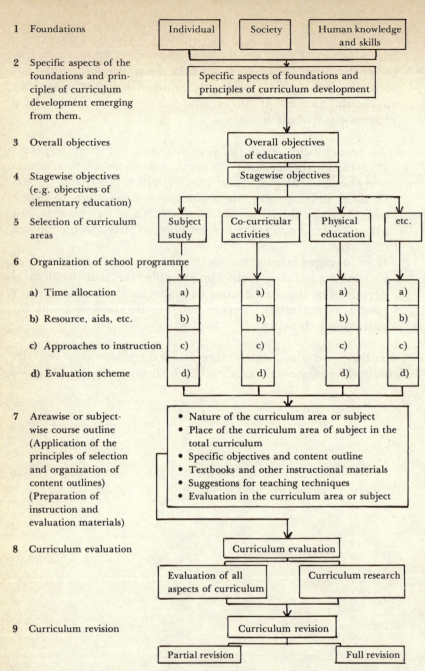

| 1 | Foundations | Individual | Society | Human knowledge and skills |

| 2 | Specific aspects of the foundations and principles of curriculum development emerging from them. | Specific aspects of foundations and principles of curriculum development |

| 3 | Overall objectives | Overall objectives of education |

| 4 | Stagewise objectives (e.g. objectives of elementary education) | Stagewise objectives |

| 5 | Selection of curriculum areas | Subject study | Co-curricular activities | Physical education | etc. |

6	Organization of school programme				
a) Time allocation	a)	a)	a)	a)
b) Resource, aids, etc.	b)	b)	b)	b)
c) Approaches to instruction	c)	c)	c)	c)
d) Evaluation scheme	d)	d)	d)	d)

| 7 | Areawise or subject-wise course outline (Application of the principles of selection and organization of content outlines) (Preparation of instruction and evaluation materials) | • Nature of the curriculum area or subject
• Place of the curriculum area of subject in the total curriculum
• Specific objectives and content outline
• Textbooks and other instructional materials
• Suggestions for teaching techniques
• Evaluation in the curriculum area or subject |

| 8 | Curriculum evaluation | Curriculum evaluation |
| | | Evaluation of all aspects of curriculum | Curriculum research |

| 9 | Curriculum revision | Curriculum revision |
| | | Partial revision | Full revision |

Fig. 4 Framework of curriculum development (Prepared by Dr R.H. Dave, Dean of Educational Development and Head of Department of Curriculum and Evaluation, NCERT, India)

128

Amalgamating these separate frameworks we obtain the following comprehensive check-list of the processes involved in curriculum development.

Situation analysis
Foundations:

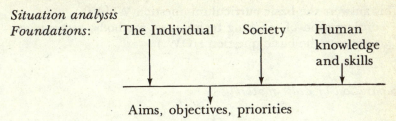

Overall objectives:

       National policy

       Different levels and types of children

       Different subjects/subject areas

↓

Stagewise objectives (e.g. objectives for elementary education, for secondary education etc.) These objectives will determine the selection of curriculum areas, of teaching-learning experiences.

↓

       Guide-lines for content/teaching-learning experiences

These goals, aims, objectives and the guide-lines for curriculum content/teaching-learning activities are translated into action in schools through *Policy and Strategy*.

    Planning a strategy for change.
    The agencies for change; co-ordination with change-agents.
    Resources in manpower, materials, time, must be correctly deployed.

↓

Curriculum Design i.e. building the programmes
This programme building will involve:
1 a survey of the chosen curriculum area by panels of teachers and others leading to a precise statement of area/subject objectives.

(Of the basic questions of curriculum development, this action
will answer the WHY.)
2   the selection and organization of learning experiences/
content; planning and building the teaching-learning units.
(This answers the basic curriculum question WHAT.)
3   consideration of teaching techniques, methods, approaches.
(This answers the basic question HOW.)

↓

Preparation of draft materials

↓

Trial and implementation
Briefing sessions, workshops, etc., with volunteer teachers from a
few pilot schools, i.e. 'pilot trial'.

↓

Trial in schools
↓

Monitoring/evaluation   Evaluation
↓

Modification of materials, objectives etc. in the
light of trials and evaluation.

↓

Further trials and modification/revision.

↓

Publication and diffusion of new materials and
widespread retraining of teachers.

↓

Continuous evaluation

Questions

1 Draw a diagram to illustrate the main processes which must be considered in curriculum development.

2 What is meant by 'situation analysis'? Discuss its importance in curriculum development.

3 Why is it important to have goals/objectives in curriculum development?

4 What do you understand by 'programme building' in curriculum development? Illustrate your remarks by a few actual examples.

5 Why are 'trials' important in curriculum development?

6 Discuss any curriculum 'trials' that may be taking place in your country now.

7 What is meant by 'evaluation' in curriculum development? Why is it important?

8 Discuss any 'evaluation' of curriculum that might be taking place in your country now.

9 Discuss some of the important factors that prevent effective implementation of a new curriculum.

10 Is your country currently engaged in curriculum development? Briefly discuss some of its main achievements to date.

11 Discuss some of the problems such curriculum development has come up against.

11　Situation Analysis

We firmly believe the world crisis in education can be overcome – if: If the people concerned candidly and systematically diagnose their educational problems and plan their educational future in the light of what they uncover in their self-diagnosis.[16e]

There was a time when all curriculum development had to begin with a specification of objectives – and 'behavioural objectives' at that. That models of curriculum development should begin with a definition of objectives is understandable: one must know where one is going and why.

Today, there is an increasing realization that the beginning of curriculum planning should rather be with 'situation analysis'.

Curriculum design should begin, not with an abstract list of objectives, but with a realistic appraisal and analysis of the situation as it exists, what changes this analysis suggests and how these changes might best be brought about bearing in mind the available resources. To alter 'what is' we first need to know 'what is'.

Skilbeck lists the many factors that must be considered if one is to obtain a true picture of the situation as it exists in any country and as it will effect decisions about the form and structure of the curriculum.

External factors:
1　Changes and trends in society which indicate tasks for schools – e.g. industrial and economic development, political directives, cultural movements, ideological changes.
2　Expectations and requirements of parents, employers.
3　Community assumptions and values including patterns of adult-child relationships.

4 Education-system requirements and challenges, e.g. policy directives, local authority pressures or expectations, curriculum projects, examinations, educational research.
5 The changing nature of the subject matter to be taught.
6 The potential contribution of teacher-support systems, e.g. teachers' centres, teacher training colleges, universities, research institutes etc.
7 Actual and anticipated flow of resources into the schools.

Internal factors:
1 Pupils – their aptitudes, abilities, attitudes, values and defined educational needs.
2 Teachers – their values, attitudes, skills, knowledge, experience, special strengths and weaknesses, their roles.
3 School ethos and structure: common assumptions and expectations including traditions, authority relationships, etc.
4 Material resources including buildings, equipment, learning materials and possibilities for enhancing these.
5 Perceived and felt problems and shortcomings in the existing curriculum.[65b]

Before one can begin effective curriculum design and planning one needs information. But 'situation analysis' is more than just collecting information; it involves identifying tasks and problems, seeking possible solutions, anticipating the difficulties and possible areas of resistance, planning the resources and the organizational changes that will be needed.

Most Third World countries have taken close stock of their educational systems.

In Fiji, an Education Commission was set up in 1969 to examine the state of education in the island. The following is a paraphrase of the Commission's findings with regard to the school curriculum.[26]

1 The curriculum is still essentially a collection of subjects, largely unrelated and taught in water-tight compartments.
2 The content of the subjects is too formal and academic to meet the needs of the majority of the children who do not proceed on to higher studies.
3 School-leaving examinations dominate the choice of subject and methods of study. 'The existing school curriculum in Fiji seems to be designed mainly to secure the passing of examina-

tions ... The frequency of examinations has also a cramping effect on sound curriculum development ... It is inevitable that in such a system of education, preparation for examinations becomes the pre-occupation of both teachers and pupils.' (Commission Report. 4.6 and 4.8)

4 Practical and aesthetic subjects are, therefore, not given sufficient time or attention. 'The whole curriculum appears to have been designed to transmit factual knowledge rather than to provide learning experience that will encourage creative activities and thus lead to an all-round physical, emotional and intellectual development of the pupils.' (4.9)

5 'What the pupil does in school neither satisfies the developing needs of the child as a child nor prepares him adequately for the world he will live in as an adult.'

This criticism of the school curriculum is today still true of many supposedly developed countries. It must be mentioned that since 1969 the Fiji school curriculum has moved a very long way towards obviating these criticisms.

It is important that members of the general public, and not only 'experts', should be invited to play their part in any 'situation analysis'. As Vaizey points out: 'Education itself is not a discipline like physics or mathematics. It is an area involving enormous numbers of people from very different backgrounds, an area in which nobody can claim a monopoly of wisdom or discovery. We must be careful to avoid saying that anybody who is not an expert in education, whatever an educationist is, hasn't a right to talk about education ...'[10f]

In Sierra Leone the educational system of the country was examined not by appointing in the first instance, an expert Commission, but by inviting the general public to a discussion and debate on the existing situation in the schools and on what changes, if any, should be introduced. This Education Review was followed by a National Conference on Curriculum and a National Seminar on Primary Teacher Education (1976).

In Zambia, a similar public debate on education and on matters affecting the school curriculum was held in 1976. As Hawes points out:

the people themselves felt they had something to say about education, about what intimately affected the lives and futures of their children. Of the 1,500 or so submissions received, more than 1,100 came from individual members of the public, the remainder coming from local and district seminars, teacher associations, parent-teacher associations, religious organizations and from the schools themselves.[36d]

In the Cameroons a research institute – The Insitute for the Reform of Primary Education – was set up in 1974 at Buea to gather information as to the most appropriate ways of preparing pupils and school leavers for integration into the life and work of the community. The Project comprises four teams working in close collaboration: two in environmental studies concerned with village technology, agriculture and social questions, a third on mathematics and the fourth on language. In his *Curriculum and Reality in African Primary Schools* (pp. 27–30) Hawes gives this account of the work of the Institute.

The team concerned with environmental studies, agricultural and social aspects made a random sample of visits throughout the two English speaking provinces of Cameroon. They interviewed teachers, headmasters, parents, chiefs and their counsellors, local farmers and final year pupils in schools in an attempt to bring out a picture of the local and school environment and of needs and aspirations of young people and adults. The wealth of information collected and most ably synthesised in the project's report was used as evidence on which to base suggestions for possible key topics round which teaching could be based. Since different communities with different needs were identified – from remote, isolated environments to well-served rural and semi-urban ones, separate community-orientated activities were suggested to suit each of these.

Teams in Mathematics and English were concerned with finding out what knowledge and what concepts children and teachers have and can master at different levels and of assessing the strengths and limitations of the environment and the cultural traditions within that environment for teaching and materials production in these two areas.

... There can be no question that the project marks an important landmark in curriculum planning in Africa. The importance of situational analysis as a preliminary to curriculum design has been recognised, investment has been made and important questions are being asked. In the sister institute

135

in the French-speaking Cameroon set up somewhat earlier at Yaounde, workers embarked more conventionally straight into a progamme of materials production and were able to announce confidently that by March 1973, 'about 47 tons of textbooks and 33 tons of documents have been produced', but you cannot profitably assess the success of a curriculum by weight; many megatons of unprofitable material have been produced (and will still be produced) all over Africa just because no preliminary study had been made to ascertain whether children and parents wanted them, could afford them, read them or understand them.

Having carried out a thorough analysis of one's situation one is now in a position to proceed to the next stage in the process of curriculum development – the stage of setting realistic objectives that can be realised. Pie-in-the-sky objectives are all too common, and Beeby, who has had very many years' experience in developing countries, sounds a word of caution against the danger of setting over-ambitious targets.

When I hear theorists talk about the task of introducing children to the computer age, of teaching them to think scientifically, to create rather than to copy, to understand principles rather than regurgitate half-digested facts, my mind goes back to village schools that I have known in many countries, to poor buildings devoid of books and equipment, to teachers partly educated, often untrained and under-paid, to children who are spending most of their time on rote memorization rather than any real understanding of what they learn. . . This is a picture all too common; this, too often, is the reality on which countries must try to build a brave new world.[41a]

Summary
Curriculum development should begin with situation analysis – a realistic appraisal and analysis of the educational situation as it exists in a particular country.

Situation analysis is more than just collecting information; it involves identifying tasks and problems and devising possible solutions.

136

Situation analysis should involve not only the 'experts', but also the general, interested public.

Questions
1   Do you feel that the educational system in your country is paying sufficient attention to the situation as it exists in your country? Discuss this.
2   What is the purpose of education in your country? Is the country's educational system succeeding in achieving the goals set for it?
3   What do you suggest still needs to be done for your educational system to achieve its goals, bearing in mind the existing conditions and situation in your country?
4   Draw up a summary 'situation analysis' of one aspect of education in your country.
5   What are the arguments for and against involving the general public in discussions about your country's educational system?

12　The Role of Objectives in Curriculum Planning

We indulge excessively in uncoordinated conferences, surveys, and studies that are on the whole highly unproductive. Our ailments are vast and complex, and they will yield only to planned, collaborative attacks focussed on clear objectives and leading to concerted action.

Julius Stratton (1964)[51a]

The case for objectives

We cannot or should not, decide on 'what' to teach or 'how' to teach until we know 'why' we are doing it.

As Professor Kerr argues: 'For curriculum planning to be rational it must start with clear and specific aims and objectives, and then, and only then, address itself to discovering the means, the content and methods, in terms of which the objectives are to be achieved. There can be no curriculum without educational objectives.'[50a]

And Professor Hirst argues that: 'It is a simple logical nonsense to pretend that a series of activities form a curriculum, or a part of a curriculum, if they are not responsibly designed to obtain specifiable objectives.'[39]

For planning to be rational, the ends or outcomes have to be stated and be defensible on rational grounds. One must be able to justify what one is doing; one must be able to give an account of why one is teaching this to that class at this particular time in this particular school.

Jamaica provides a good example of a country which decided that, rather than venture headlong into the dark of curriculum reform, as some countries have done, it would first work out what

138

its education should aim to achieve before laying down what that education should contain.[33b] The Curriculum Development Trust was set up in 1972 to produce objectives and guidelines for Primary School Grades 1–8. Four working parties were set up to ascertain:

1   What the pupils should be able to do as a result of nine years of primary education, i.e. what **skills** they should possess.
2   What the pupils should know about i.e. what **knowledge** and **insights** they should have.
3   What the pupils should feel i.e. the **attitudes** required.

Teachers at all levels were involved in this exercise to formulate the aims and objectives of primary schooling in Jamaica.

Kenya, too, realised the importance of ascertaining the goals and objectives of education first before getting down to how to implement these objectives. In 1974 it held a Workshop on the Setting of Objectives. The following year another Workshop was held to transform the objectives into content and learning experiences for the primary schools.

The objectives model of curriculum development

Characteristic of the objectives model of curriculum development is that it attempts to improve the practice of education by first obtaining clarity about the ends of education. Once we are clear about what we are seeking to achieve we can then plan more effectively the means to achieve the ends.

In 1949 Ralph Tyler, an eminent American education theorist, published a book called *The Basic Principles of Curriculum and Instruction*. On the first page he identified four fundamental questions which must be faced in any curriculum process:

1   What educational purposes should the school seek to attain? What are the objectives we hope to achieve from our teaching? What qualities of mind, what knowledge, skills, values, do we wish our pupils to acquire?

Having begun with the question of objectives, Tyler then moves on to the next steps in the curriculum development process.

139

2 What educational experiences, what subject matter, what activities, what programme of work, will best achieve these purposes?
3 How can these educational (learning) experiences be efficiently organized so as to constitute a practical guide to action?
4 How can we determine whether these desirable purposes are being attained?

These four questions supply the basis of the objectives model of curriculum development.

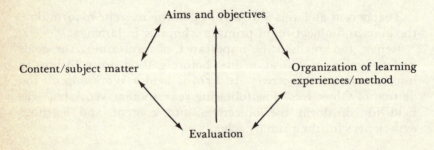

Aims and objectives

Content/subject matter

Organization of learning experiences/method

Evaluation

Fig. 5 Basic elements of the curriculum

These four basic elements of the curriculum – objectives, content, methods, evaluation – do not constitute neat, discrete categories. They form a dynamic, organic whole. They are closely inter-related and each element is influenced by, and influences, the others.

The simple four-stage curriculum model has been criticised on several grounds.

Bruner argued that leaving evaluation till the last stage of the process was like doing military intelligence after the war is over. He argued, rightly, that evaluation should take place at every stage.

Professor Kerr argued that the whole curriculum process should be, not static, but a dynamic and continuously evolving system.

Dewey pointed out that there must be a continuum of ends (objectives) and means because as we proceed factors arise which re-shape our ends-in-view (objectives); so we must not think of ends-in-view as fixed targets but as suggestions, as signposts (guides). Dewey argued for flexibility, a freedom to change ends-in-view as they interact with the means.

To meet these objectives Wheeler suggested a cyclical model instead of a linear model:

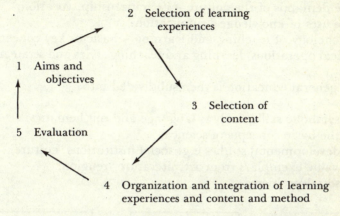

Fig. 6 A cyclical model for curriculum development[92b]

Getting the objectives

In the 'objectives' model of curriculum development the first task is that of identifying the aims and objectives, what one is hoping to achieve and why.

But how do we get our objectives in the first place? Where do they come from?

Tyler has listed five sources to which we must look for deriving objectives in education:

1 the learners themselves;
2 the needs of contemporary society;
3 the nature of the subject matter;
4 philosophy, i.e. our sets of values, etc.;
5 psychology, i.e. the way children learn.

When selecting objectives one must also consider other factors, such as the financial resources available to education, the nature of the teaching force available and so on. Otherwise one ends up with unrealistic goals which are beyond reach. The goals must be both appropriate and achievable, and not just mere wishful thinking, 'pie-in-the sky'.

Broudy, Smith and Burnett list the following as sources of objectives to develop a plan for general education.[12]

1   The demands of the culture – i.e. citizenship, vocation.
2   The uses of knowledge – application.
3   Psychology of teaching and learning – basic or key concepts, logical operations, learning and teaching styles and strategies.

The general education is then subdivided into:

a)   symbolic skills, such as language and mathematics;
b)   the basic concepts of science;
c)   developmental studies e.g. social institutions, culture;
d)   value exemplars from art, literature, religion;
e)   social problems.

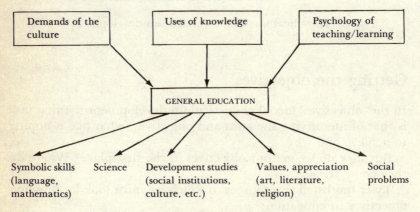

Fig. 7   Development of a plan for general education

In his model for curriculum theory Kerr regards the following as the three main sources of data for arriving at objectives:

1   The pupils – the level of development of the pupils; their needs and interests.
2   Society – 'the social conditions and problems which the children are likely to encounter.'
3   The disciplines – 'the nature of the subject matter and the

types of learning which can arise from a study of the subject matter.'

Kerr's model illustrates how the objectives are linked and interrelated to knowledge, (school) learning experiences and evaluation.

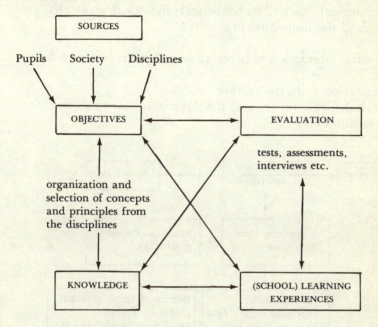

Fig. 8   Kerr's model for curriculum theory[50b]

Kerr's model goes on to show how, having decided on our objectives, we then reach, by deliberate selection and organization of concepts and principles from the various disciplines, our knowledge objective. In like manner, our objectives will determine the learning experiences that will take place. Evaluation of knowledge and school learning experiences will determine to what extent the original objectives have been achieved. The double-headed arrow linking evaluation with objectives illustrates that our original objectives may be modified in the light of what the evaluation has shown. It will be noted that double-headed arrows link all the four elements of the curriculum process, indicating their inter-relationship and dependence on each other.

Professor Lawton *(Social Change, Educational Theory and Curriculum Planning*, p. 21) uses the following sources from which to build up a curriculum:

1 Philosophical: aims, worthwhileness, the structure of knowledge, etc.
2 Sociological: social, technological and ideological changes; needs of the individual in society.

From the interaction between these two sources one makes:

3 A selection from the culture.
4 Psychological: theories of development, learning, teaching, motivation etc.

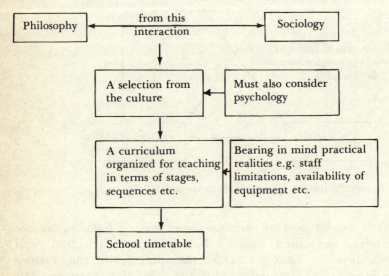

Fig. 9   Lawton's sources for building a curriculum

Goals, aims, objectives

'Goals', 'aims', 'objectives': these words are often bandied around as though they were synonymous. They are not; the words have different meanings.

144

Goals

We speak of 'goals' when we refer to a massive objective, such as, for example, the national goals of education in a country.

Aims

By 'aim' we mean a narrower, less general, more specific, statement of purpose and intention.

Professor Fafunwa provides an excellent example of aims.

The general aim of education in Africa should take cognizance of the social, economic and political needs of the continent.

To this end, African education should be an instrument for national reconstruction and should therefore help to develop the following abilities in the African youth:

1   to think effectively;
2   to communicate thought clearly;
3   to make relevant judgements;
4   to understand basic facts about health and sanitation;
5   to play one's part as a useful member of one's home, family and community;
6   to understand and appreciate one's role as a citizen;
7   to understand and appreciate one's cultural heritage;
8   to develop economic efficiency both as a consumer and as a producer of goods;
9   to acquire some vocational skill;
10   to develop ethical character;
11   to appreciate the use of leisure;
12   to recognize the dignity of labour;
13   to understand the world outside one's immediate environment;
14   to develop a scientific attitude towards problems;
15   to appreciate the need for physical preparedness; and
16   to live and act as a well-integrated individual.[24a]

We use the term 'aim' when referring to a sub-system of an education system; for example, we speak of the aims of primary education.

The Sierra Leone Educational Review Final Report, *All our Future*, 1976 (p. 7) lists the aims of primary education as:

1 Literacy in one or more languages, eventually to include literacy in at least one Sierra Leone language and in the official language, English;
2 Numeracy, i.e. computational skills in arithmetic, understanding of certain basic mathematical principles, and ability to judge the quantitative results of certain decisions and actions;
3 A rational outlook on natural and social events through observing and understanding the environments in which the students live;
4 Occupational skills at elementary level;
5 Positive attitudes towards themselves, their cultural backgrounds, towards work and the process of community and national development;
6 Positive traits of character and ethical values.

The need for more specific aims → objectives

> One of the greatest difficulties facing an educational system and the community it serves involves the task of defining its aims and setting its priorities in operational terms that are clear and meaningful.[16f]

A teacher at the chalk-face of teaching, say, social studies, might have aims such as developing a democratic way of life, developing social awareness in pupils, transmitting what is desirable in the culture. A mathematics teacher would aim 'to develop mathematical understanding.'

But such aims are too general to elicit positive action in the classroom. Words and phrases such as 'citizenship', 'the whole child', 'creative self-expression', 'a well-rounded personality', and so on, although they sound well, are mere generalities, pious hopes, often unrelated to the classroom situation and of little use as a guide in teaching.

White, in an article called 'The Curriculum Mongers', is scathing about the state of affairs in the West: 'Educational theorists have talked far too long about such woolliness as 'self-realization' or 'the whole man': teachers should forget all this claptrap and direct their thinking to the actual teaching situation, making sure that what they are doing is presented in such a way that children understand and want to learn.'[40d]

Hilda Taba points out that:

Statements that education should transmit culture, reconstruct society or provide for the fullest development of the individual stake out the broad aims. A similar function is served by statements of such aims as the development of a democratic way of life, of civic responsibility, creativity, economic self-sufficiency, of self-actualisation ... The chief function of stating aims on such general levels is to provide an orientation to the main emphasis in educational programmes. Aims at this level establish what might be described as a philosophy of education and are only a step towards translating the needs and values of society and of individuals into an educational programme. They are an insufficient guide for making the more specific decisions about curriculum development, such as what content or which learning experiences to select, or how to organize them. The general aims can be satisfied only if individuals acquire certain knowledge, skills, techniques and attitudes.[81]

In other words, to ensure that objectives are realizable and not remain mere platitudes and cliches, the broad, general aims must be broken down into more specific operational objectives.

President Nyerere, in his Address to the Dag Hammarskjöld Seminar on Education (Dar es Salaam, 1974), pointed out the need for specificity in stating objectives if they are to prove useful to the educational planner.

In 1967 I defined the purpose of education as 'to transmit from one generation to the next the accumulated wisdom and knowledge of the society, and to prepare the young people for their future membership of the society and their active participation in its maintenance or development.

Today, seven years later, I still think that this is a good definition. But it was a definition intended to cover all kinds of societies – it was designed to be universal, objective, and descriptive.

As a guide for action it therefore needs some expansion and emphasis; especially for Africans... It is imperative, especially in a young nation like ours, to analyse the purpose of education more deeply so that emphasis is placed where it is required, if we are ever to successfully attain our educational objectives.

147

Behavioural objectives – intended learning outcomes

How does one know when an aim or objective has been achieved?

Psychologists argued that most educational objectives were too general to be effective or measurable. For instance, whilst an overall, long-term aim in teaching literature might be 'to develop the child's appreciation and love of great literature', such a broad aim needs to be broken down into more short-term objectives which specify changes in the learner's behaviour that can be observed and/or measured. It will be noted emphasis is placed on some measurable or observable change in behaviour of the learner – in what he or she can do, the opinions he or she expresses, the skills he or she can show.

The adherents of the behavioural objectives school argue that objectives stated in behavioural form are clear and can be communicated to others and can be specified in advance.

In order to dispel much of the confusion that existed regarding aims, objectives, and methodology, etc. Benjamin Bloom and his co-workers at the University of Chicago produced *The Taxonomy of Educational Objectives.* This was a standard classification of educational objectives, based on 'the intended behaviour of students – the ways in which individuals are to act, think or feel as a result of participating in some unit of instruction'. The first volume (1956) dealt with the cognitive (intellectual, i.e. thinking, knowing, problem-solving) domain. The second volume (1964) dealt with the affective (emotional, i.e. feelings, interests, values) domain. A third volume deals with the psycho-motor (learning of physical skills, manual and motor) domain. The taxonomy is not so much a source of objectives as a hierarchy of educational objectives, of different instructional objectives at appropriate levels in the relevant domains. The behavioural objectives are arranged from the simplest kinds of learning to the most complex. Thus, for example, knowledge of specific facts, i.e. remembering something previously learned, is considered much simpler than the understanding of theories which, in turn, is simpler than the most complex of all, judgement and evaluation of abstract theories and of evidence.

A brief synopsis of Bloom's *Taxonomy of Educational Objectives* is given in the Appendix to this chapter.

Bloom and his associates believed such a classification would enable curriculum framers to define expected learning outcomes more clearly and would prove of great value to teachers planning curricula; they could check, for instance, that topics were not omitted or taught in their wrong logical and psychological order.

A number of criticisms can be made of Bloom's taxonomy. For example, knowledge cannot be neatly divided into three neat categories – the cognitive, the affective and the psycho-motor domains.

Another criticism made of the taxonomy is its emphasis on 'behavioural' objectives. The behaviourist school of psychologists demands objectives in terms of precise changes in pupils' behaviour which can be observed and measured at the end of a particular teaching unit. But, states of mind are not analysable into observable states. Achieving understanding, or appreciating art or literature, are very desirable educational objectives, but they do not necessarily result in a person doing or saying anything.

It is not always practicable or sensible to draw up a list of precise objectives for a complex subject like education. This could lead to a trivialisation of education – teaching more and more only of what we can predict and measure and fewer and fewer of the really important but more difficult to measure aspects of a subject. It is difficult, for example, to measure what might be called the 'expressive' objectives in a subject such as art.

Writing educational objectives

Teachers commonly write objectives in one of three ways, all of which have serious limitations.

One of the most common ways is to state objectives in terms of what a teacher is going to do, e.g. 'introduce the concept of magnetism', etc. But this format overlooks the fact that education is about learning, not teaching.

Another commonly-used method of stating objectives is to list the content of a lesson or course. This is achieved by stating the topics to be covered. Such lists are unsatisfactory for there is no indication as to what the learners are expected to do with each of the elements in the list.

A third way in which objectives are sometimes stated involves a list of generalised patterns of behaviour, but without any indication of the content involved or the context in which the behaviour applies e.g. 'a project in critical thinking'... 'to think

149

critically' – but about what? Educational objectives are sufficiently clarified only when their definition refers to both the specific behaviour and the unique content area in which this behaviour is to be applied.

An objective should contain two elements – content and behaviour; subject matter and abilities and skills.

One way of linking the two elements involved in writing objectives – content and behaviour – is to use a two-dimensional chart or grid, with the vertical axis listing content, and the horizontal axis behaviour. This technique is often used in constructing examination papers. Figure 10 shows a simple matrix used in the construction of a written examination paper in geography.

Content	Behaviour					
	Knowledge of facts	Under-standing of concepts	Applic-ation of concepts	Skills	Relevant imaginative insight	Total
Africa	4	4	6	2	4	20
World Geography	4	4	6	2	4	20
Special Regions	4	4	4	4	4	20
World Issues	8	4	2	2	4	20
Local Geo-graphical Experience	4	3	3	6	4	20
Total	24	19	21	16	20	100

Fig. 10   A matrix used to construct an examination paper in geography

Dr Robert Mager, in his book *Preparing Instructional Objectives* (1962) argues that an 'objective describes a desired outcome of the course.' In other words, it will tell you what a learner will be able to do after a learning experience. He points out that: 'when clearly defined goals are lacking, it is impossible to evaluate a course or programme efficiently, and there is no sound basis for selecting appropriate materials, content or instructional methods.'[19]

For Mager, the important point is to stress what the learner is going to do; he emphasises action verbs; you might call his objectives 'performance objectives'. He would not be happy with a verb like 'to understand', because: 'Until you describe what the learner will be **doing** when demonstrating that he 'understands' or 'appreciates' you have described very little at all ... Unless action verbs are used the situation is likely to be loaded in favour of a certain degree of fuzziness or uncertainty.'[19]

The 'process' model of curriculum design and development

The last decade has seen a decline of the 'objectives' model of curriculum design and development.

In the 'objectives' model of curriculum design, objectives are set out first and then means are taken to achieve those ends. But, as Dewey puts it, we ought not to be under some kind of tyranny of ends; we ought to be flexible and adaptive. Professor Peters argues that knowledge and understanding are worthwhile in themselves and not merely as means to ends.

The 'process' model of curriculum design, which is based on the mental process of thinking and learning, attempts to avoid starting by specifying beforehand the anticipated or desired outcomes in terms of objectives.

Peters claims that areas of knowledge are essential parts of curriculum and they can be justified intrinsically rather than just as means to ends. They can be selected as content on grounds other than the scrutiny of their specific outcomes in terms of student behaviours.

Mrs Charity James, in her book *Young Lives at Stake,* argues against planning curricula in terms of objectives. She doubts whether evaluation can really be carried out solely in terms of behavioural objectives listed in Bloom's Taxonomy. It is impossible to tell whether, for instance, a pupil has engaged in a complex act of synthesis or has displayed a feat of memory recall.

Whilst admitting that analysis can be useful, she argues that to see education in terms of discrete steps and independent units is to lose the essential wholeness of human beings and of human learning.

Mrs James' own plan for an 'open' curriculum i.e. without specified objectives, was much less concerned with knowledge and much more concerned with attitudes, values and experience, with 'enquiry and dialogue', rather than instruction and obedience; for her it is activity rather than passivity, living now rather than preparing for an adult future.[45]

Summary
The case for objectives in curriculum planning is that before one decides on 'what' to teach or 'how' to teach, one should know why one is teaching it. Curriculum planning must start with clear objectives.

For Wheeler's model of curriculum development see Fig. 6, page 141.

We get our objectives from:
1   the learners themselves;
2   society;
3   the nature of the subject matter;
4   philosophy – our sets of values etc.;
5   psychology – the way children learn.

A goal is a large, panoramic objective, e.g. the national goals of education of a country.

An aim is a narrower, more specific goal e.g. we speak of the aims of primary education etc.

For day-to-day work in the classroom these goals and aims are too large to be effective; they must be broken down into still more specific objectives.

A behavioural objective attempts to measure change in what a pupil can do, in his behaviour.

There are also 'expressive' objectives which are more difficult to measure, e.g. literary appreciation etc.

Educational objectives should be stated in terms of content and behaviour, in terms of subject matter and of abilities and skills. *The 'process' model.* Unlike the 'objectives' model of curriculum development in which the desired outcomes are first spelled out in terms of objectives, in the 'process' model of curriculum development no objectives are specified – the emphasis is on the process of learning rather than on the product.

Questions

1 Why do you need 'objectives' in curriculum design?
2 Outline, with comments, your country's goals of education.
3 Decide on a particular lesson. Now justify why you should teach that particular lesson at any particular level.
4 What are the major characteristics of the 'objectives' model of curriculum development?
5 List and comment on the main sources for obtaining the educational objectives of your country.
6 What are the differences between a goal, an aim, and an objective? Give one example of each.
7 What are the main arguments against behavioural objectives?
8 Draw up a matrix or grid, listing content and behaviour, to construct an examination paper in any one subject.
9 Write out a 'performance' objective for a lesson, emphasising exactly what the children are going to do.
10 Describe the 'process' model of curriculum development.
11 Is there any room for a 'process' model of curriculum anywhere in your country's educational system?

Appendix 12
Bloom's Taxonomy of Educational Objectives

A. The Cognitive Domain

The Main Categories	*Examples of corresponding general educational objectives*
1 Knowledge – defined as the remembering of previously learned material.	Knowledge: of specific facts of ways and means of dealing with specifics of basic concepts and principles (Knowledge represents the lowest level of learning outcomes.)
2 Comprehension – the ability to grasp the meaning of material.	Can understand facts and principles interpret (verbal material, charts, graphs) translate verbal material to mathematical formulas extrapolate

(These learning outcomes go one step beyond the simple remembering of material, and represent the lowest level of understanding).

3	Application – the ability to use learned material in new and concrete situations.	Can apply concepts and principles to new situations solve mathematical problems. (These learning outcomes require a higher level of understanding than those under comprehension).

4	Analysis – the ability to break down material into its component parts so that its structure may be understood.	Can distinguish between facts and inferences evaluate the relevancy of data analyse the organizational structure of a work (art, music, writing). (These learning outcomes represent a higher intellectual level than comprehension and application because they require an understanding of both the content and the structural form of the material).

5	Synthesis – the ability to put parts together to form a new whole.	Can write a well-organized theme propose a plan for an experiment integrate learning from different areas into a plan for solving a problem. (Learning outcomes in this area stress creative behaviours, with emphasis on the formulation of new patterns or structures.)

6	Evaluation – the ability to judge the value of material.	Can judge: the logical consistency of written material the adequacy with which conclusions are supported by data the value of a work (art, music, writing) in terms of internal and external criteria. (These learning outcomes are the highest in the cognitive hierarchy because they contain elements of all the other categories).

B. **The Affective Domain**

1	Receiving – willingness to attend.	Listens attentively. Shows sensitivity to human needs and social problems. (Receiving represents the lowest level of learning outcomes).
2	Responding – active participation. The student not only attends to a stimulus but also reacts to it.	Completes homework. Participates in class discussion. Shows interest.
3	Valuing – refers to the worth or value a student attaches to something.	Appreciates good literature (art, music). Shows concern for the welfare of others. Demonstrates a problem-solving attitude.
4	Organization – bringing together different values and building an internally consistent value system	Compares, relates and synthesises values, i.e. the development of a philosophy of life.
5	Characterisation by a value or value complex – at this level a characteristic 'life style' has been developed.	The behaviour is typical or characteristic of the student e.g. uses an objective approach in problem solving, demonstrates industry, punctuality, self-discipline etc.

C. **The Psychomotor Domain**

Writes smoothly and legibly.
Sets up laboratory equipment quickly and correctly.
Types with speed and accuracy.
Operates a power saw safely and skilfully.
Demonstrates correct form in swimming.
Demonstrates skill in driving a car.

13 Building the Programme: Writing the Teaching-Learning Units

But now we must approach the chalk-face: get down to the nitty gritty. We have our approach in terms of aims and objectives, but objectives are only the coathangers on which lessons are built. The problem for us is: What are we going to do when we face 4Z on Monday morning?[54]

In terms of the framework of curriculum construction discussed in Chapter 10 we are now at the stage of curriculum design – of building the programmes.

According to Dave's framework (Chapter 10, page 128) this will involve:

Selection of specific curriculum areas

Subjects, such as language, science, mathematics, social studies, physical education, religion, etc., and related activities and experiences, must be selected through which the overall and stagewise objectives may be achieved.

The Government of India Education Report, for example, suggests the various subjects, activities, learning experiences etc. that children should undergo at various stages (Classes I–IV; V–VIII etc.) in order to achieve its goals and objectives.[44]

> 8.15. *Standards of Attainment at the Different Stages.*
> At the lower primary stage (Classes I–IV) the child should receive instruction in basic tools of learning such as reading, writing and computation, and learn to adjust himself to his surroundings through an elementary study of his physical and social environment.

156

8.16.   At the higher primary stage (Classes V–VIII) the study of a second language will be added to that of the mother-tongue, arithmetical skill will develop into the acquisition of more difficult mathematical knowledge, environmental activities will lead to the study of natural and physical sciences, history, geography and civics, constructive and creative skills will provide the basis for practice of simple arts and crafts, and the practice of healthy living will serve as a foundation for physical education.

8.17.   The curriculum at the secondary stage should meet the needs of the adolescent as well as the needs of the democratic society in which he is expected to participate as a citizen on reaching maturity.

These curriculum areas must then be organized into a school programme. (Dave's Step 6.) This will involve considerations of:

1   time allocation, provisioning, for the various areas/subjects/experiences;
2   means, resources, aids, etc. –
textbooks and other instructional/learning materials,
resource units, kits;
appropriate supporting material;
appropriate institutional settings, e.g. laboratories, workshops, fieldwork;
3   approaches to instruction/learning –
methods, teaching techniques;
media of presentation;
4   evaluation scheme.

The Government of Fiji, for example, proposed time allocations for the various subject areas in its new Form 1–4 Curriculum, (January 1972), as shown on page 158.

Course outlines

Bearing in mind the principles for the selection and organization of content (subject matter), teaching/learning activities and experiences discussed earlier, we now reach Dave's Step 7 –

Form 1–2 level

Programme	Subjects	Number of periods per week (about 40 minutes each)
Basic Studies	English	6–8
	Mathematics	5–6
	Social Science	4–6
	Basic Science	4–6
	Home Economics/ Basic Crafts	4–6
	Total for Basic Studies =	30
Cultural Studies	Vernacular and Cultural Studies	2–4
	Art and Craft	1–2
	Music	1–2
	Physical Education	1–2
	Total for Cultural Studies =	10
	Overall Total =	40

Form 3–4 level

Programme	Subjects	Number of periods per week (about 40 minutes each)
Basic Studies	English	6–7
	Mathematics	5–6
	Social Science	4–6
	Basic Science	4–6
	Home Economics/ Basic Crafts	4–6
	Total for Basic Studies =	26
Modern Studies	Basic Economics/ Business Education	2–3
	Aspects of Modern Living	2–3
	Practical Projects	3–4
	Total for Modern Studies =	8
Cultural Studies	Vernacular/ Cultural Studies	2–3
	Art	1–2
	Music	1–2
	Physical Education	1–2
	Total for Cultural Studies =	6
	Overall Total =	40

158

producing for each specific curriculum area or subject a course outline.

Such a course outline should refer to:

1   the nature of the subject or curriculum area;
2   the place of the subject or curriculum area in the total curriculum;
3   the specific course objectives and content outline;
4   the instructional material and resources – textbooks, local newspaper articles, photographs, maps, statistics, etc.;
5   suggestions for teaching/learning techniques;
6   evaluation materials.

In addition to being specific as to objectives, course outlines should have a coherent structure. Otherwise, a curriculum can easily dissolve into an intellectual mish-mash.

Having developed course outlines in the various subject areas/disciplines, the next task is to fashion the various courses, from the broad general framework or outline covering the work to be done over several years, down to the detailed specification of what is to be done in the course of one year, one term, down to the topic(s) to be covered in one lesson.

Developing a detailed course outline

How this can be done is illustrated by the planning carried out by the Social Science Curriculum Development Committee in a developing country. (See Appendix A of this Chapter).

They begin by justifying the place of Social Science in the total curriculum.

They then consider the role of Social Science in furthering the national aims.

Then follows a statement of the broad aims of Social Science.

These broad aims are then broken down into more specific, operational aims.

Arising out of these aims will be the general learning outcomes that it is hoped will materialise.

How are these aims, objectives, learning outcomes to be achieved? This involves first fashioning the structure of the Social Science course.

The course consists of themes appropriate to the aims, with

units of study appropriate to the themes, making up a four-year Junior Secondary course.

For each year's work there are annual themes, which are then broken down to sub-themes for each term.

Form	Theme for the year	Theme for each term
1	LIVING TOGETHER	1 Family and Kinship
		2 Community and Nation
		3 Race and Migration
2	MAKING A LIVING	1 Human Needs
		2 Using Resources
		3 Competing and Co-operating
3	FREEDOM AND CONTROL	1 Rules, Regulations & Customs
		2 Sanctions
		3 Rights & Responsibilities
4	PLANNING AND CHANGING	1 Urbanisation
		2 Making Decisions
		3 Community & National Planning

These themes will guide the selection of knowledge, skills and attitudes to be incorporated in the units of study.

The units of study, the links of the connected chain making up the total course, are then prepared. We may call these the actual building bricks of the course.

Each particular 'unit' is, of course, related to the general theme for the year and to the sub-theme for the term. Thus, for Form 1, Living Together, the first sub-theme is Family and Kinship.

The Unit of study prepared for this sub-theme was entitled 'Looking at Families'.

The following is the list of the units of study for the four year course.

CORE STUDIES – TITLES FOR YEARS 1–4

Theme	Unit Number	Name of Core Study
Family and Kinship	1.1.1	Looking at Families
Community and Nation	1.2.1	Looking at Communities
Race and Migration	1.3.1	Looking at People
Human Needs	2.1.1	Wanting and Working

Using Resources	2.2.1	Managing our Environment
Competing and Co-operating	2.3.1	Working together
Rules, Regulations and Customs	3.1.1	Learning to live
Sanctions	3.2.1	Resolving Conflicts
Rights and Responsibilities	3.3.1	Freedom: Being and Becoming
Urbanisation	4.1.1	Living in Towns
Making Decisions	4.2.1	Governing and Government
Community and National Planning	4.3.1	Plans and Planning

The theme suggested for year 5 is 'Interdependence – a Global View'.

These units of study are called core units; they are compulsory. In addition to the core units there are optional *support studies*.
The support studies:
1 extend and reinforce basic concepts, skills and attitudes;
2 provide contrasts for the pupils;
3 teachers may choose which support studies they wish to teach, having regard to:
   a) the location of the school;
   b) the ability of the pupils;
   c) the interests of the teacher.

The process of building a course programme may be summarised thus:

The place of the subject in the total curriculum.
↓
The role of the subject in furthering the national aims.
↓
The broad general aims and objectives of the subject.
↓
Specific, operational aims and objectives of the subject.
↓
General learning outcomes.
↓
The structure of the course.

Aims → themes → sub-themes → units of study

Preparing the 'units' of study[78a]

'We must be clear about our aims and objectives. So before starting to write:

read through the aims of teaching the particular subject;

ask yourself: what do we hope to accomplish through this subject?

bearing in mind a particular group of pupils, ask yourself: at the end of this unit of study

1 What do we want them to know?
2 What do we want them to be able to do?
3 How do we want them to be able to feel?

Make a list of knowledge objectives
                skills objectives
                attitude objectives

i.e. state the specific learning outcomes for the particular unit.

Once we have listed the objectives for the unit of study then:

1 organize the learning experiences;
2 select the content;
3 plan the methods of teaching;
4 construct a means of evaluating.

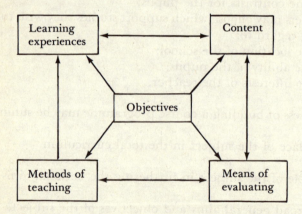

Fig. 11   A plan for preparing units of study

Criteria for:

1 *Organizing the learning experiences*
    a)   Are they feasible?
    b)   Are they varied and interesting to the pupil?
    c)   Do they help achieve the objectives?
    d)   Do they promote activity on the part of the pupils?

162

2   *Selecting the content*
    a)   Is it true?
    b)   Is it significant socially and culturally?
    c)   Does it relate to the needs, interests and level of the pupils?
    d)   Does it promote breadth and depth of understanding?
3   *Planning the methods of teaching*
    a)   Do they develop all our objectives?
    b)   Are they realistic?
    c)   Do they permit the pupils to learn by themselves?
    d)   Do they allow pupils to be active
             in gaining knowledge?
             in practising skills?
             in developing attitudes?
4   *Evaluation*: ("How well have the objectives of the unit been accomplished?").
    Evaluation can be done in several ways:
    a)   observing and describing changes in pupil behaviour;
    b)   setting tests on the content of the unit:
    c)   arranging new situations and problems for pupils: observe if they tackle them with learning and understanding;
    d)   noting 'where things went wrong' and planning improvements for next time.

Methods of teaching social science

Methods are techniques for achieving aims.
Techniques
1   Talking and chalking. (Teachers talk too much).
2   Acting in drama, role-plays and mimes. (This occurs more often in play-time than in class-time).
3   Organizing projects. (A good teacher would undertake one project even in difficult teaching conditions).
4   Individualised learning. (Using programmes and self-instructional material).
5   Problem solving.
Whichever techniques we use, it is always better for pupils to be
active – in gaining knowledge
        – in practising skills
        – in developing attitudes.

Pupils must be **doers** rather than merely **receivers** of wisdom.

The most important **activity** in any classroom is **thinking**.
Here are seven thinking skills:
  Remembering
  Translating
  Interpreting
  Applying
  Analysing
  Synthesising
  Evaluating

Note: The *organization* of our teaching is most important, *but* methodology is not more important than *aims*.

Choosing the media and materials

Aids to learning consist of more than text-books.
Consider:
1 Other printed materials – **a)** newspapers; **b)** magazines.
2 Visual materials for the class – **a)** posters, charts; **b)** slides; **c)** film-strips; **d)** films.
3 Audio materials – **a)** tape recordings; **b)** radio.
4 Real experiences – **a)** visits; **b)** field studies; **c)** simulations (games).
5 Three dimensional media – kits and models.

Designing the format of the unit

It is most important to bear in mind the abilities of the children when designing a unit. The unit must *help* them learn.
Therefore – think creatively;
           – think simply.
And *plan* for:
1 teachers' guides;
2 individual pupil materials;
3 visual and audio class materials;
4 evaluation check-list;
in order to make a packet of materials for teachers and pupils of Social Science

Now you may start writing a 'unit of study'.

164

Writing units of study

Consult the 'Notes for Writers at Form I–IV level', prepared by Graeme Coates (Department of Education, Fiji), which provide useful hints on writing units in good, clear, simple, concise English. (See Appendix B to this chapter.)

Start with Teachers' Guide. Part II.
1   Estimate the amount of class time you have.
2   Write down assumptions and objectives of this unit.
3   Plan lesson sequence taking note of the media and materials you will be using.
4   Arrange for evaluating this unit.

Then write Teachers' Guide. Part I.
1   Think of some Social Science teachers.
2   Write down the intentions of the unit.
3   Give background information to the content and the teaching skills required, so that others may teach the unit with confidence.

Now prepare teaching materials:
1   charts;
2   photographs;
3   tapes, radio programmes;
4   simulations – games.

Write
1   pupil pamphlets;
2   pupil factlets;
3   pupil workbooks.

Plan
1   An evaluation check-list for yourself, as teacher;
2   written tests for pupils;
3   oral tests;
4   "problem situations" for pupils.

Design your charts, pages and covers so that they are interesting to look at, easy to print and make, and simply aesthetically pleasing.

Put all together in a teacher's package.

FINALLY

Be prepared to start all over again, and again, and again . . .

until you are satisfied you have prepared a unit of study which will help children learn in Social Science.

The development of a Mathematics course[78A]

In the field of Mathematics the table and the diagram on pages 170 and 171, illustrate the stages in the development of a course for Forms 1 to 4, down to the first rough draft of a unit.

A trial course Forms 1 – 4   **(0) Optional**
Stated aims of the course
The course is meant for all children in a secondary school system. It must not discourage the less able nor the bright pupil. The course should:

1 enable students to have sufficient background to cope with everyday mathematical needs;
2 enable students to see the relevance of mathematics to their own particular environment;
3 develop the ability to deal analytically with situations;
4 develop creative and inventive talents;
5 develop the ability to communicate and discuss;
6 develop self-reliance;
7 provide the necessary mathematical background for the study of other subjects;
8 provide a suitable preparation for further study in mathematics;
9 give an idea of the part mathematics is playing in the development of human society.

Content

Form 1	Fractions 1, 2
	Decimals 1, 2, 3
	Area 1
	Measurement
		Money	Number
			  patterns 1
			Number
			  machines
			Co-ordinates 1
				Geoboards
				Angles

Form 2	Area 2
	Volume
	Circles
	Stats 1
		Communi-
		cations
			Number
			  patterns 2
			Problems and
			  equations
			History of
			  numbers
				Geometrical
				  instruments
				Symmetry
				Handling shapes
				Polygons

166

Form 3	Pythagoras
	Scale drawing
	Stats 2 (0)
	Clock arith (0)
	Number
	  systems (0)
		Social
		Maths
		1
			Co-ordinates 2
			Directed Nos. 1
			Directed Nos. 2
			Mathematical
			  shorthand
			Number
			  patterns 3
				Properties of shapes
				Solids and drawing
				Networks (0)
				Transformations 1 (0)

Form 4	Trigonometry 1
	Trigonometry 2
	Logs
	Probability
	  1, 2 (0)
	Stats 3 (0)
	Approximations
		Social
		maths
		2
			Co-ordinates 3
			Relations and
			  equations
			Vectors
			Matrices
				Properties of shapes
				Transformations 2 (0)

Some concepts and skills resulting from the course

Number	Symmetry	Relations	Space (2D & 3D)
1 Understanding of number and number operations 2 Skill with numbers as they occur in everyday situations (numeracy) 3 Measurement 4 Approximations and estimations 5 An introduction to 'aids' to computation	1 Symmetry in shapes (2D) 2 Approximate symmetry in nature 3 Symmetry in patterns of numbers 4 Symmetry in events 5 Symmetry in operations	'All maths is about relations' 1 Pictorial representation (graphs) 2 Analysis of situations to uncover relationships	1 Knowledge of and experience with common shapes 2 Ability to imagine and draw common shapes 3 Analysis of movement of shapes 4 Analysis of patterns in shapes

In the study of maths the need should automatically arise to:

1 Have a new vocabulary – 'words'
2 Develop a symbolic mathematical vocabulary. This new vocabulary and use of symbols is a tool to 'aid' understanding. If not controlled it becomes 'jargon' and inhibits understanding.

Writing the units

Who is to write the 'units'?

In general, experienced teachers form the best panel of writers. They know the type of language to use for particular groups of children; they know what activities or skills teachers are able or unable to perform as part of regular teaching.

The expertise of teachers should be supplemented by that of other experts and specialists. Attagara describes the co-operation between experts from several disciplines in developing and writing new curricular materials in the United States thus: 'In almost every academic discipline, teams of subject-matter specialists joined hands and minds with psychologists on learning theory to produce the "new mathematics", the "discovery method in science", the "audio-lingual" approach to language, and the "anthropological" and "problem-solving" process in the social sciences.'[5b]

But having written the first draft of a unit, this is only the beginning of a long process. After small-scale informal classroom trials and discussions the draft material is revised. The revised draft is then circulated to a wider group of people for comments and is tried out by more teachers and more pupils. These further classroom trials provide further feedback for revision.

The operational stages in developing the teaching/learning materials may be summarised:

1 Produce the units.
2 Trial the units in selected 'pilot' schools. } *Phase One*
3 The units are evaluated and re-written. }
4 Units retrialled, evaluated and amended (if necessary). *Phase Two*
5 Units produced in final form, perhaps commercially, for use in all/more schools.

Trialling of new materials and techniques

No matter how experienced an engineering team is, or how diligently they may have worked in developing a new industrial product, it is inconceivable that an industrial company should proceed with the mass production of the product without a field try-out. Unfortunately, educational systems are not so careful and new programmes have frequently been disseminated without actual field try-out.[53]

Pilot trials should form the standard procedure before any innovation is put into the schools *en masse*. Howson outlines the logistic steps that should be followed:

In the first year the project team will have to write and pre-test the first form materials and to begin to train the teachers in the pilot schools; in the second year it will have to prepare and pre-test second form materials, test the draft first year materials and later begin to prepare a revised version of them, and to train teachers from the pilot and associated schools. The third year will see increased in-service training commitments, the preparation and testing of third form materials, testing and subsequent rewriting of second form materials and final testing of first form materials prior to preparation of a published version. Unless this vast increase in work has been foreseen and steps taken to meet it, the preparation and testing of the materials has necessarily to suffer with possibly disastrous results for the project... It is necessary to allow at least $n + 2$ years for the life of a project established to prepare materials for n school years.[41b]

Teachers should play a vital role in such trialling. It helps both the curriculum developers and the evaluators if teachers are really involved in trialling and evaluating the material. It helps both the evaluation and teachers if they are not merely required to fill in forms, send them back and hear no more until the next set of questions arrives.

Feedback is of vital importance for the success of any new venture.

Those schools not included in the pilot-stage of the innovation may be brought into the scheme in a later, second-phase, operation, following one or two years after the first trials –

WRITING A MATHEMATICS UNIT

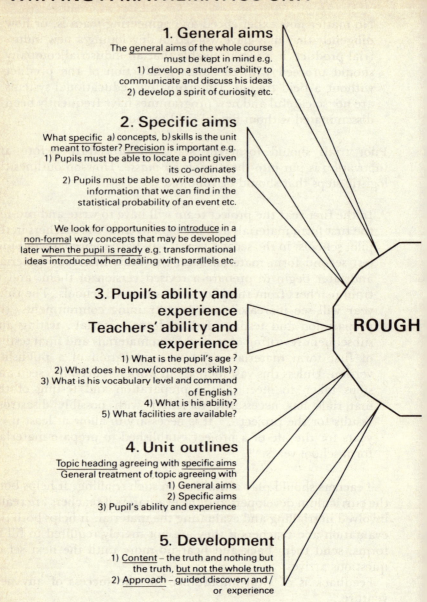

1. General aims
The general aims of the whole course must be kept in mind e.g.
1) develop a student's ability to communicate and discuss his ideas
2) develop a spirit of curiosity etc.

2. Specific aims
What specific a) concepts, b) skills is the unit meant to foster? Precision is important e.g.
1) Pupils must be able to locate a point given its co-ordinates
2) Pupils must be able to write down the information that we can find in the statistical probability of an event etc.

We look for opportunities to introduce in a non-formal way concepts that may be developed later when the pupil is ready e.g. transformational ideas introduced when dealing with parallels etc.

3. Pupil's ability and experience
Teachers' ability and experience
1) What is the pupil's age?
2) What does he know (concepts or skills)?
3) What is his vocabulary level and command of English?
4) What is his ability?
5) What facilities are available?

4. Unit outlines
Topic heading agreeing with specific aims
General treatment of topic agreeing with
1) General aims
2) Specific aims
3) Pupil's ability and experience

5. Development
1) Content – the truth and nothing but the truth, but not the whole truth
2) Approach – guided discovery and / or experience

ROUGH

Fig. 12   Writing a Mathematics unit

170

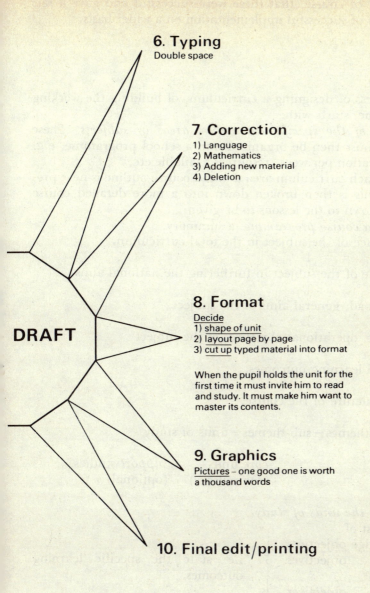

6. Typing
Double space

7. Correction
1) Language
2) Mathematics
3) Adding new material
4) Deletion

DRAFT

8. Format

Decide
1) shape of unit
2) layout page by page
3) cut up typed material into format

When the pupil holds the unit for the
first time it must invite him to read
and study. It must make him want to
master its contents.

9. Graphics

Pictures – one good one is worth
a thousand words

10. Final edit/printing

171

assuming, of course, that these were successful and gave a fair indication of successful implementation on a wider basis.

Summary
The process of designing a curriculum, of building the working programme, starts with:
Selection of the specific curriculum areas or subjects. These subjects must then be organized into a school programme, e.g. time allocation per week, resources available etc.

From each curriculum area a broad course outline is next prepared. This is then broken down into a more detailed course outline, down to the lessons to be given.
Building a course programme: a summary.

The place of the subject in the total curriculum.
↓
The role of the subject in furthering the national aims.
↓
The broad, general aims of the subject.
↓
Specific, operational objectives of the subject.
↓
General learning outcomes.
↓
The structure of the course.

Aims → themes → sub-themes → units of study

core units   *support* studies
(compulsory)   (optional)

Preparing the units of study
Make a list of
   knowledge objectives
   skills   objectives   i.e. state the specific learning outcomes.
   attitude   objectives
Then: organize the learning experiences,
      select the content,
      plan the methods of teaching,
      construct a means of evaluating the unit.

The steps in developing the teaching/learning materials:
1 Produce the units.
2 Trial them in 'pilot' schools. – VERY IMPORTANT
3 Re-write units in the light of the trials.
4 Further trials and modification if necessary.
Make the teachers partners in all this work. Feedback from them is very important.

Questions
1 Choose a particular subject or curriculum area. Justify its place in the school curriculum.
2 How does this subject help to further the national goals of your country?
3 What would you say are the broad aims of teaching this particular subject?
4 List some of the general learning outcomes you would expect from teaching this subject.
5 Develop a brief course outline for one term's work in a particular curriculum area or subject.
6 List the stages involved in preparing teaching/learning materials from start to finished products.
7 Why is 'trialling' so important in curriculum design?
8 As a group project in association with your colleagues attempt to produce a Unit of Study which could be used in the schools.

Appendix 13A
Social Science[78a]

Why Social Science?
A. **The world is changing rapidly**
1 The Population Explosion means
   - many more children for schools
   - pressure on human and physical resources
   - changing social relationships
   - need to learn new social skills.
2 The Data Explosion means
   - there is now so much more to learn
   - we have to be selective
   - we have to learn how to select

- we have to learn how to learn in a world packed with information
3 The New Technological Revolution means
  - communications are more rapid
  - more people can travel more easily
  - more specific skills are required
  - we can pollute our environment more easily and quickly
  - more information can be processed very rapidly
  - we can destroy the human race.
4 Political changes in the region mean
  - more people share in the responsibility of government
  - national identities need to be established
  - national aspirations need to be encouraged.
5 Educational Changes – there is now a regional University. This means
  - selection procedures for further education will change
  - examinations for higher education and school leaving certificate will also change.

B. **Individual hopes, needs, attitudes and life-views are changing very rapidly.**
  - towns are growing, village life is changing
  - old customs are vanishing
  - tribal and family groups are reforming
  - people's values are changing.

The aims of a modern curriculum at a national level are:
1 To better prepare the peoples to cope with modern life – modern in the sense of present and on-going, while,
2 Retaining as much of their indigenous culture and their way of life which is essential to the development of a people's identity.
Hence Social Science to help further these aims.
Appropriate aims of Social Science
That pupils should:
1 Be knowledgeable about their cultural inheritance.
2 Appreciate and understand the changes now occurring in their country's social and economic life.
3 Adapt to the changes without losing their cultural identity.
4 Be committed to play, with reasonable efficiency, imagination and integrity, a role appropriate to a member of a contemporary community in a rapidly changing world.

5   Appreciate the diversity yet interdependence of peoples in the national and international communities.

In short,
- pupils should be well-informed about their society;
- able to think intelligently about it;
- put it in world perspective;
- and be interested and concerned about it.

In order to achieve these aims pupils must develop:

1   Knowledge and understanding
    through the practice of
2   Skills – both thinking and social
    and hold positive
3   Attitudes towards others, themselves and learning.

The general learning outcomes sought for are:

Social: That pupils should:

1   be tolerant, and have understanding and goodwill for others;
2   be able to co-operate with others;
3   be confident and have self-esteem;
4   have a sense of responsibility;
5   hold attitudes favourable to the social, economic and cultural development of their country;
6   be willing to accept social changes within a system of law and order;
7   increase their own self understanding in relation to other individuals, social groups and society;
8   respect individual and human rights;
9   observe and become committed to democratic processes in decision making;
10 function as innovators in society so that they may promote peace and harmony, justice and understanding;
11 acquire attitudes and knowledge which will lead to active participation in community and national life.

Intellectual: That pupils should:

1   develop a capacity to learn and acquire skills to communicate their learning;
2   note that experimentation and systematic obeservation are the basis of objective knowledge;
3   be able to calculate, analyse and infer in order to make sound judgements;
4   think critically and desire to learn continually;
5   understand the processes of interaction between man and man, and man and his environment;

6 be aware of the need for a rational appraisal and use of resources for development at community, national and international levels;

7 learn and use elementary skills of enquiry in field research;

8 be knowledgeable about the past but have a sense of the unfinished business of man's evolution;

Specific learning outcomes

These will be stated for each unit of study, and will be developed from the general learning outcomes defined above, and related to each termly theme.

Specific learning outcomes for *core* units must be stated before support study units are written.

Appendix 13B

Notes for Writers at Form I–IV Level[78b]

1 *Simple sentences:*
Use simple one-clause sentences, in preference to two or three-clause sentences.

2 *Sentence length:*
Try to keep your sentences to about 16 words, or a maximum of two lines.

3 *Tenses, voices, commands:*
Be consistent in your use of tenses.
a) The past tense is probably the most valuable for writing.
b) Sometimes the present simple is appropriate – e.g. The retailer sells rice in small quantities.
c) Writers may find the passive voice useful – e.g. The taro was grown in a swamp.
(Note, however, that from the point of view of style the active voice is more direct and vigorous).
d) The imperative is useful for giving instructions or commands – e.g. 'Take a piece of string which is 50 cm long. Tie the two ends together'.

4 *Vocabulary:*
Use simple one, two or three-syllabled words wherever possible. Use only essential technical terms. Introduce only a few new words amongst a number of known words.

5 *Joining sentences:*
The children in Form I will be familiar with the following conjunctions, if you want to vary your sentence patterns.

a) and/but/or/so – use freely.
b) Noun clause conjuctions – how/how many/what/when/where/which/who/if/that.
e.g. 'He asked the captain how many men were on board the ship.'
c) Adjectival clause conjunctions – that/which/who/whom.
e.g. 'The men who killed the villagers escaped into the bush.'
d) Adverbial clause conjunctions – after/as/as soon as/because/before/if/until/when/while.
e.g. 'He came here in 1960, when he was only about 10'.

Prepositions and participles:
Avoid unusual idiomatic uses. These little words are one of the biggest problems because they reflect English idioms –
e.g. 'up'   I'm fed up with your attitude/Line up everybody/Tidy up that cupboard/Jump up there/Tie up that parcel, etc.
e.g. 'for'   Ice-creams for 5 boys/ice-creams for 5 cents/Ice-creams for lunch, etc.

The articles 'a' and 'the':
Make sure you use these accurately. When in doubt refer to an English speaker, but be consistent.

Don't string phrases together at the beginning of sentences.
This seems to be a major fault with writers at this level. Get to the subject early. Place phrases at the ends of sentences. Avoid inversion.

Participal phrases:
Form I children are not used to reading or using sentences which contain participal phrases e.g. 'Driving down the road, he saw his brother'.
e.g. 'Not wishing to annoy the other chiefs whose support he needed, the King agreed to their demands', is difficult for Form I. It is better to say: 'The King agreed to the demands of the chiefs because he wanted their support'.

Prepositional Phrases: Again, get to the subject early.
e.g. 'At Davuilevu about twelve miles to the north-east of the town near where the steel bridge is today lived the old priest', is difficult for Form I. It is better to say, 'The old priest lived at Davuilevu, about twelve miles north-east of the town'.

14 Strategies of Curriculum Innovation and Implementation

> The problem of innovation is not a matter of supplying the appropriate technical information, but rather a matter of changing attitudes, skills, values and relationships. Change in attitudes is just as necessary as change in products ... Innovation is defined as activating forces within the system to alter it.[18]

> Innovative and creative change has to be introduced by voluntary action and not by expert preaching or governmental decrees.[90]

In 1969 Ronald Havelock, of the University of Michigan, made an exhaustive study of how innovation, whether in education, or science, or agriculture, or industry, came about. He identified three main models of innovation.

1 *The Research, Development and Diffusion Model* (R, D and D), where an idea or practice is conceived at the head or centre, for example, at a central planning unit or curriculum development centre, and then fed into the system.
2 *The Social Interaction Model* (SI),
   where change proceeds through contacts, formal and informal, among interested individuals or groups of people.
3 *The Problem-Solving Method* (P–S),
   where individuals are themselves involved in conceiving, initiating and developing innovation at the local level.

The Research, Development and Diffusion Model

This is the model usually adopted in the first wave of curriculum development. The R, D and D model is effective where curriculum development has to be on a large scale, where ideas have to reach geographically dispersed and isolated users and where those who will be implementing the changes (the teachers) are often lacking in knowledge and expertise. This is the situation in many developing countries and hence the model has been used extensively in curriculum reform movements in these countries.

The Research, Development and Diffusion approach is a highly organized, rational, approach to innovation, founded on the following logical sequence of activities in the evolution and application of an innovation.

1 Basic research (as in industry) by a central project team which develops a new curriculum, devises and designs prototype materials etc.
2 Field trials. The development and testing of the prototype materials in a number of trial schools, followed by redesign and revision in the light of these trials.
3 Mass production of the (modified) prototypes.
4 The planned mass dissemination or diffusion of the innovation, by courses, conferences, workshops, etc.
5 Implementation of the innovation by the users (the schools, teachers, pupils).

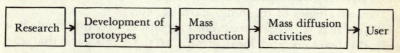

Fig. 13   The Research, Development and Diffusion Model

Characteristic of the R, D and D approach is a development agency at the centre which produces packaged solutions for users at the periphery (schools and teachers). Hence, this approach is also known as the 'centre-periphery' approach. It is typical of the situation in many developing countries, where, for example, a national curriculum development agency at the centre (Ministry of Education, University, Teacher Training College) develops curricular programmes for the schools, at the periphery.

The advantage of a central agency, such as a national Curriculum Development Centre, is that it can harness the efforts of experts and talented teachers for the benefit of the whole system. Furthermore, such a system can ensure that national priorities are given adequate emphasis. A strong case can be made for such development centres as against leaving so vital a task to the whims and fancies of ad hoc committees.

Moreover, curriculum development centres can take a leading role in the crucially important task of training and re-training of teachers for their new tasks.

The R, D and D model has several *advantages*.

1 The innovation developed is not some chance, ad-hoc change, but is based on research and relevant data, and on the principles of curriculum development.

2 The materials and prototypes, produced by specialists and experts, can be expected to be of high quality.

3 These matrials are tested before diffusion on a large scale.

Among the *disadvantages* are:

1 The high initial development costs, though it is hoped these are compensated by the resulting quality and efficiency in the long term.

2 Teachers are involved in the development process only to a limited extent; by and large they are the passive recipients of materials developed for them at some distant agency.

3 Because of the high degree of centralisation, there is a danger of failing to take account of local needs and variations.

4 This model of innovation is effective in the case of materials production, such as pupils' texts, teachers' guides, etc. but it is not very appropriate to other types of innovations, such as new strategies of teaching/learning, etc.

Whilst it is true that materials can ensure dissemination, it is only the teachers and local groups at the chalk-face that can ensure implementation of the innovation.

With regard to the second of the disadvantages listed above, the university scientists who set about transforming science teaching methods in the United States to a large extent ignored the teachers and deliberately set out to develop 'teacher-proof' curricular materials – materials that could be used in the hands of any teacher, even the incompetent. But what the scientists did not appreciate was that pupils take their cue from teachers, not from materials. The teacher cannot be ignored. No matter how carefully the pupils' work-cards and texts might be structured, what is learned is, in the long run, the product of teacher-learner interaction. As Bruner commented: 'The efforts to make the curriculum teacher-proof was like trying to make love people-proof'.

By involving as many teachers as possible in the curriculum development process this disadvantage can, to some extent, be mitigated. By involving the teachers closely they are not forced to dance to a tune composed and played by people remote from their problems.

A variation of this 'centre-periphery model' is the 'proliferation of centres' model. In this model the primary centre becomes a trainer of trainers, those being trained setting up their own centres in their regions or school districts, where they pass on the central message, the content, of the innovation to be diffused, the new methods, techniques, ideas to be adopted. The primary centre is thus able to concentrate on training or re-educating the change agents, on deployment, support, monitoring and general management.

The Social-Interaction Model

As against the 'theory-into-practice' R, D and D model, the Social-Interaction Model (S-I) employs a different pattern of operation: awareness – interest – evaluation – trial – adoption.

Social interaction is the usual way by which ideas and practices are diffused through society – by informal contacts between interested individuals and groups. This was, and still is, the basis of tribal education, as for example, in Africa.[49]

The S-I model emphasises diffusion, the movement of messages from person to person and system to system. It stresses the importance of interpersonal networks of information, of opinion leadership, personal contact and social integration.

The strategy usually takes the form of convincing a respected administrator or teacher of the usefulness of a new device or practice, and then enabling colleagues to come and see for themselves the new practitioner using the innovation.

A great advantage of this model of innovation is that it is a 'natural' process. One of the disadvantages is that it involves individuals rather than groups or organizations and it is these latter that generally have to implement innovations. Also, the process, being informal and unplanned, can be slow. But such an unplanned approach can be made more systematic by structuring and co-ordinating the contacts between groups and individuals interested in curriculum development. In the past this was done through courses and conferences, by visits to schools, by inspectors, and so on. Here the central agency acts merely as a co-ordinator or communicator of ideas, rather than being itself the generator of ideas. This model is also called a 'periphery-

periphery' model. Ideas are generated at the periphery and communicated, via the centre, to other points on the periphery.

The Problem-Solving Model

This is based on the assumption that innovation is part of a problem-solving process which takes place inside the user or client system, be it a school, the teacher or even the student himself. Whereas in the R, D and D model the innovative initiative comes from the 'centre', in this problem-solving model the initiative comes from the periphery – the school/client. Innovators at the periphery set about solving their own problems. Unlike the R, D and D model, innovations are not specified in advance but arise from the needs of the client/schools. 'The problem-solving model is built round the user of the innovation. It assumes the user has a definite need and that innovation satisfies that need. Thus the process is from problem to diagnosis of a need then to trial and

Among the *advantages* of the Problem-Solving Model are:
adoption. Emphasis is on client-centred collaboration rather than on manipulation from without'.[43]

The following steps are characteristic of the P-S model.
1   A need is identified.
2   This need is translated into a problem which is then diagnosed.
3   This diagnosis leads to a search for solutions.
4   The possible solutions are evaluated. The innovation which seems to provide the best solution is then tested for its effectiveness.

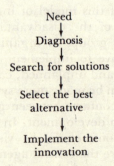

Need
↓
Diagnosis
↓
Search for solutions
↓
Select the best
alternative
↓
Implement the
innovation

One might call this a periphery-centre approach to innovation.

182

1   The innovations are initiated, generated and applied by the teachers and schools themselves on the basis of their needs. Such innovation will have strong user commitment and the best chance for long-term survival. Whereas in the R, D and D and the S-I models, the receiver (the teacher) is generally a passive figure in the innovation process, in the P-S model he is actively involved in finding an innovation to solve his own unique problem.

2   It is flexible enough to encompass all types of innovations – materials, methods, groupings of pupils etc.

3   The chosen innovation (solution) is geared to the particular circumstances of the school/client.

Among the *disadvantages* may be listed:

1   Being local and limited in size, the quality of the innovation (in the way of materials, for instance) may not be as good as that which a large central curriculum development centre could provide.

2   Though appropriate to the needs of the school, the particular innovation may not necessarily be based on sound theory or practice.

3   Such innovations usually take up a considerable amount of the teachers' time.

The Linkage Model

In an effort to overcome the weaknesses of the three models outlined above, yet drawing upon their strengths, Havelock has proposed a fourth model – the Linkage Model – which combines aspects of all three models by using linkage procedures and agencies intermediate between the centres of curriculum change and the schools, which mediate and link together all the parties involved in the innovation process.

These linkage agencies could be teachers' centres, colleges of education, universities, regional resource centres, and such like, which provide linkage by giving support and advice, providing resources, such as curriculum materials from a central agency, by running in-service courses, seminars, visits, by providing a service to trial schools after the main development team has withdrawn, by proposing innovations tried and tested elsewhere to users with similar or related problems.

Failure to implement innovation

Curriculum design becomes curriculum proper when it is adopted in the classroom. But there is often a mismatch between the 'official' curriculum and the 'actual' curriculum of the classroom. Comprehensive schools are established but they do not necessarily provide comprehensive education – they still stream their pupils by ability as did the 'grammar', 'secondary modern' and 'technical' schools they were designed to replace. The change is superficial, not fundamental. Similarly, 'inter-disciplinary' teaching founders when teachers maintain a single discipline approach, when firm disciplinary boundaries are jealously guarded. We may pay our respects to 'discovery learning' but in so many schools 'chalk and talk' still prevails, theory dominates over practice, and practical work, if undertaken, is often just a cookery-book exercise. Modern language courses devised to encourage active pupil-participation are still taught by passive rote learning. 'Cuisenaire' rods are used as a glorious abacus rather than as media for introducing number concepts in a new way. We have merely exchanged new rote for old rote.

Innovations cross the thresholds of schools, but their adoption is often short-lived. Then, as Eric Hoyle points out, ' "tissue-rejection" occurs – the carefully developed materials gather dust in cupboards, the new ideas slowly lapse away, they fail to become a permanent and effectively functioning part of the school – they are not institutionalised'.[42]

'Campaigns' in education are more easy to launch than to maintain and sustain. But unless they are maintained and sustained they become mere memories. So often, innovation lasts only as long as the outside funding (the soft money) does; as soon as the institution has to continue the innovation on its own local budget the innovation is discarded.

Bhuntin Attagara of Thailand succinctly describes what has happened in many cases in developing countries when external funding is ended. 'How often has unrestrained excitement at the start of a project ended up, three or five years later and one or ten million dollars later, as just another project.'[5c]

Reasons for the gap between aims avowed and achieved

There are many reasons for the discrepancy between the intent of curriculum projects and what actually happens in the classroom, between the theory and the practice, between desire and actual achievement, between plan and execution.

Among the chief of these reasons is resistance to change springing from tradition. As the Unesco pamphlet *Educational Planning: a world survey of problems and prospects*, (1970) states (p. 79):

There is practically complete agreement in theory on the view that great changes are inevitable, but in practice, every positive innovation encounters the most vigorous opposition. Education is a realm of tradition, and resistance to change springs up in the most varied quarters, ranging from the teachers themselves, the administrators, the parents, the pupils and students, to political, professional, confessional and cultural circles. Several countries note that socio-psychological resistance to reform is the major problem, perhaps more stubborn, than the financial problem itself.

The task of curriculum innovation and implementation involves changing the attitudes of people. In the words of another Unesco pamphlet:

The sound common sense of the countryman, the wisdom of generations which has been handed down to him and his instinct for self-preservation all incline him to put his trust mainly in traditional methods, however mediocre the results. He is, conversely, suspicious of innovation. He must, therefore, be convinced of the advantages of the new approach to education, the effectiveness of which will in fact depend on his participation, understanding and personal support.[89c]

The importance of parental co-operation in educational innovation is borne out by the comment of an experienced Ghanaian official who suggested that drastic change in primary education should never be attempted until the parents had been prepared for the change through 'continuing' education, perhaps using the village primary schools as community centres.

Griffiths writes: 'Parents, as elsewhere in the world, are concerned with success in examinations. They are likely to be suspicious of change, particularly when it involves their children spending time in scientific experiments, making things, drawing, visiting, etc., all of which takes up time better spent on getting on with their 3 Rs'.[28d]

Change is a long drawn-out process which begins in the minds of men. An innovation that is at odds with existing values and practices will certainly encounter initial difficulties. In a society that demands unquestioning respect and obedience to elders, where their word is to be accepted without query, it will be difficult to introduce methods of teaching and learning that positively encourage questioning and thinking for oneself.

In Africa, as Fafunwa points out: 'the average African parent still believes that the child is to be seen not heard'.[23e]

Another reason why innovations fail 'to catch on', 'to take', is the sheer inertia of any large educational undertaking. Educational practices are generally very deeply entrenched. And because they have prevailed for decades, not to say centuries, they are the harder to change.

Professor Mort of Teachers College, Columbia University, said, somewhat provocatively, that it takes about fifty years for a good idea in education to be generally accepted and another fifty years for it to be implemented – by which time it is obsolete, or it has vanished in a cloud of good intentions. As an example, the concept of the comprehensive school was suggested in Sweden in the 1880s. But it was not till the 1930s that the educational change was finally put into practice.

Trying to achieve too much, too fast, can have the opposite result. Hawes describes such a case thus: 'The 'New Primary Approach' (to teaching English) in Kenya derived from a research project carried out in 25 Asian schools in Nairobi . . . The extension went too far too fast. The time available for in-service training was cut and cut again. Supervision arrangements broke down. There were pained complaints about pseudo-literacy or even illiteracy in the upper classes.'[36e]

Sometimes the planned change may be just too ambitious at that point in the country's development. It was in 1967 that Tanzania adopted the policy of Education for Self-Reliance. The author of an article in the *Daily News*, Dar es Salaam, January 6, 1975, admits that Tanzania has not succeeded in implementing all the changes it would have liked in its educational system.

It is true we have succeeded in making a number of changes. For instance, all the syllabi in all the schools and higher education institutions have been changed. At the moment all the syllabi in our places of learning emphasise Tanzania environment, and not the environment of foreign countries. At the same time, [attempts] are made to ensure that the youth learn by doing . . .

. . . Nevertheless, we must accept that many of the objectives we [set for ourselves] have not been realised as intended. We have been afraid to bring about a revolution to free ourselves from the system we have inherited.

And the Chairman of the Office of Educational and Cultural Research and Development in Indonesia warns 'Radical changes in quality of teaching and learning take a long time to be accomplished. Large changes without sufficient time for preparation have often proved more harmful than useful. The practice itself is more like using slogans and changing names than actually changing substances. Courses can be added and deleted in practically no time; however, teacher and student practices may not change at all in the process.'[74]

Summary
The main strategies for innovation would seem to be:
1 *The Research, Development and Diffusion Model* (R, D and D), where an idea or innovation is conceived at the head or centre, e.g. a curriculum planning unit, and then fed into the educational system.
2 *The Social-Interaction (SI) Model,* where innovation is brought about through contacts between interested individuals and groups.
3 *The Problem-Solving Method* (P-S), where the people themselves initiate and develop innovation at the local level to solve their own problems.
4 *The Linkage Model,* where intermediate agencies, e.g. teacher's centres etc., link together the centre and the schools involved in the innovation process.

Innovations must be sustained and institutionalised, if they are to be more than fleeting memories.

The task of curriculum innovation and implementation involves changing the attitudes of people.

Questions

1   List the main strategies for introducing change into the curricula of schools.
2   Which, if any, of these strategies has been used in your country? Give a brief description.
3   Outline the main stages involved in the R, D and D approach.
4   What are the main advantages of the R, D and D strategy in curriculum development?
5   What are the main disadvantages of the R, D and D approach?
6   Briefly describe the Social-Interaction model of change.
7   How would you use it to bring about any particular change in the schools in your country?
8   What are the advantages and disadvantages of the S-I model?
9   List the main steps in the Problem-Solving Model of curriculum innovation.
10 Give one example of how this P-S approach has been, or could be, used to bring about change at the local level.
11 What are the advantages of the Problem-Solving model of innovation?
12 What are the disadvantages?
13 Describe the Linkage Model of innovation.
14 Give an example of the use of the Linkage Model of change in your country's educational system.
15 Give one example of where the curriculum in the classroom is different from the curriculum proposed.
16 Are there any such mismatches between curriculum avowed and curriculum achieved in your schools? Why do you suppose this has happened? How could matters be remedied?
17 Describe any one project in your country that has proved either successful or unsuccessful.
18 What are the main factors which hinder innovation taking place in the schools?
19 How can these inhibiting factors best be overcome?

15 Innovation and the Teacher

Curricula or method innovations invariably founder because they are formulated in vacuo by curriculum development experts and then imposed on schools where unprepared teachers, with neither the inclination nor knowledge to implement them, make impolite noises concerning these bothersome innovations and proceed with the business of preparing their pupils for public examinations. Manifestly, educational change can only succeed when teachers are sufficiently impressed by the validity of the new approach and thoroughly grounded in the techniques necessary for its implementation. In short, the teacher is the key to educational innovation.[2]

The teacher – the key to educational innovation

Whether an innovation succeeds, takes root, depends in the long run on the teacher; he is the 'adopting unit'. Specialists and experts may select the objectives and plan the general advance, but it is the teachers in the class who are the assault troops. No genuine innovation occurs unless the teachers are personally committed to ensuring its success. Innovation must start at the teacher's level. In the final analysis it is he or she who has to operationalize on the innovation at the classroom level. And Beeby reminds us:

What many schools of thought tend to forget is the nature of the teacher, and especially the below-average teacher. More brave and imaginative ventures in education have foundered on the limitations of the mediocre teacher than on limitations of the average child. I have seen 'progressive' methods in a classroom used brilliantly, and I have seen the same methods in the hands of another teacher lead only to amicable chaos. I have witnessed superb lessons in the new mathematics, but I have sat in misery while a teacher blundered through a lesson on operating in base seven that left utter confusion in the children's minds and mine.[41c]

A curriculum is only as good as the quality of its teachers. Positively, a curriculum is enriched by the creativity and imagination of the best teachers; negatively it is vitiated by the limitations of poor teachers and poor teacher training.

A National Workshop on Primary Education, organized by the Nigeria Education Research Council, April 26–May 8, 1971, pointed out in its Conclusions the crucial importance of teachers in the development plans of the nation: 'That there is a danger and self-deception for our country to fail to understand the important role and place of teachers in the development of our country. Poorly trained, discontented and frustrated teachers cannot bring about the required economic, cultural and moral rejuvenation necessary for a better future for our country.'[59]

Bortei Doku, in his article on 'Innovations in Elementary School Science Teaching and Teacher Training in Ghana' describes how: 'the teachers' own lack of scientific knowledge was a handicap, as shown by one who interpreted "lime water" as juice from the citrus fruit.'[70]

In the competition for good quality recruits education tends to lose out because other competitors, (e.g. industry), with large purses set the standards for attractive salaries and so education often ends up with a high proportion of 'second choice' candidates.

Hawes and Aarons deal with the strategies one can adopt when faced with a large, unqualified and untrained teaching force.

In many cases, where schools are remote and teachers not too well trained the alternatives are clear: either
1   to restrict content, teach it well, relate it to the local community and thus achieve understanding and hopefully lay the basis of further learning; or
2   to go through the masquerade of teaching 'at' the children following the offical syllabus and series of recommended books which as the children pass from class to class become

190

increasingly imcomprehensible to more and more learners.[37a]

Involvement of the teacher

Involvement of the teacher in educational reform and innovation is crucial. The teacher is, indeed, the heart of the matter. You cannot proceed without the full co-operation of teachers and the local authorities. Teacher skills and attitude count for a great deal more in curriculum renewal than do changes in content and methods.

In the last analysis, any curriculum reform comes through decisions by the teachers in the classroom. They know the local situation, the local dynamics. Unless teachers are available and willing to participate in curriculum development there is no future for it. That is why they must be totally involved in the curriculum development process. It was in order to encourage the fullest co-operation and interest of teachers in the process of curriculum development that a seminar on Primary Teacher Education held in 1976 at the Institute of Education, Sierra Leone, recommended that studies of curriculum development might be introduced into the programmes of the professional training of teachers.

If an innovation is to be anything more than a passing novelty then the teachers concerned must be involved from the start. And their involvement must be genuine, not just a matter of their being told what to do and why, but a proper participation in planning and decisions. There must be 'shared endeavour' between all those working on new programmes. Instead of the arrogant 'we-know-what's-good-for-you' attitude, the teachers must be consulted rather than told what to do, they must be respected rather than patronised. Teachers, on the whole, are not against reforms as much as they are offended at the way they are presented to them, not to mention imposed on them.

P.A.I. Obanya of the University of Ibadan describes the 'hostile' reaction of Nigerian teachers to a new French language syllabus.[63]

In 1971 the West African Examinations Council introduced a new syllabus for the School Certificate Examination in French. The syllabus was considered revolutionary in its shift from a stress on literacy to one on oracy. However, the syllabus was not received well. This reaction was not due to any shift in emphasis. As Obanya says: 'Initial "hostile" reaction to the "new French" syllabus was due to a failure on the part of the innovators to ensure adequate participation by school teachers during the planning stages'.

The African Social Studies Programme was not going to repeat this mistake. 'The African Social Studies Programme has considered it necessary to involve people at different levels of the educational system as much as possible in the process of innovation in social studies'.[66]

Professor Fafunwa points out that if teachers are to be fully involved in the process of educational change they must understand the principles behind and the reasons for change. 'If the curriculum in Africa is to be drastically changed, as many people seem to agree, the change can occur more realistically and more effectively only if the teacher is fully involved in the process of change, and to be fully involved, he must be fully oriented as to the whys and wherefores of the change.'[23f]

Not only must the teacher understand the reasons behind the change or innovation, he must fully appreciate the philosophy underlying the innovation. If the intention is to introduce more discovery/enquiry - oriented teaching/learning in the classroom, the teacher must fully comprehend the rationale behind this methodology - otherwise he ends up 'lecturing' or talking to the pupils and giving them the answer because by that method he will cover the syllabus more quickly - or so he thinks. No change in practice, no change in the curriculum has any meaning unless the teacher understands it and accepts it. As Beeby points out 'if the teacher does not understand the new method, or if he refuses to accept it other than superficially, instructions will be of no avail. At the best he will go on doing in effect what he has always done, and at worst he will produce some travesty of modern teaching . . . A teacher using a technique that he has accepted but not understood can, by some strange inverted alchemy, turn the most shining idea to lead.'[41d]

This is true. But one must accept that it is extremely difficult to change old educational habits. The average teacher has a very great capacity for going on doing the same thing under a different name. Some teachers are reluctant to see changes come. That is a natural reaction. Many of the teachers would like to follow the path of least resistance. They want to do things as they used to do them during the last so many years. Many teachers often lack the necessary skills and knowledge to carry out an innovation. They are understandably reluctant to break new ground. They lack the sense of inner security so necessary in good teaching.

With well-educated and thoroughly trained teachers, the most broad and general suggestions as to methods will suffice, but with less intellectually sophisticated teachers it is often necessary to be much more detailed and specific in the instructions.

In countries where there is a large corps of unqualified or little-trained teachers it is essential that materials such as teachers' guides and handbooks should be made as detailed as possible, without 'talking down' to the teachers. Some new projects have attempted to prepare 'user-proof' materials, guaranteed to work even in the hands of the most incompetent receivers, where most of the problems of the user are anticipated and catered for as far as possible. The U.S.S.R. has developed such 'teacher-proof' packages, complete with very detailed handbooks and instructions, in its science-teaching programmes. It is these 'teacher-proof' kits that led Prof. John Lewis to state that: 'in Russia they have very many bad science teachers but very few bad science lessons'.

J. Alles, referring to the work of the Sri Lanka Curriculum Development Centre, describes how one can cater for teachers with less experience, background and qualifications.

To take account of the number of teachers with limited professional background it was thought necessary to prepare detailed classroom materials and to mount an extensive in-service education programme. Not only did the writing teams prepare the students' texts but they also provided teachers with detailed instructions on how the texts should be used – a typical course was divided up into individual lessons and teachers' guides devoted up to two or three pages to a single lesson. The schemes of work also indicated the types of questions to be put to the pupil. This manner of working meant teachers had a preferred sequence of teaching presented to them. This did not necessarily imply a shelving of the teachers' freedom and initiative. Interested teachers had the privilege of making variations.[41e]

He goes on to explain the accompanying in-service programme.

The in-service education programme has been based on the use of a cohort of 'teacher-leaders' who act as intermediaries between the writing team and the bulk of the teachers in the field. These 'teacher-leaders' are selected on a district basis and have frequent opportunities to meet the writing teams who communicate to them the main features of a new course, its underlying thinking, proposed sequence of content etc. Teacher-leaders in turn convey these ideas to a group of thirty to fifty teachers in the area.[41e]

V.L. Griffiths outlines how inexperienced teachers may be assisted, from considerable help in the early stages of their career, to the time when they are more experienced and so need less 'spoon-feeding.'

The first step may be to offer teachers a single unvarying course for use in primary schools, but as they gain confidence with this they must be given alternative courses and materials and encouraged to use their own judgement in deciding between them. Then, by degrees, one should enrich the material until the teachers, by this time much better educated, can exercise an intelligent and informed choice of methods and materials to suit the particular children in their care.[28e]

Beeby details the many difficulties involved when trying to implement new programmes with an inadequately trained teaching force.

Poorly educated teachers can teach only what they know, and so they cling to the textbook and depend on the narrow, formal framework of the system to give them their sense of security. When in doubt, they fall back on the ways in which they were themselves taught a generation earlier.

To ask such teachers to take a wider view of society's needs and to adapt their teaching boldly to them is like snatching the life-jacket from a poor swimmer. Within reasonable limits the change can be made, but not by official fiat alone. New and more intelligent supports must be offered to the mass of average teachers as well as new freedom for the adventurous few. This means syllabuses and examinations prepared with expert assistance, textbooks and teachers' guides detailed enough to be of day-to-day help, new methods of supervision, in-service training courses throughout the whole country, more education and longer training courses for new entrants to the profession and a fresh outlook on education for all those in authority in the school system.[10g]

He continues:

Again, the conditions of work in the schools are often not conducive to the adoption of new methods and techniques in teaching. The internal organization of the school is sometimes too authoritarian or mechanical, the average headmaster is too indifferent and apathetic, and the facilities are often too poor for the teacher to undertake any kind of creative work.[101h]

One can perhaps sympathise with the attitude of those who, because of their lack of education and experience and discouraged by adverse circumstances, are reluctant to change. But there is another group of teachers who have to be 'converted'. These are the complacent ones. They know they are doing a good job. They have been doing it for the last twenty years and they are damned if they are going to change for anybody else especially since adopting an innovation generally means considerably increasing their work-load. Moreover, innovation 'de-skills' the experienced teacher; it makes his experience and expertise irrelevant. He was an excellent teacher of traditional mathematics; now along comes the 'new' mathematics. He feels lost and insecure. He has to give up his piece of professional estate in which he had invested his professional competence. His confidence is under-mined. That is why it is important to involve him from the start in decisions and planning – that will preserve his confidence and decrease his anxiety.

In Britain, the retraining of experienced teachers is one of the most crucial components of curriculum development.

The experienced teacher will not want to lose the security of his well-tried established ways. So in the clash between old and new, we must appeal not only to his head but to his heart as well. In short, innovations must be accompanied by incentives if teachers are to give up their 'professional estate'. Kenya has introduced a scheme whereby teachers who participate in curriculum development work, in local research, in community activities, can have such work recognised for promotion purposes.

It is not only the teachers who must be closely involved in

curriculum change and innovation – the headmasters and principals of schools also have a key role to play in curriculum innovation and implementation.

Hawes describes how the crucial role of headmasters in curriculum change was recognised when the Bunumbu project was started in Sierra Leone. At Bunumbu the role of the headmasters 'was taken seriously and a full one year course organized so that they could fully understand the implications of the very different task which faces them and in which they, possibly more than any other set of people, can help or hinder success.'[35a]

In addition to teachers and head-teachers, the school supervisors and inspectors must also be involved in the process of curriculum reform if their active co-operation is to be won. To secure the co-operation of the supervisional staff it is necessary to involve them in activities of programme development and of teacher pre-service and in-service training. Without their co-operation programme implementation becomes extremely difficult, if not impossible.

In the past the school-inspector was a man who came from the top to see that orders were being carried out. Today his role is a more liberal one and in some respects reverses his former role: he can be the feed-back agent who carries suggestions and ideas from below to guide and re-orientate those involved in the decision-making processes at the top. Sympathetic and understanding school supervisors and inspectors can help raise the productivity of the teachers they come in contact with.

Another group who must be brought into consultation are local development officers, not only because they may contribute useful ideas to the curriculum, but also because, unless they appreciate the change in attitude that is being attempted, they may well be critical of the first products of the reformed schools. This is particularly likely where development officers are accustomed to having their views accepted by local people and are unused to being asked 'why?'.

Involvement – how?

Kerr states that: 'real reform can only be achieved through a full measure of teacher involvement'.[40e]

This is true. But how does one get such involvement? Kerr argues that:

196

the road to this kind of involvement seems to be, first, to interest the teachers in a particular line of development – not usually difficult; then to bring teachers together in circumstances which will create a willingness to enter with confidence into a commitment to work as a member of a curriculum group; and finally to arrange for provision of all resources and specialist help for which the group asks. The conventional method of in-service provision through conferences and short courses of lectures rarely provides all three conditions for total involvement – interest, commitment and resources.[40e]

Banks describes how involvement of the teacher in curriculum development is sought in Britain:

Generally in the months before the trial schools begin to use the materials, some (or in some cases all) of the trial school teachers attend a one-week briefing conference, mainly staffed by the project team and led by the director. This is the occasion when the first attempt is made to 'convert' teachers, some of whom may not come in a sympathetic frame of mind, to the desirability and practicability of the new curriculum.

These meetings are greatly helped if the project team have got ready in time for them a reasonable sample of the trial teaching materials the teachers are expected to start with in the autumn.[40f]

'Education Centres' or 'teachers' centres' are coming to be established more and more in most developing countries. These serve many purposes – from providing facilities for courses, for local curriculum development, for local production of resource materials, to being a social centre where teachers can meet and mutually discuss. Such centres can be the hub and pivot of curriculum innovation. In Kenya, for example, interesting and local booklets on local history are prepared at teachers' centres, supported in some instances by collections of artifacts.[36f]

In many countries, cheap and simple cards and booklets in reading and arithmetic are made by teachers' groups. The booklets are usually very short, often no more than two sheets of foolscap paper stapled together and folded to make an eight-page book.[36g]

Courses: in-service training

The more conventional way of introducing teachers to new ideas and techniques and methodologies in education is by courses, ranging from a few days to several weeks.

In-service courses are usually held during the school vacations so that teachers are not absent during school time. But, as Hawes points out: 'Too many in-service courses are still very sorry affairs, vague "how-to-be-a-good-teacher" courses, often patronising in tone and sometimes providing a living example of those didactic methods they so urgently want teachers to avoid'.[36h]

Enlightened in-service training is crucial. In the case of science, for instance, the same principles and techniques of exploration and enquiry that hold for the learners hold just as much for teachers.

All curriculum development must be seen against the shortage of teachers, the inexperience of teachers, and, in many cases, the isolation of teachers. One must ensure that curriculum change does not outrun the capabilities of teachers.

Several countries have had great success with their schemes of 'master teachers' – selected local persons trained especially to conduct in-service courses and so pass on the message of the new ideas and techniques and methodologies. These 'master teachers' work as links between the curriculum design team at the centre and the teacher in the classroom. In many cases these key personnel then in turn organize in-service training for other teachers in their region or state, thus achieving a 'multiplier effect'.

Hawes gives several examples where decentralisation and the use of the 'multiplier effect' have been effectively used by making use of local 'curriculum implementers'.

In Tanzania they are called 'itinerant teacher educators', in Northern Nigeria 'mobile teacher trainers', in Ghana 'local subject organizers'. In each case they have proved a potentially effective instrument for channelling productive local suggestions and for achieving sensible modifications in centrally designed materials. Meetings and feedback sessions in which they share local experiences have proved very valuable.[36f]

He describes how the six states in northern Nigeria connected with the Primary Education Improvement Projects have developed a system of Mobile Teacher Tráiners (M.T.Ts). Each M.T.T. is usually responsible for only six to ten schools. The M.T.T. provides on-the-job training for teachers and also assists in curriculum development and evaluation. Since he is responsible for a small number of schools he is able to get to know his teachers very well. 'Moreover, since he is not an inspector and has no fixed status in the education hierarchy he can thus easily gain the confidence of those he works with'.[36j]

Hawes continues: 'Central curricula are not only adopted but gradually adapted to suit local needs through the constant intervention of those knowledgeable and enthusiastic field workers'.[36j] 'In this way', as Hawes points out, 'implementation of the programme will revolve around people rather than bits of paper'.[35b]

Two other factors very important in implementing any new curricula are the examination and the school inspection systems. Attempts at introducing new ideas are often hampered by examinations that are largely irrelevant and a rigid system of inspection that clutters up the inspectors with so many administrative details that they have not the time to help teachers improve the quality and the relevance of their teaching.

A new kind of teacher

There is no area in which there is more urgent and continuing need for reform than that of the professional education of teachers. We must prepare teachers who are not only good classroom operators but also community leaders. They must be trained not only in the techniques of teaching young people but also in adult education and group dynamics. They must be sensitized to the imperative need for national integration and economic development. They need to have a deep conception of the nature of society and of their own role in influencing the shaping of social goals. They need to know much more than those things which immediately impinge on the academic welfare of their pupils. They need a deep understanding of the main social, political and economic problems of their countries and the role which education can play in alleviating, if not eliminating those problems.

199

(*Innovation NOW! International Perspectives on Innovation in Teacher Education.* International Council on Education for Teaching. U.S.A. 1972. p. 27)

In many developing countries the role of the teacher is changing, especially in primary schools, from being only a teacher of the 3 Rs to one of community worker and change-agent. In Gujerat State, for example, the training of teachers includes training them for their roles as rural-construction workers. In a case study describing the activities by students 'in the service of the nation' the authors mention: relief work during the floods of the Tapi River; relief for Bangladesh refugees; work in the jails of Madhya Pradesh to 'socialise' the Chambal dacoits who voluntarily surrendered etc.[91c]

In such ways the gap between the classrooms, whether in schools or in training colleges, and the life of the community is reduced.

The significant role that teachers can play in changing the life of the community led to the establishment of the Rural Teacher Training School in Zinder, in Nigeria. The broader role of teachers as community leaders and as catalysts in the ruralization policy forms the back-ground against which the training of the teachers is carried out. Since the teachers of the future must be deeply conscious of the environment in which they and their pupils are to live and to work, their training is based on a practical approach to the humanities and the natural sciences, founded on application in hygiene, food, or the problem of water. The practical part of their training involves their active participation in the social and economic life of the region. The inspectors of the primary schools in the district are also given in-service training at the college.

Not only is the teacher's role changing in his relations with the local community, the pedagogy behind his profession is also changing. Instead of being an encyclopaedic Mr Know-All, a transmitter of knowledge, the teacher of the future will be the creator of desirable learning situations, helping his pupils to gain entry into the commonwealth of knowledge. Lawton foresees that 'the teacher-pupil relationship will be more of a collaborative learning experience, based on mutual respect rather than domination. In the same vein, the role of the inspector will change from that of a supervisor to one of professional co-operation'.[51b]

In the past the basic duty of the teacher was to teach the 3 Rs

and some additional factual knowledge. It was perhaps understandable that he should resist any such ideas as encouraging his
pupils to find out things for themselves. To him it was a waste of
time, when he could so easily just tell them the answers. Again, if
the enquiry method is adopted the poorly-educated and ill-
equipped teacher will feel reluctant to expose himself too often to
a situation when he is unable to deal with his pupils' questions.
The methods of training teachers must also change if the teachers
of the future are to change so as to accept a more vigorous
leadership in their communities and in the professional execution
of their teaching role. Teachers in training who are encouraged
to learn and to find out things for themselves are much more
likely to adopt similar 'discovery' strategies with their pupils when
they get into the classroom.

The teacher training colleges

> Of all the educational problems that beset the African
> countries today, none is as persistent or as compelling as the
> one relating to the training of a competent teacher.
> (A. Fafunwa, *New Perspectives in African Education*,
> 1967. p. 82)

The training and re-training of teachers is crucial. But, as W.M.
Zaki of the Ministry of Education, Pakistan, states, the teacher
training colleges themselves are, in many instances, in need of
reform. 'Teacher training programmes have remained unfruitful
and ill-adapted to the changing needs of the profession.'[96]

In many training colleges, including those in the developed
countries, the educational philosophies of the twentieth century
are taught by the methods of the nineteenth. In both pre-service
and in-service teacher education, the predominant mode of
instruction is still the lecture. And since teachers tend to teach the
way they were taught, not the way they were taught to teach,
these didactic methods are continued in the schools.

Senteza Kajubi argues rightly that teacher training institutions
should set a better example and lead by practising what they
preach. 'It is equally important for teacher training institutions to
demonstrate through their own teaching and involvement in
community affairs the principles and methods which they advocate, instead of, as they do at present, merely teaching about how
to teach.'[47a]

201

The curriculum of the teacher training colleges

The long-range implications of teacher education are of crucial significance. The teachers trained during the 1980s will be the senior teachers and the educational leaders in the twenty-first century. Thus, teacher education must be designed not for former programmes of education, nor even for present programmes of education, but rather to prepare teachers for future programmes of education.

But no one is too sure about what this teacher education for the twenty-first century should be.

The Unesco pamphlet *Educational Planning*, in 1970, pinpoints some dilemmas (p. 131):

There is far from being unanimity as to the purpose and content of ordinary education. The champions of general culture rightly maintain that the teacher's role is not to condition the children, but to awaken their interest and that he must consequently be given a very wide range of general culture. The partisans of vocational training maintain with equal justice that it is necessary to choose priorities and that to begin with the teacher must be trained for specific tasks. The dilemma is particularly serious in developing countries and in primary, junior and secondary technical education. One possible solution would be to apply the centres of interest method to teacher training. In this case the centre of interest would be the actual curriculum which the future teacher would have to teach. General culture would consist in studying the key points of the curriculum more thoroughly and in examining questions arising from the practical problems of school life.

The first published statement on education by Dr Nnandi Azikiwe, who was to become Nigeria's first President, is found in his book *Renascent Africa*. In this he writes:

I therefore feel that the system of education which encourages the existence of a privileged class of aphabetists has no prospects of producing real leaders to guide and counsel the type of Africans that must come with their own tomorrow.

All I have said can be summed up in these words: *Africans have been mis-educated. They need mental emancipation so as to be re-educated* to the real needs of Renascent Africa.[6]

With a view to remedying this state of affairs the Foundation for African Education, Incorporated, was set up in the early 'fifties' to establish an International College of West Africa. The bulletin for the Proposed International College states;

It is the conviction of the Foundation that unless West Africa in particular and Africa in general evolve an educational system that is indigenous to their environment, and unless they attempt to design their curricula according to their social, economic and political needs, education, whether primary, secondary or higher, will continue to be mere intellectual ornamentation. The curriculum, the Foundation believes, is not only a group of subjects to be mastered, but also the totality of the students' experience and environment.

This International College was to include a College of Education for the training of teachers. The curriculum of this College of Education was to be as follows:

The Curriculum

The curriculum is an undergraduate curriculum and is based on the assumption that the teacher should have a broad and liberal education, that he should be master of the subject or group of subjects which he expects to teach and that this training should be paralleled by practical and professional education which will enable the teacher-in-training to acquire a knowledge of the learner, the learning situation and the learning process, as well as familiarity with the problems to be met and new meaning to the subjects of instruction.

Education

The academic curriculum is made up of two integral parts:
A.   The General Education courses are designed to help our students to appreciate what it means to be a responsible, participating citizen in a democratic society, to recognise the interdependence of the different peoples of the world and to foster international understanding; to understand common phenomena in their physical environment and apply habits of scientific thought to both personal and civic problems; to appreciate the ideas of others and to express their own

effectively; to co-operate intelligently in solving community health problems; and to choose socially useful and personally satisfying vocations.

To meet these needs all students are required to take the following background courses during the first two years in College:

1 Nigerian Government
2 Community and Personal Hygiene
3 African History and Civilization
4 Biological Science
5 Physical Science
6 Humanities (Philosophy, Literature, Religion, Arts)
7 Economics
8 Rural Sociology
9 Communication
10 Physical Education
11 Two African Languages, besides the one spoken by the student (Hausa, Ibo, Yoruba, Tiv, Swahili, French, Spanish, Kanuri, Ibibio, Edo, Idoma, Nupe, Ga, Fanti).

B. Each student will major in one of the following teaching subjects provided he has demonstrated sufficient aptitude for such a discipline:

Biology, Physics, Chemistry, Economics,
Languages – African, English and French,
Geography, History, Home Economics, Industrial Arts,
Mathematics, Psychology, Commercial Arts and
Journalism.[23g]

The dreams of Dr Azikiwe and of the Foundation for African Education were realised in 1960 with the founding of the University of Nigeria, Nsukka.

Today many teacher education programmes continue to be very conventional in approach, organized around content rather than skill-building. Understandably there are calls for a systematic overhaul of traditional teacher training programmes, the emphasis to be placed on skill-building rather than on content courses, such as History of Education etc., important as these may have been in past teacher education programmes.[38]

New horizons in teacher education

Teacher training institutes must be an aggressive force for change in education, not a reflection of the status quo. Educational institutions must become the laboratories of reform.

(International Conference on the World Crisis in Education,
Williamsburg, 1967, Summary Report.)

Teacher training colleges must become deeply involved in research and experimentation and themselves become centres of innovation. Many teachers' colleges today make use of the 'new' technology in their programmes. Micro-teaching, programmed instruction, team-teaching, film, radio and television are all increasingly being used in the preparation of teachers. Moreover, the teachers themselves are being trained to become efficient users of these new technologies and techniques which are increasingly becoming the tools of the trade.

One of the great problems facing most developing countries is the need to train or upgrade more and more teachers more cheaply.

With a view to reaching the large numbers of unqualified and poorly-qualified teachers, particularly those in the remote areas, several countries are using distance-teaching techniques of various kinds – radio and television with linked residential courses, correspondence courses, programmed instruction etc. In this way teachers even in the most inaccessible areas can benefit from the work and influence of the very best teachers. As the new technologies, like satellite communication, open up new horizons for bringing good teaching to students in all corners of a country, so the curricula and methods of teaching will have to adapt to these new techniques of instruction.

An example of the use of one of these new techniques and technologies – correspondence education – in the preparation of teachers is given in the Appendix to this chapter.

Correspondence instruction is probably the most economic method of education. The average cost per student decreases as enrolments mount so that more time and money can be spent on improving the quality of the lessons.

Correspondence education is of considerable value since it does not remove or segregate students from the general social and economic life of the country. It enables working people to attain

205

country is occupied by the Kalahari Desert or bushveld – the difficulties of communication, the widely dispersed population, all added to the difficulties of training and upgrading the unqualified teachers. It was felt that correspondence education offered a means of reaching teachers even in the most remote parts of the country on an equal footing with those in the more populated towns.

Professor L.J. Lewis suggested that the solution to the untrained teacher problem in Botswana lay in an in-service approach based on correspondence education plus residential courses. He recommended that:

> provision be made for a two-year in-service course for un-qualified teachers, comprising three short residential periods of intensive instruction followed by private study conducted through correspondence using programmed learning materials, to be assessed by cumulative records of work done both at residential courses and during the periods of private study. Teachers who complete the course of study satisfactorily to be awarded the status of elementary qualified teachers.[93]

The proposal to combine short-term residential courses with correspondence work was an attempt to accelerate the pace of training with minimal disturbance to the existing system. Teachers, already in very short supply, would only be absent from their schools for a period of 18 weeks spread over two years, some of this time falling during the school vacations. But, as White points out, 'given the overall shortage of teachers, finding replacements for even this time posed a major problem; but at least the dimensions of the problem were manageable. It would have been patently impossible, without inflicting a serious handicap on the educational system, to have found replacement teachers while unqualified staff attended say a three-year residential course.'[93]

The Ministry of Education made one amendment to the Lewis proposal. The Ministry felt that in view of the initial low academic base of most of the untrained teachers the course of training should extend over three, not two, years. For each of the three years students would spend six weeks in college, followed by forty-six weeks of correspondence education.

Building of the College began in Francistown in 1967 and the first 671 students for upgrading were admitted in 1968.

recordings, slides, films and so on; in fact, anything that might prove of value to teachers. Such collections will constitute banks of materials on which teachers can draw.

In Appendix A of this chapter, the setting up and operation of a Science Equipment Resource Centre is described briefly.

When a teacher has tools to hand his confidence, his effectiveness, his 'productivity' all increase. With better tools, his professional capabilities are more fully utilised and he accomplishes larger and better results.

Local production of equipment

Much can be done with limited funds and unlimited imagination. . . . The energy and expertise now locked up in homes and factories and perhaps even jails could be applied to educational needs at relatively little cost. [16g]

In the past many countries have expended scarce funds on importing equipment and other resource materials from abroad. This can be a very expensive business, so many countries have set up their own local equipment production units to provide low cost equipment.

Several have established mobile servicing units that travel from school to school, helping to service their broken equipment etc. In many countries teachers are provided with kits, or tool boxes, containing basic tools and instruments to help the teachers to produce inexpensive instructional materials on their own.

The Teaching Aids Production Unit of Francistown Teachers' College in Botswana provides workshop facilities and designs prototypes for locally produced equipment. These 'semi-manufactured materials' in kit form are later assembled by teachers in local workshops.

Hawes describes how the Primary Education Improvement Project in Northern Nigeria persuaded a match factory to turn out large quantities of matches without heads in boxes at a very reasonable cost; these match-sticks were then used for counting, construction, decoration and design.

Many people argue that perhaps the time has come for a change of strategy – that we should build our courses round what is available in the way of teaching materials and resources rather

213

hole continuous through the nodes. With careful bending this can be used for siphoning when neither straws nor rubber tubes are available.

Beware of extravagant and harmful investment in 'gadgets'. A bicycle can be used to provide endless lessons in physics. In many developing countries, older children are encouraged to produce materials for their younger colleagues, as, for example, in writing and copying out stories and reading cards, making drawing books from scrap-paper and newsprint; making and cutting out number and reading games; making toys and simple games equipment.

With a view to increasing the availability of reading materials Benue State, in Nigeria, operates a 'hidden library scheme'. From a prepared list each parent buys a different book for his child, and children then exchange books.

The 'new' educational technologies

Many developing countries are today investing in the 'new' educational technologies, such as instruction by radio and television, programmed instruction etc. The Ivory Coast, for example, operates a nation-wide programme of instruction by television. The initial outlay is high in cost but this is offset by the huge audiences that can be reached so effectively.

Bhuntin Attagara argues the case for more widespread use of the new media and technologies.

Far too few funds are currently allocated for educational media especially in developing countries. Our need is for both sophisticated and unsophisticated materials. Many of our schools have no electricity, and some have no floors. In many cases teachers, with good hearts, in lonely and remote outposts would give anything for several simple books, a few wall-charts, an occasional visit by a supervisor, and maybe most of all, a nearby well.

On the other side, the overhead projector, video-tape, sound laboratories, programmed materials, radio and television have a real and powerful role to play in bringing more confidently and rapidly developing countries into the fast-moving decades ahead. Too many educational projects have given only peripheral consideration to media and technology. Where there is perceptive planning and discriminating selection, educational media and technology can make a significant impact on the quality and quantity of learning and teaching.[5b]

Experience of the educational use of newer media, such as radio and television, in developing countries is still meagre, and so far, not very encouraging. This is possibly because their use within a school system has often been looked on as a side-show and adopted for reasons of prestige rather than educational value.

Before embarking on adopting the new technologies in education countries should ensure that they have the resources in personnel and facilities to meet the technical problems that may arise. How often does one come across expensive, sophisticated apparatus lying rusting or dust-covered in cupboards because adequate servicing and maintenance facilities are lacking?

But not all new media and technologies need involve expensive initial outlays. For example, Senteza Kajubi, of the Institute of Education in Nairobi, states 'a more systematic and regular use of self-instructional correspondence materials through newspapers seems to have great potentialities which are worth examining in developing countries'.[47b]

This would be inexpensive. And the developing countries must search for other cheap but effective new technologies to meet the problems caused by exploding population increases with progressively diminishing resources.

Summary
For curriculum innovation to succeed the teachers must have the tools for the job. There must be a ready and continuing supply of teaching/learning materials with adequate support services.

Local production of equipment is to be preferred to the expense of importing items of equipment. The supply of teachers' kits/tool boxes will encourage teachers to make their own equipment when they can.

Courses should be developed around whatever equipment and materials are readily available locally.

Producing one's own teaching materials can ensure that they are relevant, flexible and adaptable.

An efficient mechanism for the distribution of teaching/

217

17 Evaluation

I believe educational evaluation, in its broad interpretation, is the sole means for ensuring the progressive and enlightened development of the people the educational system serves. Goals are often too readily set and aims too ambitiously expressed and unless a systematic (scientific) examination is made of the methods utilised to achieve these ends, there is the danger that progress may be slowed or even upset.

(Michael Kinunda, Commissioner of National Education, Tanzania. Speech at African Regional Seminar on Education Evaluation, Dar es Salaam, 1975)

Evaluation is among the most important processes in curriculum development. It enables one to determine to what extent, if at all, the objectives of a programme have been achieved. This implies, of course, first that the aims and objectives are known and specified clearly. If the learning experiences and activities and the resulting behaviour patterns expected are clearly laid down then one can measure these objectively – by tests or examinations administered by the teacher or by self-assessment by pupils themselves.

Lawton suggests[51c] that there are two major aspects of evaluation –

1 'valuing' – determining the value or worthwhileness of a particular programme or course or educational system, and
2 'measuring' – determining the actual educational outcomes and comparing them with the intended outcomes e.g. measuring the extent to which a pupil has learnt as a result of a particular programme.

220

The criteria of evaluation

Evaluation should be based on a number of criteria:

Consistency with objectives

If one of the objectives of a course or programme is the understanding of principles, then the evaluation should assess or measure such understanding and not merely memorisation of facts. If development of particular attitudes is desired the evaluative procedure should look for evidence that such attitudes have been developed.

There is often a large discrepancy between what appears in syllabuses and outlines of work, high on rhetoric, and what obtains in reality. Thus we have courses ostensibly dedicated to the building of good citizenship – yet measured or evaluated in terms of knowledge of government structure. We have courses devoted to 'appreciation' of literature – and evaluated by knowledge of authors' names and movements and literary types.

Maybe it is desired to introduce a 'practical bias' into the curriculum. But if some subsequently administered examination contains no element of 'practical' assessment, it is likely this element will be given low priority in the teaching, resulting in failure to achieve the desired objective. Some evaluation of manual ability should be included to ensure that the intended practical bias in the curriculum is realised. In the same way, the most obvious way to find out if a pupil has or has not understood a concept or idea, say in science, is to present him with a situation so chosen that he cannot deal with it successfully unless he has grasped the concept.

Validity and reliability

Validity implies that there should be agreement between what the evaluation instrument (e.g. an examination or test) measures and the function it is intended to measure, i.e. that the test measures what it set out to measure.

Reliability implies that the evaluation instrument (e.g. test) should give the same results when administered at different times.

Continuity

Evaluation should be a continuous process and an integral part of curriculum development and classroom instruction. Evaluation provides feedback and on the basis of such feedback weaknesses in the curriculum or instruction can be identified and remedied. Feedback introduces a dynamic element into curriculum development; evaluation leads to a recycling of the process of curriculum development, the 'plan-in-action' being modified as suggested by the results achieved.

Monitoring – or feedback and control – is a very important aspect of the curriculum development process. Monitoring is the internal modification of function as a result of feedback from within the system. This is what one does, almost unconsciously, when one drives a car – continually making small adjustments to keep the car on the right path. If a system is allowed to function without continuous monitoring there is a danger of failure and even chaos.

Formative evaluation is the name given to the continuous evaluation which takes place during the life of a programme or project.

Summative evaluation refers to an evaluation at the end of a programme.

Formative evaluation is more important than summative evaluation since one needs to modify things as they develop rather than wringing one's hands when things have gone wrong. Evaluation is a fundamental part of curriculum development, not an appendage or extra. Its purpose is to collect facts the course developers can use to do a better job.

The greatest service of evaluation is to identify aspects of a course where revision is necessary. Evaluation therefore needs to be formative and on-going. To be influential in course improvement, evidence must become available midway in curriculum development, not in the home stretch, when the developer is naturally reluctant to reconsider or scrap a finished body of materials and techniques.

Evaluation, used to improve the course while it is still fluid, contributes more to improvement of education than evaluation used to appraise a product already placed on the market.

Many countries now adopt a plan of 'rolling reform' – the notion of continuous reform of their education systems. The Ivory

Coast, for example, has established a central research institution which undertakes this 'rolling reform'.

Comprehensiveness

This criterion implies that all the objectives of the curriculum be evaluated, not only some. Often evaluation is concerned only with assessing objectives in the cognitive domain and usually only the lower objectives at that, such as the recall of facts. That is why examinations have come in for much criticism – that they only test memory and recall of facts. Objectives such as attitudes of co-operation, of commitment, of self-reliance, are just as important. If the goals of a school include, for example, along with mastery of subject matter, such important 'side-effects' as the spirit of self-reliance, of enquiry, of loyalty, of commitment to true citizenship, then these things must also be kept in view in any evaluation of the school's work. Unless a school keeps trying to find out how well it is succeeding in its purpose, the purpose itself is likely to atrophy.

In education, evaluation refers to the process of determining the degree to which the objectives of an educational activity or enterprise have been achieved.

Such evaluation can relate to:

1 The broader administrative and general aspects of an educational system – judging how good the school system is, how relevant its programmes are, etc.

2 Course improvement – assessing the state of instructional methods, of the intrinsic worth of the instructional materials – which are satisfactory, which are not, – where change is needed, etc.

In the Appendix is a simple questionnaire that was sent out to teachers engaged on Class 7/8 Basic Science trials in order to obtain feedback on various aspects of the course.

3 Individual pupils – identifying needs of the pupil so as to plan his learning better; judging pupil merit for purposes of selection or grouping; acquainting the pupil with his own progress and deficiencies. Testing and teaching are inseparable aspects and not two different enterprises as one might be led to believe by current practices in education. Frequent information about student performance should be the basis on which the teacher decides on the next instructional step. Feedback provides

information to teachers as to how successful they are in achieving their teaching objectives. When a teacher gets data constantly as to what is 'working' and what is not, what is already mastered and what is still to be learned, he should be able to teach with much greater precision.

But it is not the teacher alone who needs the diagnosis. After each bit of evaluation the student, too, should know better where he stands and how to move ahead.

The student should see evaluation as an aid, not as a trap to catch him out. It is essential that the pupil must be freed from a feeling of failure. His knowledge should be assessed so as to show not what he cannot do, but what he can do. This is especially true for the less able student. So often the sole purpose of evaluation appears to him 'to catch him out', to show-up as many as possible of his errors and weaknesses.

Special mention should be made of diagnostic testing and remedial teaching. The subject of mathematics lends itself easily to the construction of diagnostic tests which emphasize the use of testing for the improvement of the pupil's achievement rather than just measuring it. Mathematics is largely a sequential subject and hence it is essential for the child to understand a certain set of relationships and concepts before he can understand the next higher relationship or concept. It is therefore necessary to evaluate the pupil's understanding by the use of diagnostic tests.

These tests should be accompanied by remedial measures where necessary, which may be in the form of graded exercises, explanation of certain facts or processes accompanied by suitable illustrations.

Some dangers of 'narrow' evaluation

Williams has rightly said that 'we have developed a preoccupation with everlastingly grading everything in sight . . . The student has been marked and graded day after day until the getting of good marks has become a goal itself, with intrinsic learning left a very bad second'.[40g]

Such narrow, myopic, preoccupation with grading is condemned because

in its gross exaggeration of the more mechanical, easier-to-measure features of education, it virtually blots the broader, more fundamental objectives out of sight ... Evaluation has been so tragically successful in concentrating attention and energy on the narrowest objectives that marks and grades based on those objectives become almost an obsession. And all that falls outside the marking-grading system suffers.[40g]

Whenever possible the pupils should be more personally involved in the evaluation/diagnosis process, especially of their own work. At present the teacher does the evaluating or marking and returns the pupils' papers with a grade and masses of red corrections – which only helps to discourage the pupils further.

Examinations

The undue importance that is given to examinations and certificates in English-speaking Africa is so alarming that one wonders whether what obtains in most countries of Africa today can be called a system of education or a system of examinations.[23h]

Examinations are probably the most commonly adopted means for evaluating the progress or otherwise of pupils. And examinations have a profound influence on what is taught in schools. Hawes reports that: 'the effects of the examination on the primary school curriculum, described as the "backwash effect", are massive and on the whole disheartening'.[36o]

Writing of conditions in Benue and Plateau States in Nigeria he says:

In classes 6 and 7 the curriculum is very much affected by examinations. Children are 'prepared' for the Common Entrance examination taken in December; examinations for private institutions (business colleges etc.) in March, and First School Leaving Certificate in June. Emphasis is given to practice of multiple answer questions, to English and Mathematics and factual knowledge for the 'General Knowledge' paper, all to the exclusion of much else in the curriculum.[37b]

The greater freedom of the primary school in Britain, with its more enlightened curriculum and approach, stems from the abolition of the 11 + examination, formerly used as an exami-

225

nation to select pupils at the age of 11 for entry to grammar, secondary modern or technical schools.

As long ago as 1952 the Secondary Education Commission in the United Kingdom enumerated the defects of examinations.[10h]

> The examinations today dictate the curriculum instead of following it, prevent any experimentation, hamper the proper treatment of subjects and sound methods of teaching, foster a dull uniformity rather than originality, encourage the average pupil to concentrate too rigidly upon too narrow a field and thus help him to develop wrong values in education. Pupils assess education in terms of success in examinations. Teachers, recognising the importance of the external examination to the individual pupils, are constrained to relate their teaching to an examination which can test only a narrow field of the pupil's interests and capacities and so inevitably neglect qualities which are more important though less tangible.

Admittedly, examinations can be good servants of an educational system, but they should never be allowed to become its master. In other words, the curriculum should dictate the content and objectives of examinations, not the other way round. It is unsound educational practice to allow an examination to determine what students need to learn and hence what they will be taught.

In *Education for Self-Reliance* (1967) President Nyerere wrote:

> Further, at the present time our curriculum and syllabus are geared to the examinations set – only to a very limited extent does the reverse situation apply . . . And the examinations our children at present sit are themselves geared to an international standard and practice which has developed regardless of our particular problems and needs. What we need to do now is think first about the education we want to provide, and when that thinking is complete think about whether some form of examination is an appropriate way of closing an educational phase. Then such an examination should be designed to fit the education which has been provided . . .

He appreciates the constraining effects that examinations as we know them have; but he is equally determined not to be bound by such a strait-jacket.

One difficulty in the way of this kind of re-organization is the present examination system; if pupils spend more of their time on learning to do practical work, and on contributing to their own upkeep in the development of the community, they will not be able to take the present kind of examinations – at least within the same time period. It is, however, difficult to see why the present examination system should be regarded as sacrosanct . . . There is no reason why Tanzania should not combine an examination, which is based on things we teach, with a teacher and pupil assessment of work done for the school and community . . .

A child is unlikely to learn less academically if his studies are related to the life he sees around him.

The President's suggestion is now in operation in Tanzania. In the examination to determine who goes on to secondary school from primary school, cumulative records of performance and teachers' reports are considered along with examination marks.

Examinations are what you make them. It is not that examinations are good or bad but that they are used in the wrong places and in the wrong way.

Hawes instances cases of this, where, for example, the selection examinations for entry to secondary schools are often set by the wrong people testing the wrong things: 'Those involved in setting the examination may lack direct experience of primary schools and their curriculum. They think more, perhaps, in terms of what knowledge and skills they would hope to find in a secondary school entrant rather than of those one might expect from a child who had successfully completed a primary school course.'[36o]

Speaking of Sierra Leone he points out that if the examination for entry to the teacher training colleges was more of a school-leaving examination and less of an entrance examination this would encourage more locally-based and creative teaching in the schools, rather than cramming.[35c]

John Deakin, after pointing out that 'external' examinations are helpful in maintaining nationally acceptable common standards of attainment, also goes on to explain that: 'examination syllabuses merely lay down in varying degrees of detail, what will be examined: they do not prevent the teaching of additional topics nor do they require the adoption of any particular methods of teaching'.[20]

The fault is not all with examinations. Dissatisfaction with examinations has sometimes led to calls for their abolition. But this would be a case of throwing out the baby with the bathwater.

Though many criticisms can be levelled at examinations for exerting a constraining influence on the curriculum, examinations can also be a source for good. They can have a broadening influence on the curriculum by demanding passes in a wide range of subjects or by assessing field-work as well as theory in subjects like geography and biology. They can also introduce balance into a curriculum, by demanding that science or mathematics or a language, for example, must be passed.

Whilst in Britain changes in public examinations have usually followed in the wake of curriculum development, in many developing countries public examinations have been used as a lever to bring about curriculum change.

The West African Examinations Council, which was set up in 1953 to serve Ghana, Nigeria, Sierra Leone and the Gambia, has used its examination to influence teaching for the better. By making practical tests compulsory in science subjects and by proposing a compulsory oral test in English Language it has encouraged more practical work in the schools and greater attention to spoken English and to more effective methods of teaching the language.

Thus the much abused examination system can be a very effective instrument of change, making respectable and acceptable changes which would otherwise be viewed with suspicion. In Kenya, too, as Hawes points out:

> a very useful innovation in mathematics as in science has been a major attempt to influence teaching through the design of examination questions. For the first time in both subjects conscientious efforts have been made to isolate the different forms of reasoning and processes of thought (as against recall of information) and to construct items (multiple-choice questions) to test these. . . .
>
> The use of item analysis as an attempt to diagnose weaknesses and improve both examination design and teaching efficiency is significant.[34]

Examinations or tests should be used both to throw light on the ways in which teaching can be improved and also to guide the reappraisal of objectives.

228

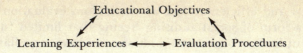

Educational Objectives

Learning Experiences ←→ Evaluation Procedures

Local examinations

When a developing country assumes responsibility for setting its own examinations it has a marvellous opportunity to change the curriculum and syllabuses in ways best suited to its own environment, needs and circumstances.

In the past most former British colonies took the Cambridge Overseas School Certificate and G.C.E. Examinations; some still do. But increasingly there has been a movement away from a strong centralized overseas examination system to local and regional examining boards, such as the West African Examinations Council mentioned above. In some cases assessment by schools is being used increasingly for certification purposes.

Before localisation of the examination systems much of what was taught was based on the U.K. scene; history, for example, was often a case of '1066, King Henry VIII and all that'. Localisation provided the opportunity for radical reform. When the West African Examinations Council started operation it introduced two papers in African History – 'History of West Africa AD 1000 to the Present Day' and 'History of Africa in the Nineteenth and Twentieth Centuries.' These were introduced on an optional basis. At first very few schools took these subjects because there were no textbooks. However, the existence of such a syllabus stimulated authors to write the necessary books. Two particularly valuable textbooks were produced at a writing workshop held at the University of Ibadan in 1965. All West African pupils now study history relevant to their own society. In the same way a paper on 'West African Government' replaced 'British Constitution' at '0' Level. The English Literature syllabuses likewise came to be changed to permit study of West African authors.

Deakin observes that in the introduction of objective tests the West African Examinations Council was years ahead of its counterparts in the U.K. by ensuring that the tests effectively covered the entire syllabus thus obviating 'question-spotting' or coaching certain topics only, as often used to happen.

Examinations also have a useful part to play in ensuring

standards and efficiency. Just as curriculum evaluation can be seen as a form of social auditing, seeing that limited funds are usefully utilised, so, too, examinations can have a similar effect. 'Countries which do not have country-wide examinations tend to have very many poor schools.'[16h]

Other techniques of evaluation

Evaluation of achievement is usually done by means of paper-and-pencil/pen tests or examinations. The reason for this is partly that such tests can be objective and dependable, they are economical of time, easy to administer, they can be marked in standard scores which allow comparisons of various kinds to be made.

Of the paper-and-pencil tests used in schools the essay type is the commonest. The demerits of the essay type test are well known, e.g. the field covered is limited (only four or five questions to be answered); there is a danger of question spotting and cramming; it is difficult to maintain consistency in marking; the verbally fluent are at an advantage; marking often tends to be subjective and impressionistic. Some educators reply that the essay type test has its value in allowing students to develop ideas, to express themselves; that such tests often demand insight and understanding.

Objective or 'new-type' tests are coming to be used more and more. Among the merits of objective tests are the fact that a much wider content can be tested; the marking is objective; there is a high degree of validity and reliability. There are many varieties of objective tests:
    multiple choice,
    true/false,
    ranking,
    completion,
    matching,
    classification.
However, constructing good objective tests is not easy. Moreover, the objective test seems to be appropriate mainly to the testing of factual information.

Another limitation of objective tests is that they do not adequately measure the more 'intangible' qualities such as attitudes, values, creativity, etc.

To get evidence about the development of intangible traits and behaviours it is usually necessary to employ informal techniques in addition to formal paper-and-pencil tests. Such informal techniques include:

observation,
interviews,
case study,
record cards,
questionnaires,
interest inventories,
attitude scales,
surveys,
work produced by students, etc.

Testing should be integrated with teaching whenever possible and be made a continuous process. Many evidences about the pupils' achievement are available at the time of teaching itself. During the classroom discussion or field trip or group work, the teacher can find out the progress of the class and even of the individual students.

The written examination should not be the sole technique of evaluation. Appropriate techniques of evaluation should be used according to differing instructional objectives. This may, in science for instance, include the testing of practical skills, use of observation techniques, and evaluation of pupil products and records. A continuous evaluation of learning activities such as evaluating the pupil's progress in collecting and classifying data, separating the irrelevant from the relevant, identifying inter-relationships, power of reasoning and formulation of arguments, keenness in making observations, and evaluation of other aspects of scientific understanding, skills and attitudes should be prac-tised by the teacher using appropriate techniques. All these evaluation procedures should ultimately lead to better learning on the part of the pupil and better teaching and curriculum revision on the part of the teacher and the school.

Simple assessment charts like the following can be very effective in providing the teacher with valuable information on his pupils.

Assessment charts need not be elaborate affairs. The simple chart, in Fig. 14 for example, sets out just four types of objective and the extent to which they have been met, using

1 - a simple yes/no scale
or 2 - a three point scale
or 3 - a verbal/descriptive scale.

231

The techniques of evaluation used by the new C.S.E. examination in Britain include amongst others, objective testing, projects or individual studies, course work and continuous assessment of course work and pupil performance over a period of one or two years prior to the examination. Assessment of project work can constitute the major or even sole basis of grading the pupils.

All these relatively new strategies of evaluation have proved stimulating and effective.

Topic:

Unit of Work	Understands facts and principles	Knows sources of information	Can communicate	Interest
1	Yes	Yes	No	Yes
2	B	B	C	A
3	Fairly well	Quite good	Weak	High

Fig. 14 A simple assessment chart

Summary

Evaluation is the process of determining the degree to which the objectives of an educational activity or enterprise have been achieved.

Evaluation has two aspects:

1 valuing – determining the value or worthwhileness of a particular programme or course or educational system; and

2 measuring – determining the actual educational outcomes and comparing them with the intended outcomes e.g. measuring the extent to which a pupil has learnt as a result of a particular experience.

Evaluation should be a continuous process. Evaluation provides feedback. On the basis of such feedback weaknesses in a curriculum can be identified and remedied. Feedback provides information to teachers as to how successful they are in their teaching.

Formative evaluation takes place during the life of a programme or project.

Summative evaluation takes place at the end of a programme. Formative evaluation is more important since it gives you a chance to rectify things that may have gone wrong.

232

Diagnostic tests are a useful means of finding out where weaknesses may lie: such weaknesses can be rectified by remedial teaching.

Beware of a very 'narrow' view of evaluation where getting good marks becomes the be-all and end-all of the education process.

Evaluation should cover not only the quantitative aspects of education, but also the qualitative aspects e.g. attitudes, behaviour etc. by classroom observations, checklists, etc.

Examinations should be designed to reflect the education given. They should not dictate the syllabus or curriculum or methods of teaching/learning.

Other types of evaluation, apart from examinations, are objective tests (e.g. multiple-choice, true-false etc.), course work, continuous assessment, cumulative records of performance, projects.

Local examinations provide an excellent opportunity to countries to change the curriculum and syllabuses in ways best suited to their own environment and circumstances.

Questions

1 What do you understand by the word 'evaluation'?
2 What are some of the criteria for evaluation to be effective?
3 What is the difference between 'formative' and 'summative' evaluation? Give one example of each.
4 Which is more important – 'formative' or 'summative' evaluation? Say why.
5 List some of the advantages and disadvantages of evaluation.
6 Briefly describe how you would evaluate
   a) an education system;
   b) a particular course;
   c) individual pupils.
7 Describe any evaluation that you or your country has been involved in.
8 Give an example of diagnostic testing and remedial teaching.
9 List the good points of examinations.
10 List any bad points of examinations.
11 Can you find any faults with the examination systems in your country? How could these faults be rectified?
12 Argue the case for either external examinations or for local examinations.

13 Describe any localisation of examinations that you are familiar with.
14 Give examples of some 'new' techniques of evaluation.
15 Devise a 'new' type of test for use in a class after one or two lessons on a particular topic.

Appendix 17

Questionnaire to obtain feedback on Teachers' Handbook and general course content

Responses

1 Some lessons are more interesting than others. The pupils are happy, they enjoy their work and seem to understand it well. Choose one or two of the most interesting lessons you taught, and say why they were interesting.

1 Lesson No.
   Reasons:
   Lesson No.
   Reasons:

2 Some lessons are not so interesting. The pupils are dissatisfied, impatient or bored with the work. Choose one or two of the least interesting lessons you taught, and say why they were so.

2 Lesson No.
   Reasons:
   Lesson No.
   Reasons:

3 Some lessons are more difficult for the teacher than others. He finds the work hard to explain, to demonstrate or to present. He may become anxious, worried or confused and seek for help. Choose one or two such lessons and say why they were so.

3 Lesson No.
   Reasons:
   Lesson No.
   Reasons:

4 Some lessons have too much work for the time, others not enough work, and others are just about right. Give your general opinion about the length of the lessons in the course, and specific examples

4 Our Basic Science periods contain _____ minutes.
   Tick One
   In general, the work is
   Too much for the class time...
   Just right for the class time...

of too-long, too-short, and just right lessons.

Not enough for the class time...
A lesson with too much work was No...
A lesson with the right amount of work was No...
A lesson with not enough work was No...

5   The main book you used was the Teachers' Handbook. Give your honest opinion about this book under the headings provided.

5   a) The size of the pages.
    b) The size and clarity of the print.
    c) The way each page is set out in two columns.
    d) The illustrations and diagrams.
    e) The way of arranging under headings 'aims', 'materials', etc.
    f) Ease of handling and referring to during the lesson.
    g) The clarity and simplicity of the English used in the text.
    Other

18   New Horizons in Education

Traditional education: its merits

Professor Fafunwa, Professor of Education in the University of Ife, Nigeria, writes:

> In the Old African society the purpose of education was clear. Functionalism was the main guiding principle of education. The African society regarded education as a means to an end and not as an end itself. Education was generally for an immediate induction into the society and a preparation for adulthood ... Children were involved in practical farming, fishing, weaving, cooking, carving, knitting, and so on ... Traditional African education was an integrated experience. It combined physical training with character building and manual activity with intellectual training. At the end of each stage, demarcated either by age level or years of exposure, the child was given a practical test relevant to his experience and level of development and in terms of the job to be done. This was a continuous assessment which eventually culminated in a 'passing out' ceremony, or initiation into adulthood ... The curriculum was relevant to the needs of the society. Unemployment, if it existed at all, was minimal and very few young men roamed the villages and towns.[24b]

Judith Evans comments:

> In the traditional society, all aspects of education are an integral part of daily life ... Children take part in adult activities to the full extent of their age and ability. Education is a joint enterprise: the adults are eager to teach, the children

eager to learn ... In traditional education emphasis is on learning by doing rather than by teaching, and there is no departmentalization of the curriculum. In traditional societies education and life are co-determined.[22c]

President Jomo Kenyatta, in his book *Facing Mount Kenya* provides an excellent case for espousing all that was valuable in traditional African education.

Whatever the shortcomings one must agree that such traditional education was a real education which achieved its objectives, limited though these might have been.

'Colonial' education

But then came colonisation by the European powers. Things changed – and, in many respects, for the worse.

Many developing countries attest that the Western influence on the curricula of their schools has been and often still is an obstacle to the development of more relevant, more appropriate, school programmes.

President Nyerere, in *Education for Self-Reliance*, writes:

The education provided by the colonial government in the two countries which now form Tanzania had a different purpose. It was not designed to prepare young people for the service of their own country; instead, it was motivated by a desire to inculcate the values of the colonial society and to train individuals for the service of the colonial state.

Tanzania inherited in full measure the colonial educational tradition common to African countries which had been under British rule. The tradition was basically a bookish one, deriving from both the concepts of nineteenth and early twentieth century European schooling and the logic of an elitist system which was designed to produce catechists, schoolmasters and clerks for commerce and Government service ... This colonial tradition has led to serious consequences.

For the truth is that many of the people in Tanzania have come to regard education as meaning that a man is too precious for the rough and hard life which the masses of our people still live.

Everything we do stresses book learning and underestimates the value to our society of traditional knowledge and the wisdom which is often acquired by intelligent men and women as they experience life, even without their being able to read at all.

Yet at present our pupils learn to despise even their own parents because they are old-fashioned and ignorant; there is nothing in our existing educational system which suggests to the pupil that he can learn important things about farming from his elders ... And from school he acquires knowledge unrelated to agricultural life. He gets the worst of both systems!

There are almost 25,000 students in secondary schools now; they do not learn as they work, they simply learn.

An example of this non-productive, elitist attitude is typified in the following statement of a Tanzanian youth of seventeen who had been asked to list his 'aspirations' for life. 'Up to this time I like mostly to play football, learning mathematics and physics and also to be employed in any office so that I can obtain some money for my school needs. Then I don't want to look after cows, goats or sheep because this work gives me hard labour.'[65c]

Education in many developing countries was organized solely to produce white collar workers in the administration. The only 'industry' was administration and that is non-productive.

As René Dumont says in his *False Start in Africa* (1966), p. 78, 'As at presently conceived administration will be the ruin of these countries.'

A report by a Cameroonian Planning Group in 1962 refers to a criticism applicable, not only to schooling in the Cameroons, but to education in many developing countries. 'The most serious criticism of present-day (Cameroonian) primary education is that it leads to nothing practical, that it takes the child out of his environment and that it is, in consequence, a factor of individual maladjustment and social imbalance.'[11b]

The bookish, elitist, academic education transplanted by the metropolitan colonial powers did little for the industrial and economic development of many of the developing countries. This is borne out by these remarks of a Ugandan: 'Under colonial rule, those who took technical education were treated with disdain when clerks and interpreters were what the colonial rulers needed most. Now with independence the former colonies find they have a serious lack of technicians, artisans, etc.'[11c]

238

The pervasive hold on the people of the 'foreign transposed' systems of education is well put by Howson.

> In spite of sporadic and often misdirected efforts to adapt education to local conditions, education will not achieve its promise so long as the transposed British system, with its emphasis on selection by rigid examinations, heavily loaded towards measurement of rote learning, is the sole means in so many developing countries of escape from poverty, drudgery and village life to wealth, an office job and the city.[41f]

The increasing irrelevance or inappropriateness of much of the inherited European systems of education to citizens in developing countries has led to widespread re-examination and re-statement of education aims.

'Educational institutions are not exportable'

There is a tendency for us to be obsessed by the body of knowledge that we acquired in our learning at whatever stage we imbibed it. This, in turn, often leads us to believe that knowledge somehow has quality if imported from the West.

As will be shown presently, adaptation of what is good from another society is unobjectionable. But where harm can result is when a complete educational system, developed for a particular society, is taken over or transplanted in a society quite different in many major respects. The Report of the Third Commonwealth Education Conference pointed out the danger of importation, lock, stock and barrel. 'The adoption by one country of a curriculum evolved by another without regard to differences in social, economic and cultural background could have unfortunate results. Adaptation is different from adoption.'

The goals and aspirations of Third World countries are very different in many cases from those in other countries, and so it would hardly be appropriate for them to adopt educational systems developed for countries with quite different aims and priorities and emphases.

During 1966/7 Beevers sent out a questionnaire relating to educational goals to over five hundred experienced educationists drawn from 53 developing countries. He analysed the replies he

239

received from 513 of these experienced educators, representing a response of over 85 per cent.

The goal that was chosen most was: 'To help children develop minds which can cope with the problems of living in a rapidly changing world'. This goal was selected by 377 out of the 513 who replied to the questionnaire.

The goals, in the order in which they were selected most, are listed below.

Analysis of significant goals[11d]

Rank

1* To help children develop minds which can cope with the problems of living in a rapidly changing world.

2 To help pupils develop the skills of logical thinking (e.g. observing ... etc. ... decision making).

3 * To help pupils to develop as competent citizens who contribute to the development of their community.

4 * To develop national unity.

5 To help pupils to develop to their highest capability.

6 * To develop citizenship qualities in the pupil.

7 * To help pupils acquire an education particularly suited to their needs and capabilities in a rural society.

8 To develop in pupils an enquiring and experimental attitude.

9 * To help pupils develop social rather than selfish attitudes.

10 * To develop cultural understanding between differing groups within the community.

11 * The improvement of health and sanitation in the community.

12 * To develop for society an education which will change with the advent of new knowledge and new problems.

13 To help pupils at all levels develop the capacity for problem solving.

14 (As a way through the vast stock of knowledge of today and the future) to help pupils develop an attitude for acquiring and using knowledge on a continuing basis.

15 To help pupils develop as resourceful people aware of their own potential.

16 To develop in pupils regular and constructive habits of work.

* Societal goals.

240

The goals with the lowest score (each 19 out of 513, and hence not included in the list above) were: 'To develop in pupils a delight in the imagination'. 'To help pupils develop an appreciation of music'. Both these goals would probably have achieved a much higher rating in Western societies.

It is revealing, too, that there is a greater emphasis on societal goals – nine out of the top twelve goals, marked with an asterisk, – than would probably be the case in societies in developed countries. A quarter of the goals, all societal, would probably not figure in a statement of goals for the U.K., for example;

to develop national unity;
to help pupils acquire an education suited to their needs and capabilities in a rural society;
the improvement of health and sanitation in the community.

In contrast to Western societies which would probably stress the individual and personal achievement, the sample from the developing countries stressed one principal factor – community life.

It would seem that since the goals in more affluent countries differ significantly from those in developing societies the curricula in these would need to be significantly different too. And yet, in the past, metropolitan countries have tended to export their educational systems lock, stock and barrel, rather than encouraging a local product geared to the indigenous societies. No wonder the complaint has been raised, loud and clear, as to the inappropriateness of the educational systems introduced by the colonial authorities.

Professor Fafunwa remarks:

The syllabi of most of the subjects taught are replicas of the English, French or Portuguese syllabi. Under such conditions the students that Africa will produce will be those who are African in blood but English, French or Portuguese in opinion, morals and intellect. Consequently, they will tend to be 'misfits' in their own society. Unquestionably, wholesale curriculum reconstruction is well over-due in Africa and we mean that a radical change both in content and in orientation is needed.[23d]

He refers to the youths of today who are the products of the colonial secondary schools as 'marginal men – they belong neither to Europe nor to Africa'.[23k]

241

In nearly all cases Western institutions have been aped rather than adapted for societal innovation.

Many absurdities can and do arise when developing countries adopt globally the elaborate educational systems of Western countries. There is the case of a university in a poor country in Africa which had established a course in European medieval law.

Hawes gives several examples of importations, lock, stock and barrel, of European educational systems and practices.

> The basic patterns are inherited from colonial times and often (at some remove) from the English Board Schools of the early 1900s; hence the 3 term year, the 5 day week, the 6 or 7 year cycle, the age 5 or 6 entry, the 40 minute period.
>
> Until recently nobody stopped to consider the rationale for these practices. They were accepted uncritically as part of the school package.[36p]

Not only can one not import or export educational systems haphazardly from country to country without running the risk of 'rejection' but one must also recognise the implications for curriculum arising from regional, cultural, linguistic differences within one and the same country. President Nyerere realizes this only too well in his book *Socialism and Rural Development*.

> It is essential to realize that within the unity of Tanzania there is also such diversity that it would be foolish for someone in Dar-es-Salaam to draw up a blueprint ... for every corner of our large country ... Principles of action can be set out, but the application of these principles must take into account the different geographical and geological conditions in different areas, and also the local variations in the basically similar traditional structures.

The question of 'standards'

> Educational standards are not universal. They are interconnected and interact with the particular society in which they develop. They can be neither high nor low in the void, for their true purpose is to serve and inspire the society in which they function.[3b]

It is perhaps understandable that the yard-sticks of Western culture should be accepted in many circles. Western culture is still dominant and its most characteristic achievements – science and technology – are likely to remain a feature of whatever civilisation may succeed it.

Difficulties and discrepancies arise in trying to transplant the 'standards' of one society, in a particular stage of development, to another society in a different stage of development. This has occurred in many former British colonies, torn between maintaining British 'standards' and between evolving an educational system more relevant to their future development. Academic standards, some say, are universal and sacrosanct; once they are allowed to slip they may take generations to recover. So we should tie our curricula and standards, as most of the French ex-colonies have done, to those of a few universities of world standing.

Fafunwa points out how inappropriate – and ridiculous – it can be to slavishly hold on to the academic standards pertaining to a quite different culture and set of circumstances. 'Without attempting to be ridiculous, it is like asking a man in Africa to wear a woollen suit as being the usual international dress while he is struggling to save money to purchase khaki or a light cotton dress'.[23i]

There are no magic international 'standards' of education, no 'modern' or 'old-fashioned' curricula, only standards and curricula which prove efficient and relevant to the needs of a society. If educational 'standards' are to make any sense and serve any useful purpose they must be considered as relative, rather than as hallowed and monolithic. They must be viewed as being relative to the particular purpose, place and time of the student clientele. Any other basis for judging standards and quality is pointless in terms of a nation's development. Every nation can and should have its own relevant standards of excellence, suited to its own conditions and needs. But these standards will not be static, they will be like moving targets, the standards of educational performance being constantly readjusted as knowledge, technology and the country itself advance.

There are, of course, certain instances when 'international standards' must apply – as for instance in the training of nuclear physicists or commercial jet pilots.

Self-reliance in education

Whilst one accepts that education may not be an exportable commodity, this does not exclude the mutual advantage that can accrue from co-operation between countries in matters educational, as, indeed, in all matters. While educational strategies are substantially national, involving a nation's own sovereign choices, they may at the same time draw ideas from the international context and benefit from useful examples contained in the wealth of educational experience in all countries.

This is what many countries have done and are doing. As President Nyerere of Tanzania states in his *Socialism and Rural Development*: 'We must take our traditional system, correct its shortcomings, and adapt to its service the things we learn from the technologically developed societies of other continents.'[62]

Professor Fafunwa, too, argues for judicious adaptation of what might prove to be valuable from other nations. 'While an educational system in its entirety cannot and should not be transferred from one cultural environment to another, the underlying ideas and principles can be carefully studied and sensibly modified and adapted to suit new conditions and changes.'[23j]

The Unesco booklet *Educational Trends in 1970* (pp. 25–26) outlines the major directions in the move away from foreign imported educational systems, practices and ideas.

> Essentially, the move is towards a broader, environmental-oriented curriculum in the primary school and increasing regard at the secondary level for pupils' vocational needs in the light of the country's economic development – for example, emphasis on ruralization in the educational policies of the majority of African states. In implementation of these policies, the authorities have been led to the sources of the national community's way of life – cultural as well as economic – for curricula, teaching methods and preparation of teachers have all to be worked out afresh. They cannot easily be derived from experience elsewhere . . .

The importance of environmental studies has been exemplified in a number of countries by attention to newer aspects of problems – pollution, population control – with a demand that curricula take account of such issues.

244

Hawes confirms this change to a more environment-oriented emphasis in the education programmes of countries in Africa.

> Alongside the priority placed on language and communication ... I detect a concern that curriculum materials in all school subjects should be 'development orientated', should reflect concern over such matters as health, nutrition, food production, conservation of resources and the co-operation and enquiry-mindedness necessary to achieve these. There are no separate 'development education' or 'self-reliance' periods. The knowledge, skills and attitudes necessary for these purposes are woven into the fabric of Language, Mathematics, Social Studies and Science.[36q]

Samir Amin, of the Arab Republic of Egypt, and Director of the African Institute of Economic Development and Planning, Dakar, in an article 'What Education for What Development?' also confirms the change in direction to a more relevant, indigenous education pattern.

> Hence we can see clearly the outlines both of a self-oriented development strategy and of an education radically different from the borrowed (i.e. Western) model. The strategy must start with a direct definition of the needs of the masses, without reference to the European model; it must necessarily be egalitarian; it must help to awaken a capacity for autonomous technological innovation.[4]

The way ahead

> Education follows the laws of every human undertaking, growing old and gathering dead wood. To remain a living organism, capable of satisfying with intelligence and vigour the requirements of individuals and developing countries, it must avoid the pitfalls of complacency and routine. It must constantly question its objectives, its content and its methods.[25]

> If education is to help change the world and to help brighten the lives of more and more people, it must begin by changing and brightening itself.[10i]

As society changes the curriculum also needs to change. There is a constant need to review curriculum if it is to retain value in a changing society. The dinosaurs of old did not (or could not) adapt to changing situations and environments; they perished. The same analogy can be applied to education.

The 1962 Unesco Conference on Secondary School Curriculum, held in Tananarive, emphasised the need for curriculum change in Africa.

> The attainment of Independence in Africa now makes it necessary to re-examine a type of education which in many African countries was formerly designed to 'assimilate' young Africans to the culture of the Metropolitan countries. Curriculum reform is a corollary of political emancipation – cultural emancipation being the means by which the 'African Personality' can be asserted. This calls for re-discovery of the African cultural heritage and the transmission of that culture to African adolescents in secondary schools.[87]

New situations bring new opportunities. But as Professor Fafunwa points out;

> curriculum reconstruction cannot take place in a vacumn. Curriculum change must indeed be predicated on a sound philosophy of education. The African nations and communities must come to grips with the following issues:
>
> 1 What kind of African society do we envisage now and in future? Is it a socialist, capitalist, islamic, christian, animist state?
> 2 What is a given African society's views on values, freedom, culture, ethics, common citizenship and the individual; or state the issues in broader terms?
> 3 What is a given African society's position on politics and education, the state and education, religion and moral education, the school and the social order, etc?
> 4 What can we learn from traditional African education?
>
> If we can answer the above questions satisfactorily, we should be able to see our way clear to tackling the next question; What do all these mean in terms of their educational implications, that is, in terms of educational goals, structure, organization, curriculum and finally, as these again relate to the preparation of the teacher?[24a]

246

President Nyerere, for one, made explicit the kind of society he wanted and the educational implications of this.

At the Dag Hammerskjöld Seminar on Education held in Dar es Salaam in 1974 the President stated quite firmly:

We leaders will be – and should be – criticised in the future if we now refuse to acknowlege the need for change.

We will be, and we should be, condemned by later generations if we do not act now to try to find and institute an educational system which will liberate Africa's young people . . .

We have the position where a formal school system, devised and operated without reference to the society in which its graduates will live, is of little use as an instrument of liberation for the people of Africa. And at the same time learning just by living and doing in the existing society would leave us so backward socially, and technologically, that human liberation in the foreseeable future is out of the question.

Somehow we have to combine the two systems. We have to integrate formal education with the society. And we have to use education as a catalyst for change in that society. That is the task. It is one which various African nations, or groups within nations, have been trying to fulfil over the last decade . . . [82b]

Summary

The old system of traditional education had much to recommend it – its purpose was clear; education was regarded as a means, not an end, by itself. Since the education was functional unemployment was minimal; there was no drift to the towns and cities.

This system was replaced in many developing countries by colonialist systems of education, which were bookish, academic, elitist, with the emphasis not on work but simply on learning to qualify for white collar jobs in administration. Little emphasis was placed on education for industrial and economic development with the result that today there is a serious shortage of technicians, artisans etc.

The increasing inappropriateness of this kind of education has led to demands for a re-examination of education in developing countries in order to meet the changing challenges of the future.

Educational institutions, including 'standards', are not

exportable. One can certainly adapt what is relevant and appropriate and useful from other educational systems. But one should not adopt foreign systems and practices wholesale.

Education in developing countries is moving away from foreign imported systems to more relevant indigenous patterns. It is increasingly more environment-and development- oriented as instanced by concern with real life problems – pollution, health, food, population control, conservation.

As society changes the curriculum also needs to change. There is a constant need to review and re-examine education. Unless it adapts to changing situations it will perish – as did the dinosaurs of old.

Questions

1   Is your country's system of education 'traditional' or 'colonial/ westernised' or a mixture of both or quite different to these types?
2   Are there any remnants of 'traditional' education in your country? Describe these.
3   Are there any aspects of 'traditional' education in your country which you feel should be abolished or encouraged? Say why.
4   What would you say are the advantages of 'traditional' education?
5   What are the disadvantages, if any, of traditional education?
6   Do you feel your country would be better off if it had a 'traditional' pattern of education? Say why.
7   Do you think your country has gained by adopting parts of a 'colonial' pattern of education? Explain.
8   What are some of the drawbacks your country suffers from because of the education system left behind by the former colonial powers?
9   List any advantages and disadvantages of the old 'colonial' system of education.
10   Give some examples of educational practices your country has adopted from other countries which you feel have been a) beneficial   b) harmful.
11   List some educational practices your country has adapted from other countries which have proved beneficial to your country.

12 Are any 'standards' used in your schools still borrowed from abroad? Are they appropriate to the needs of your society?
13 Give examples of 'local' standards introduced by your school system as being more appropriate to your society's needs.
14 State the main ways in which your country's education system has moved away from 'foreign' patterns and practices of education.
15 Outline the ways in which your country's educational system should be changed to meet the challenges of the future.

Bibliography and References

1 E. T. ABIOLA, 'Understanding the African School Child,' *West African Journal of Education*. (Ibadan: Feb. 1971) (pp. 64–66)

2 S. ADAMS, 'The Introduction of Social Studies at Junior Secondary Level in Sierra Leone', In J.A. Ponsioen (ed) *Educational Innovations in Africa*. (Institute of Social Studies, The Hague: 1970) (p. 210)

3 M. ADISESHIAH, *Let My Country Awake*. (Unesco, Paris: 1970) a (p. 84); b (89).

4 S. AMIN, 'What Education for What Development?' In *Prospects*: *A Quarterly Review of Education*. Vol. V. No. 1. (Unesco, Paris: 1972) (p. 52)

5 BHUNTIN ATTAGARA, 'Concerning Goals and Methods,' In *Prospects*. Vol. III. No. 1. (Unesco, Paris: 1973) a (84, 85); b (90); c (84)

6 DR N. AZIKIWE, *Renascent Africa*. (Ziks Press, Lagos: 1937) (pp. 134–135).

7 M. K. BACCHUS, 'Secondary School Curriculum and Social Change in an Emergent Nation,' *Journal of Curriculum Studies*. Vol. 7. No. 2. (Collins: Nov. 1975.) (p. 120)

8 G. H. BANTOCK, 'Towards a Theory of Popular Education,' *Times Educational Supplement*. (Mar. 12 and 19, 1971) In R. HOOPER (ed) *The Curriculum: Context, Design and Development*. (Oliver and Boyd. Edinburgh: 1971) (p. 251)

9 C. E. BEEBY, *The Quality of Education in Developing Countries*. (Harvard University Press, Camb. Mass: 1966) (p. 37, 31–32)

10 C. E. BEEBY, (ed) *The Qualitative Aspects of Educational Planning*. (Unesco, Paris: 1969) a (117); b (190); c (194); d (198); e (298); f (113); g (50); h (211); i (35).

11 R. BEEVERS, *Curriculum Change in Developing Countries*. (M. Ed. Thesis. University of Leicester: 1968) a (82); b (12); c (133); d (123 et seq.)

12 H. S. BROUDY, B. O. SMITH AND J. R. BURNETT, *Democracy and*

Excellence in American Secondary Education, (Rand McNally, Chicago, Ill: 1964)

13 J. S. BRUNER, *Toward a Theory of Instruction*, (Harvard University Press, Camb., Mass: 1966)

14 K. BUCHANAN, *Reflections on Education in the Third World*, (Spokesman Books, Nottingham: 1975) (pp. 28-29)

15 CENTRAL ADVISORY COUNCIL FOR EDUCATION, *Half Our Future*, (H.M.S.O., London: 1964) (p. 29)

16 P. E. COOMBS, *The World Educational Crisis*, (Oxford University Press, New York: 1968) a (171); b (139); c (108); d (115); e (16); f (104); g (181); h (85).

17 P. E. COOMBS, In C. E. BEEBY, *The Qualitative Aspects of Educational Planning*. (pp. 17, 18)

18 PER DALIN, *Case studies in Educational Innovation. IV*, (Organization for Economic Co-operation and Development: 1970) (pp. 44-51)

19 I. K. DAVIES, (Referring to Robert Mager) 'Writing General Objectives and Writing Specific Objectives', in *Curriculum Design*, Editors Golby, Greenwold, West (Croom Helm Publishers, London, 1977) (pp. 323, 322)

20 J. DEAKIN, *Examinations and the Secondary School Curriculum*, In A. G. Howson (ed) *Developing a New Curriculum*, (Heinemann, London: 1972) (p. 112)

21 RENÉ DUMONT, *False Start in Africa*, (Deutsch, London: 1966)

22 JUDITH EVANS, *Children in Africa*, (Centre for Education in Africa. Teachers' College, Columbia University, New York: 1970) a (29); b (21); c (41)

23 A. B. FAFUNWA, *New Perspectives in African Education*, (Macmillan, Lagos: 1967) a (56); b (69); c (61, 63); d (64); e (16); f (99); g (129); h (46); i (114); j (113); j (6); k (53).

24 A. B. FAFUNWA, 'Some Guiding Principles of Education in Africa,' *West African Journal of Education*. (Ibadan: 15 Feb. 1971) a (6 -7); b (5)

25 E. FAURE *(et al) Learning to Be*, (Unesco, Paris: 1972) (p. 79)

26 FIJI, 'Report of the Fiji Education Commission,' (Ministry of Education, Suva: 1969)

27 PAULO FRIERE, *The Pedagogy of the Oppressed*, (Sheed and Ward, London: 1972) (pp. 57-58)

28 V. L. GRIFFITHS, *The Problems of Rural Education*, (Unesco, Paris: 1968) a (16-17); b (17-18); c (26); d (32); e (37)

29 D. HAMILTON, *Curriculum Evaluation*, (Open Books, London: 1976) a (75-84); b (78)

30 F. HARBISON, *Critical Manpower Problems in Nigerian Agricultural and Rural Development*, (Education and World Affairs Nigeria Project Task Force. New York: May 1967) In P. E. COOMBS, *The World Educational Crisis*. (p. 81)

31   A. HARRIS, *(et al) Curriculum Innovation*, (Croom Helm, London: 1975) (p. 378)

31A A. HARRIS, *Intuition and the Arts of Teaching*, (Open University, Course E203, Unit 18) (p. 77)

32   R. G. HAVELOCK, *Planning for Innovation through the Dissemination and Utilisation of Knowledge*, (University of Michigan, Ann Arbor: 1971)

33   H. HAWES, *Curriculum and Curriculum Development in Jamaica*, (Institute of Education. University of London: 1976) a (39); b (21)

34   H. HAWES, *Curriculum and Curriculum Development in Kenya*, (Institute of Education. London: 1976) (pp. 31, 42)

35   H. HAWES, *Curriculum and Curriculum Development in Sierra Leone*, (Institute of Education, London: 1976) a (25); b (21); c (29)

36   H. HAWES, *Curriculum and Reality in African Primary Schools*, (Longman, London: 1979) a (164); b (163); c (88); d (121); e (55); f (63); g (153); h (124/125); j (127); k (21); l (119); m (152); n (146); o (101); p (74); q (182)

37   H. HAWES AND A. AARONS, *Curriculum and Curriculum Development in Nigeria*, (Institute of Education, London: 1976) a (71); b (52)

38   J. A. HENDRY, 'Teacher Education and Curriculum Development,' (Swaziland: 1979).

39   P. HIRST, *Knowledge and the Curriculum*, (Routledge, London: 1974)

40   R. HOOPER, (ed) *The Curriculum: Context, Design and Development*, (Oliver and Boyd, Edinburgh: 1971) a (210-211); b (495); c (191); d (277); e (196-197); f (438); g (325-335).

41   A. G. HOWSON, (ed) *Developing a New Curriculum*, (Heinemann, London: 1972) a (41-42); b (22); c (45); d (46); e (83-84); f (61).

42   ERIC HOYLE, *Strategies of Curriculum Development*, (In Open University Course E203; Unit 23. Open University Press, Milton Keynes: 1976) (p. 48)

43   A. M. HUBERMAN, *Understanding Change in Education: an Introduction*, (Unesco/I.B.E. Paris: 1973) (p. 62)

44   India, *Report of the Education Commission (1964-1966)*, (Delhi: 1966)

45   MRS CHARITY JAMES, *Young Lives at Stake*, (Collins, London: 1968)

46   M. JOHNSON, *Curriculum Development: A Comparative Study*, (National Foundation for Educational Research Publishing Co., Windsor: 1974) (p. 8)

47   W. SENTEZA KAJUBI, 'Educational Priorities in Africa', In *Prospects*: Vol. III. No. 1. (Unesco, Paris: 1973) a (82); b (80).

48   KENYA, *A Land of Contrasts*, (Ministry of Education and Ministry of Information and Broadcasting, Nairobi: 1979) (p. 43)

49   JOMO KENYATTA, *Facing Mount Kenya*, (Secker and Warburg,

253

London: 1938)

50   J. F. KERR, (ed), *Changing the Curriculum*, (University of London Press, London: 1968) a (42); b (20)

51   D. LAWTON, *Social Change, Educational Theory and Curriculum Planning*, (University of London Press, London: 1973) a (422); b (47); c (65); d (46)

52   W. A. LEWIS, In C. E. BEEBY, *The Qualitative Aspects of Educational Planning*, (Unesco, Paris: 1969) a (82); b (62)

53   A. LEWY, *The Development, Evaluation and Implementation of the Curriculum*, (International Institute of Educational Planning, Paris: 1975) (p. 15)

54   B. MACDONALD AND R. WALKER, *Changing the Curriculum*, (Open Books, London: 1976) (p. 63)

55   E. MIDWINTER, *Social Environment and the Urban School*, (Ward, Lock Ltd. London: 1972)

56   G. MILNER, 'Cultural Arrogance', (Private paper. Apia, Western Samoa: 1973)

57   R. W. MORRIS, 'The Role of Languages in Learning Mathematics', In *Prospects*. Vol. VIII. No. 1. (Unesco, Paris: 1978)

58   A. MOUMOURI, 'The Return to National Languages and Cultures', In *Prospects*. Vol. V. No. 1. (Unesco, Paris: 1975) (p. 65)

59   NIGERIA EDUCATION RESEARCH COUNCIL, *Guidelines on Primary School Curriculum*, (Report: National Workshop on Primary Education, April–May 1971, Ibadan: 1973) (p. 343)

60   NIGERIA, *National Policy on Education*, (Federal Ministry of Education, Lagos: 1981)

61   JULIUS NYERERE, *Education for Self-Reliance*, (Govt. Printer, Dar es Salaam: 1967)

62   JULIUS NYERERE, 'Socialism and Rural Development', In *Ujamaa*: *Essays on Socialism*, (Oxford University Press, Dar es Salaam: 1968)

63   P. A. I. OBANYA, 'Nigerian Teachers' Reception of a New French Syllabus,' *Journal of Curriculum Studies*. Vol. 6. No. 2. (Collins, London: Nov. 1974) (p. 171)

64   R. OGBONNA OHUCHE, 'Piaget and the Mende of Sierra Leone', *Journal of Experimental Education*. Vol. 39. No. 4. (Wisconsin: 1971) (p. 75)

65   THE OPEN UNIVERSITY, *Curriculum Design and Development*. (*Course E203*), (Open University Press, Milton Keynes: 1976) a (Unit 14, p. 38); b (Unit 26, pp. 96–97); c (Leaflet: 'Some Further Comments' (on Tanzania), (p. 6); d (Unit 4, pp. 66–67)

66   D. V. OWIREDU, 'The African Social Studies Programme', In J. A. PONSIOEN (ed) *Educational Innovations in Africa*. (p. 214)

67   PAKISTAN, *Report of the Curriculum Committee for Secondary Education*, (Ministry of Education, Rawalpindi: 1960)

68   FRANKLIN PARKER, 'Curriculum for Man in an International

World', (Contributions to International Education Year Conference. Kansas State University: 1970) (p. 61)

69   P. H. PHENIX, *Realms of Meaning*, (McGraw - Hill, New York: 1964)

70   J. A. PONSIOEN, (ed) *Educational Innovations in Africa*, (Institute of Social Studies, The Hague: 1972) (p. 230)

71   J. R. PRINCE, *Science Concepts in a Pacific Culture*, (Angus and Robertson, Sydney: 1969) (p. 33)

72   D. R. PRICE-WILLIAMS, (ed) *Cross-Cultural Studies*, (Penguin, London: 1969) a (5); b (117-129); c (85); d (21, 202-209); e (253); f (259).

73   C. SANGER, *Project Impact: An Experiment in Mass Primary Education in the Philippines and Proyek Pamang in Indonesia*, (International Development Research Centre, Ottawa: 1977) (p. 21)

74   SETIJADI, *Educational Planning - Indonesia*, (Bulletin: Unesco Regional Office for Education in Asia, Bangkok: No. 16) (p. 29)

75   B. SHAW, *Visual Symbols Survey: a report on the recognition of drawings in Kenya*. (Centre for Educational Development Overseas, London: 1969)

76   M. D. SHIPMAN, *Inside a Curriculum Project*, (Methuen, London: 1974) (p. 170)

77   SIERRA LEONE, *Educational Review, Final Report: All Our Future*, (Govt. Printer, Freetown: 1976)

78   SOUTH PACIFIC, *Social Science in the South Pacific*, P. Hart *et al*. (Unesco Curriculum Development Unit, University of the South Pacific, Fiji: 1972) a (Introduction for Teachers); b (Notes for Writers at Form I - IV Level. Graeme Coates.)

78A SOUTH PACIFIC, *Mathematics*. E. Leaton *et al*. (Unesco Curriculum Development Unit, University of the South Pacific, Fiji: 1972)

79   SRI LANKA, *Curriculum for Development*, Final Report. (Subregional Unesco Curriculum Workshop. Colombo: Oct. 1976) a (81); b (52-61)

80   SRI LANKA, *Asian Expert Seminar on the Development of Science and Mathematics Concepts in Children*. 29 May-10 June, 1972, Final Report. (Unesco Regional Office for Education in Asia, Bangkok) (p. 52)

81   H. TABA, *Curriculum Development*: Theory and Practice, (Harcourt and Brace, New York: 1962) (p. 196)

82   TANZANIA, a 'The Purpose of Education', (In *The Daily News*, Dar es Salaam: 6 Jan. 1975)
b Dag Hammerskjöld Seminar on Education. (*The Daily News*, Dar es Salaam: 21 May, 1974)

83   P. H. TAYLOR, *Curriculum Development. A Comparative Study*, (National Foundation for Educational Research, Windsor: 1974) (p. 190)

84   THAILAND, *Current and Projected Secondary Education Pro-*

grammes for Thailand: a Manpower and Educational Development Project, (Ministry of Education, Thailand: 1966) (p. 104)

85 R. TYLER, *The Basic Principles of Curriculum and Instruction*, (University of Chicago Press, Chicago, Ill: 1949)

86 UGANDA, *Report of the Uganda Education Commission*, (Kampala: 1964)

87 UNESCO, *The Adaptation of the General Secondary School Curriculum in Africa*, Conference Report. (Tananarive: July, 1962) (p. 5)

88 UNESCO, *Educational Planning*: *a World Survey of Problems and Prospects*, (Unesco, Paris: 1970)

89 UNESCO, *Education in a Rural Environment*, (Unesco, Paris: 1974) a (51); b (30); c (59).

90 UNESCO, *Prospects*: *A Quarterly Review of Education*, Vol. III. No. 1. (Unesco. Paris: 1973) (p. 17)

91 UNESCO, a Bulletin. Vol. II. No. 1. (Sep. 1976) (p. 86); b Bulletin Vol. III. No. 2. (Mar. 1969) (p. 28); c Bulletin No. 18. 'Some Aspects of Science Education in the Asian Region', (18 June, 1977) (p. 218) (Regional Office for Education in Asia, Bangkok)

92 D. K. WHEELER, *The Curriculum Process*, (University of London Press, London: 1971) a (chaps. 7-9); b (30)

93 C. J. B. WHITE, 'The Training of Unqualified Teachers, through Correspondence Education in Botswana', In J. A. PONSIOEN (ed) *Educational Innovations in Africa*, (pp. 185/186)

94 JOHN WHITE, 'The Curriculum Mongers: education in reverse', (*New Society*, London: No. 336. 6 Mar, 1969) Reprinted in R. HOOPER. *The Curriculum*: *Context, Design and Development*. (pp. 273-280)

95 JOHN WHITE, *Towards a Compulsory Curriculum*, (Routledge and Kegan Paul Ltd., London: 1973) (pp. 75-76)

95A A. N. WHITEHEAD, The Aims of Education and other Essays. (Seventh Impression). Benn, London: 1970 (pp. 28-30)

96 W. M. ZAKI, *Education Planning in Pakistan*, (Unesco Regional Office for Education in Asia, Bangkok: Bulletin No. 16. June 1975) (p. 101)

Index

259